Nazi Victory
Crete 1941

Nazi Victory
Crete 1941

David A. Thomas

STEIN AND DAY/*Publishers*/New York

'There are some who say we should never fight without superior or at least ample air support, and ask when this lesson will be learned. But suppose you cannot have it. The questions which have to be settled are not always questions between what is good and bad; very often it is a choice between two very terrible alternatives. Must you, if you cannot have this essential and desirable air support, yield important key points one after the other?

'The further question arises as to what would happen if you allowed the enemy to advance or overrun without cost to himself the most precious and valuable strategic points. Suppose we had never gone to Greece and never attempted to defend Crete: Where would the Germans be now?'

The Prime Minister, Winston S. Churchill in an
address to the House of Commons, June 10th, 1941

Contents

List of Illustrations

Following page 124

1. Admiral Sir Andrew Cunningham, Commander-in-Chief of the Mediterranean Fleet (Imperial War Museum).
2. Rear Admiral I. G. S. Glennie (Imperial War Museum).
3. Rear Admiral H. B. Rawlings (Imperial War Museum).
4. The assault ship *Glenearn* (Imperial War Museum).
5. The Italian destroyer *Sagittario* (Major Aldo Fraccaroli).
6. Lieutenant Fulgosi of the *Sagittario* and Commander Mimbelli of the *Lupo* (Ufficio Storico Marina Militare).
7. Lieutenant Colonel Dinort (Ullstein Bilderdienst).
8. Major Walter Enneccerus (Ullstein Bilderdienst).
9. General Wolfram Freiherr von Richthoven, commander of *Fliegerkorps VIII* (Ullstein Bilderdienst).
10. A Junkers 87 Stuka dive-bomber (Imperial War Museum).
11. Suda Bay after a *Luftwaffe* attack (Imperial War Museum).
12. The battleship *Warspite* under air attack on May 22nd (Ullstein Bilderdienst).
13. HM cruiser *Fiji* (Imperial War Museum).
14. *Luftwaffe* pilot's photograph of the cruiser *Gloucester* (Imperial War Museum).
15. A sequence of photographs from a German pilot's film of the sinking of the *Gloucester* (Imperial War Museum).
16. Captain H. M. L. Waller RAN of the *Stuart* with Lieutenant-Commander R. Rhoades on the *Vendetta*'s bridge (Australian War Memorial).
17. Captain Sir Philip Bowyer-Smith and officers on the bridge of his cruiser HMAS *Perth* (Australian War Memorial).
18. The Australian destroyer *Nizam* returns to Alexandria

5

crowded with troops from Crete (Australian War Memorial).
19. The destroyer *Kipling* is welcomed into Alexandria (Imperial War Museum).
20. The destroyer *Kimberley* (Imperial War Museum).
21. Admiral Rawlings's flagship, the cruiser *Orion* (Imperial War Museum).
22. HM destroyer *Nubian* preparing to leave harbour to escort a convoy from Suda Bay (Imperial War Museum).
23. Yeoman of Signals, the commanding officer of the destroyer *Hotspur,* Lieutenant-Commander Cecil P. F. Brown, Lieutenant C. G. Forsberg, Lieutenant L. P. Tillie and Lieutenant Hugh Hodgkinson (Imperial War Museum).

MAPS AND CHARTS

Acknowledgements

A GREAT NUMBER of people have given their time and help in the compilation of this book. Others have guided me in my researches and have pointed the way for further investigation. To all these helpers, who come from the United States, Western Germany, Italy, Switzerland, Greece, Australia and the United Kingdom, I am indebted.

Admiral Karlgeorg Schüster, the Admiral commanding Axis naval forces at the time of the Cretan campaign, has been kind and courteous in his correspondence though unable to help in detail 'because at the end of the last war I lost all records, notices, reports, personal notes of all kinds, either in my bombed-out house in Berlin or in US prisoner-of-war camps'.

A German friend, the naval historian Günter Schomaekers, generously provided me with valuable facts, procured information and thoughtfully directed lines of further research.

Admiraglio de Squadra Carlo Paladini, Director of the *Ufficio Storico della Marina Militare,* generously donated volumes of the official history of the Italian Navy in World War II and provided me with photographs and biographical data.

Captain N. Stathakis of the Royal Hellenic Navy, the Armed Forces Attaché in London, and Admiral T. Michael have been kind and helpful. But other official Greek sources have shown a marked reluctance to cooperate. Thus, the efforts of the Greek Navy in opposing the German attacks on Greece and Crete go unrecorded.

I am indebted to Mr Frank Kennerley, Borough Librarian of Redbridge, and to his staff for their unfailing help and kindnesses.

The staff of the photographic library of the Imperial War

Museum, Mr M. Brennan, Mr R. E. Squires, and Mr E. Hine deserve praise for their customary patience and help in identifying and locating illustrations.

Commander Hugh Hodgkinson kindly provided information and drew upon his experiences in the Cretan battles to proffer advice: 'Destroyer captains in the Mediterranean in 1941,' he wrote, 'were living under conditions never asked before of commanders. They knew that a single misjudgement might mean the loss of half their crew. My captain . . . had seen the entire bows of his previous destroyer HMS *Gallant* disappear before his eyes (when struck by a mine) and the stern end towed into Malta. He had known the loss of life among his ship's company. He was in desperate need of rest and recovery and yet he came straight across to command the *Hotspur*. . . . As the months of sleepless strain increased he continued to handle the *Hotspur* with wonderful skill; he was retained in command for six months including the terrible experience of Crete . . . I would therefore impress very deeply upon you that your book should stress the appalling strain under which particularly the destroyer captains lived.' I hope I have heeded this advice.

Thanks are due to Messrs Glen Line Limited for unearthing a copy of their booklet about the war service of HMS *Glengyle;* to the Office of the High Commissioner for Australia in London; to Mr W. R. Lancaster, Director of the Australian War Memorial, Canberra for procuring photographs, and to G. Hermon Gill, official naval historian for the Australian Navy.

The Department of the Navy, Washington, the Department of the Army, Washington and the *Bundesarchiv* in Bonn have kindly provided information. Ullstein GMBH of Berlin were helpful in locating some German photographs for me.

The United States Naval Institute, Annapolis, continue to maintain their high standard of cooperation and assistance, for which I thank them. Major Aldo Fraccaroli, an Italian Naval Reserve officer and eminent naval historian, drew upon his vast library of photographs and generously provided advice.

For their translation services I am grateful to Mr P. Hetherington and to Mr and Mrs L. Cariss. Peter Smith, author of *Stuka At War,* kindly offered help, for which I am grateful.

Rear Admiral P. N. Buckley of the Naval Historical Branch, Ministry of Defence, kindly verified facts and provided useful information.

Thanks are due to many authors and publishers who have kindly consented to my quoting from their works. I gladly acknowledge the following: *A Sailor's Odyssey* by Viscount Cunningham of Hyndhope, Hutchinson & Co (Publishers); *Greek Tragedy '41* by A. Heckstall-Smith and Vice Admiral H. T. Baillie-Grohman, Anthony Blond; *HMS Warspite* by Captain S. Roskill, Collins; *Without Prejudice* by Lord Tedder, Cassell & Co; *Hitler's War Directives* edited by H. R. Trevor-Roper, Sidgwick & Jackson; *Climax in Crete* by Theodore Stephanides, Faber & Faber; *Before the Tide Turned* by Hugh Hodgkinson, George G. Harrap; *The Luftwaffe War Diaries* by Cajus Bekker, Macdonald & Co (Publishers); *The Second World War* by Winston S. Churchill, Cassell & Co; *Victory at Sea* by Lieutenant-Commander P. Kemp, Muller.

The Director of Publications and Her Majesty's Stationery Office have kindly granted permission to quote from the following: *The War at Sea 1939–1945* by Captain S. Roskill; *The Mediterranean Fleet; Medical History of the Second World War* by J. L. S. Coulter; *Despatch* by Admiral Sir Andrew Cunningham and *Reports* by Vice Admiral Pridham-Wippell and Rear Admiral H. T. Baillie-Grohman published in a supplement to *The London Gazette.*

Finally, I should like to acknowledge the efforts of Miss Avril Damant and Mrs M. Braund for their help with my typescript.

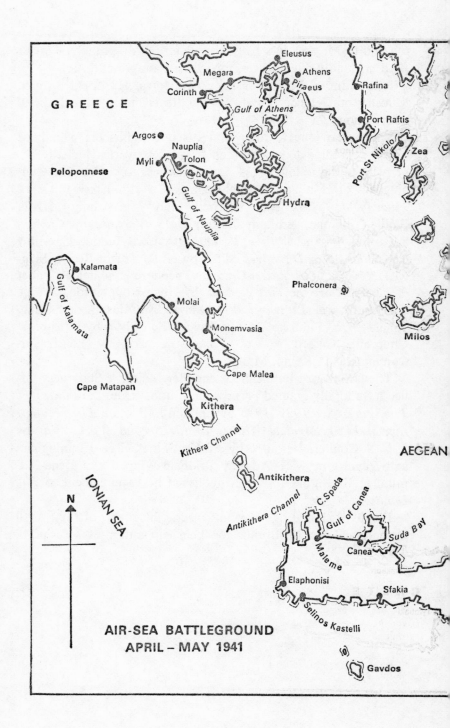

GREECE

Peloponnese

Corinth

Megara

Eleusus

Athens

Piraeus

Rafina

Port Raftis

Gulf of Athens

Argos

Nauplia

Myli

Tolon

Gulf of Nauplia

Hydra

Port St Nikolo

Zea

Kalamata

Gulf of Kalamata

Molai

Monemvasia

Phalconera

Milos

Cape Malea

Cape Matapan

Kithera

Kithera Channel

AEGEAN

Antikithera

Antikithera Channel

C.Spada

Gulf of Canea

Suda Bay

Maleme

Canea

IONIAN SEA

N

Elaphonisi

Sfakia

Selinos Kastelli

AIR-SEA BATTLEGROUND
APRIL – MAY 1941

Gavdos

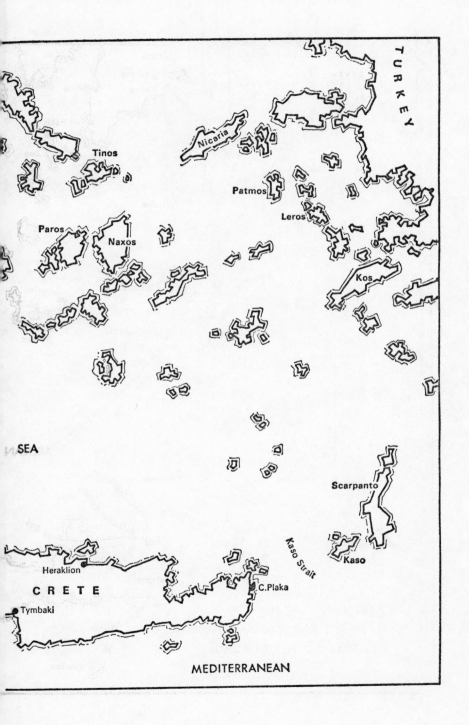

TURKEY

Tinos

Nicaria

Patmos

Leros

Paros

Naxos

Kos

SEA

Scarpanto

Kaso Strait

Heraklion

Kaso

CRETE

C.Plaka

Tymbaki

MEDITERRANEAN

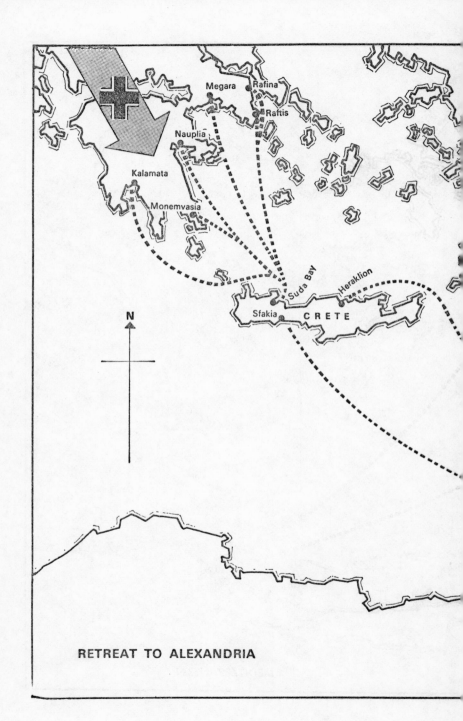

N

RETREAT TO ALEXANDRIA

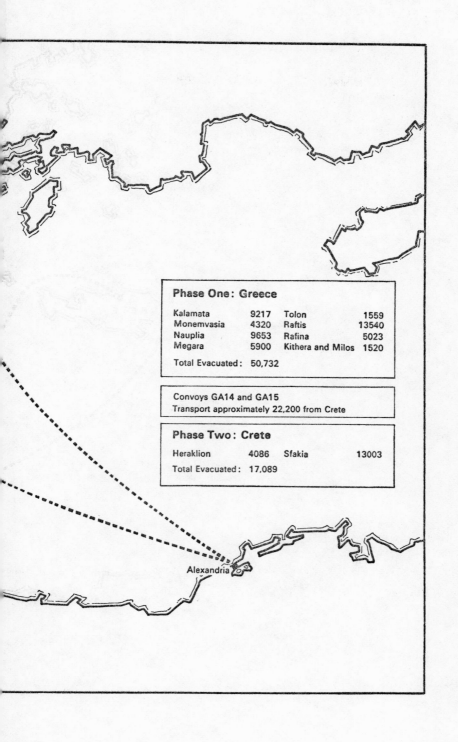

Phase One: Greece

Kalamata	9217	Tolon	1559
Monemvasia	4320	Raftis	13540
Nauplia	9653	Rafina	5023
Megara	5900	Kithera and Milos	1520

Total Evacuated: 50,732

Convoys GA14 and GA15
Transport approximately 22,200 from Crete

Phase Two: Crete

Heraklion	4086	Sfakia	13003

Total Evacuated: 17,089

Alexandria

Preface

THIS BOOK IS a chronicle of naval defeat. It aims to reconstruct in detail the series of naval operations in and about the waters of Greece and Crete during the six-week period starting April 22nd until June 1st, 1941.

The circumstances of the naval engagements and battles, poorly-documented and confused in many reports, now merit critical reviewing and recounting with the added benefit of historical detachment. The battles which will be related were almost exclusively contested between warships of the Royal Navy and aircraft of the German *Luftwaffe*. They proved to be a series of sustained aerial bombardments the like of which no navy in the world had experienced before. Not until the *Kamikaze* suicide missions of the Japanese pilots at Okinawa four years later was the severity of the Mediterranean ordeal to be surpassed.

For the first time in naval history a fleet with plenty of sea-room for manœuvre was to come to grips with an enemy air fleet. The sheer magnitude of the Cretan battles dwarfed the Norwegian confrontation, and the Japanese despatch of the *Repulse* and the *Prince of Wales* in the Gulf of Siam was achieved by a relatively small force of aircraft and contained little of the drama which surrounded the prolonged ordeal that the Mediterranean Fleet endured at the hands of two *Luftwaffe Fliegerkorps*. The outcome of the Cretan battles, predicted in the inter-war years, gave overwhelming victory to the *Luftwaffe*. The Royal Navy withdrew from Crete bombed to defeat.

*

The Battle for Crete falls conveniently into two phases as far as the Mediterranean Fleet is concerned. Phase 1 consisted of defence: the prevention of seaborne landings. Phase 2 was escape:

15

the evacuation of British and Allied troops to Egypt, more than 400 miles away. Both phases demanded a large number of warships operating hundreds of miles from their base with little or no fighter protection against the relentless attacks of the *Luftwaffe*. Only darkness afforded respite from the intensity of the aerial bombardment. But in the Mediterranean the early summer days are long and the skies dazzlingly bright with sunshine. The Royal Navy strived hard to evade the *Luftwaffe* and minimise losses but because of the ferocity and accuracy of the German attacks the British losses were heavy.

Admiral Sir Andrew B. Cunningham, Commander-in-Chief of the Mediterranean Fleet, subsequently reported in his *Despatch*[1] that the losses were so great that they could be compared with those which might conceivably be incurred during a major fleet action. Yet in this instance one of the opposing fleets consisted solely of aircraft.

Three cruisers and eight destroyers were sunk. But equally serious from the British viewpoint was the damage suffered by the remaining ships of the Fleet. Two battleships suffered: the famous *Warspite,* Cunningham's own flagship, and the *Barham,* both of them majestic veterans of World War I, and representing half the battleship strength of the Mediterranean Fleet. The aircraft carrier *Formidable,* a recent and vital acquisition by the Fleet, was damaged and taken out of service. Five cruisers were seriously damaged and seven destroyers suffered damage in varying degrees.

The toll in human life was even more distressing. More than 2,000 officers and men of the Royal Navy were killed or lost at sea during the battles and nearly another 500 were wounded.

*

One of the most significant aspects of all the naval activity during the period under review was the complete absence of an opposing fleet. At no time during the Greek and Crete evacuations did the Italian Navy manage to cast off the caution induced by

[1] *The Battle of Crete* by Admiral Cunningham, Supplement to *The London Gazette,* May 24th, 1948, HMSO.

the defeat at Matapan and leave the security of its ports. History has few parallels to match this resolute decision by the Italian *Supermarina* to avoid naval combat while enjoying—on paper at any rate—superiority over the opposing fleet.

The Mediterranean Fleet, and indeed the Royal Navy itself, had suffered such grievous losses in the first nineteen months of the war at sea that a major naval defeat in the Mediterranean at this time might have led directly to the evacuation of British naval units from the Eastern basin. Such an abdication of British admiralty would have opened the gates to untold riches in the Middle East for the Axis powers. A British presence in the Eastern Mediterranean was, in fact, a lynchpin of British strategy in the whole Middle East theatre, and upon it depended the nourishment of Malta, the sustenance of her armies in the desert of North Africa and the maintenance of her oil supplies for the war effort. But even these measureless prizes were not enough to tempt the Italian Fleet.

Now, with the benefit of hindsight we can ask: why did the Italian Commander-in-Chief Afloat, Admiral Angelo Iachino, or *Supermarina,* fail to take advantage of the Royal Navy's weakness and strike? Now, if ever, was the time. Now, if only to redeem the lost prestige from the defeat at Cape Matapan, was the time to foray south and seek out the enemy. But the opportunity was ignored. It was never to present itself again to such advantage. Instead, it was the Mediterranean Fleet which risked command of the sea by venturing into the perilous waters of Crete during this crucial period of the war: risked it and very nearly lost it. It was a calculated risk of Nelsonian proportions.

At a time when, together with the officers and men under his command, he endured conditions almost beyond human endurance with incredible fortitude, Admiral Cunningham resolved that the evacuation of troops from Crete must go on despite the losses and privations. 'It takes the Navy three years to build a new ship,' he declared to his Staff. 'It will take three hundred to build a new tradition. The evacuation will continue.'

In his memoirs[2] Cunningham refers to the six-week period of tragedy in Cretan waters as 'a disastrous period in our naval history, a period of great tension and anxiety such as I have never experienced before or since'.

Exactly how great was the tension and anxiety for the Commander-in-Chief is difficult to communicate now. It is important to remember that while we are only concerned here with an investigation into the naval aspect of the Greek and Cretan entanglements, for Cunningham, Crete was only part of a total picture that embraced many other equally important issues. It was his concern to sustain the besieged garrison of Malta, in the face of unremitting aerial bombardment, by fighting convoys through the Narrows to the beleagured island, operations which took on the importance of major fleet actions. He had to blockade the Axis forces on the Libyan coast and to maintain the supply of the British desert armies and the fortress of Tobruk. The Mediterranean Fleet had to be kept at almost instant readiness to sally out to intercept and engage an enemy battle fleet should it venture out to sea. It was his concern to operate the 10th Submarine Flotilla from Malta's Lazaretto Creek and even at times to station an offensive squadron of cruisers and destroyers at Malta.

Admiral Cunningham also held himself and the ships under his command in readiness to undertake any other hazardous operation that the Admiralty might order, such as a naval bombardment of an enemy port or the ill-advised recommendation to scuttle the battleship *Barham* in the port of Tripoli, a project which upon sober reflection was happily abandoned.

There were additional tasks thrust upon the Mediterranean Fleet, brought about by the ebb and flow of war: such a task was the transportation and the escorting of an army of 58,000 troops to Greece and then, within a short month of completing this huge task, the dispiriting duty of rescuing them all and evacuating them to Crete and Egypt. Cunningham bore all these ordeals with characteristic courage and sturdy defiance. He had an enor-

[2] *A Sailor's Odyssey* by Admiral of the Fleet Viscount Cunningham of Hyndhope, Hutchinson, 1951.

mous capacity to deal with adversity. He dominated the naval scene in the Mediterranean like an Olympian figure, towering over his adversaries and colleagues. One eminent naval historian[3] declared that the ultimate triumph of the Mediterranean Fleet was due 'to his relentless tenacity in holding the Eastern Mediterranean throughout those pregnant months when defeat was staring us in the face, to his unfailing grasp of the essential meaning of maritime power, to his courage in adversity and brilliance in victory'.

What, then, was achieved by this Olympian figure and the naval sacrifices at Crete? The British feared that the occupation of the island would act as the first stepping stone in an offensive against British interests in the Middle East. With Crete now safely neutralised Hitler could take one step across to Cyprus, a further stride would take him to the lush oilfields of Syria and Iraq while another would encompass even Persia. The pipe dream did not stop there. On the southern front Rommel's *Afrika Korps,* now enjoying virtual command of the desert air, could apply the other claw of a pincer movement to take into its grip the fleet base of Alexandria, the capital Cairo and one of the greatest prizes of all, the Suez Canal. With Wavell having failed to relieve invested Tobruk at the end of May and the Germans having advanced to Halfaya, the claws of the pincer seemed likely to clamp together with frightening finality.

Cunningham's Mediterranean Fleet, now in desperate straits, viewed the prospect of survival despondently for the hard-learned and unwelcome lesson had been driven home powerfully, that the war in the Middle East and the Eastern Mediterranean hinged more and more upon the possession of airfields. Because the Germans understood this lesson and linked their tactics to a domination of the air, the dangers for the Mediterranean Fleet loomed larger than ever.

Almost every naval departure from Alexandria was now exposed to risk. The *Luftwaffe* in Crete now commanded the northern flank. The *Luftwaffe* in Cyrenaica now commanded the

[3] Lieutenant-Commander Peter Kemp: see his *Victory at Sea,* Frederick Muller, 1958.

southern flank. Each British warship leaving Alexandria had to run the gauntlet of *Luftwaffe* attacks.

Nor could the presence of the Italian Fleet, disinclined though it might be to venture out to sea, be discounted. Its four battleships and twelve cruisers, with supporting destroyers and submarines, posed a latent threat even greater than before the Cretan battles.

But in fact none of these fears came to pass. The German attack upon Russia in June 1941 changed events in the Mediterranean dramatically. Cyprus no longer became a serious target. The plan to invade Malta in the summer of 1942—Operation Hercules—was put aside. Alexandria, Cairo and the Suez Canal were spared. The insurrectionary government of Iraq was put down. Syria and Persia remained unscathed. Crete, hard-won at the cost of the lives of thousands of young Germans, proved useless to the victors, save as a latent threat to the Mediterranean's northern flank.

The losers could claim, with some justification, that the Crete operation delayed the German attack upon Russia by one month, and thus prevented the fall of Moscow before the snows of 1941 engulfed the advancing German divisions.

The *Luftwaffe,* committed in strength to the Russian front, could spare nothing to exploit the victory of Crete and the advantage of the island's geographical position. Perhaps as a consolation the Germans might put the island to good use as a forward staging post for their supplies to North Africa. But even this modest benefit was denied them for the ironic, tragi-comic reason that the Greek railways were quite incapable of handling the necessary traffic to transport the stores.

The island of Crete, after its bloody and convulsive battle, reposed—perhaps deservedly—for the rest of the war in a peaceful, undisturbed sleep.

CHAPTER 1

Mediterranean
Background

By THE SPRING of 1941 British fortunes in World War II were reaching their nadir. Victor of campaigns which surpassed those of Napoleon nearly a century-and-a-half before, Hitler stood like a Colossus, undisputed conqueror of the continent of Europe. Even those countries which still lay outside his military occupation were, nevertheless, subject to Hitler's influence, and rested in uneasy accommodation with the dictator.

Nations toppled like empty bottles. In the uneasy late 'thirties, the Saar, Austria and Czechoslovakia had submitted to the German invaders without opposition. Poland, in September 1939, was the first nation to offer organised military resistance to Hitler's aggression and her courageous action embroiled the world in war. With traditional patriotism the Poles fought doggedly in defence of their native land, but the Stuka bombers and the Panzer divisions crushed the opposition with a violent, convulsive display of arms.

A few months later the German tanks clattered and rumbled throught the streets of Denmark, while simultaneously the battle for Norway developed as the Norwegians fought to repel the German invaders. But this campaign, which lay finely balanced for some days, culminated in the evacuation of the small British force hastily transported to Scandinavia to give support to the Norwegian forces. It was the first major British clash of arms with the Germans since 1918. And it was a defeat experienced in the coldness of a Norwegian spring.

Further south, within a few short weeks of the Norwegian victory, the *Wehrmacht* demonstrated its power in another display of ruthlessness as more armoured divisions thundered into Holland and Belgium and France. As the cool spring of 1940 gave way to early summer, the days grew hotter and drier. Resistance by the Belgians and the Dutch was ferocious but brief and no sooner had their forces been swept aside than the full weight of the German war machine was hurled upon the French armies and the smaller British Expeditionary Force, which reeled back like flotsam and jetsam on an advancing wave. The BEF elbowed its way through streams of refugees towards the sea and rescue. France collapsed. The BEF was snatched from ignominious surrender from the beaches of Dunkirk, a nine days wonder made possible by the British command of the sea.

The Nazi swastika fluttered confidently over the capitals of Europe and Hitler extracted vengeance from the French in a railway compartment in the forest of Compiègne.

England, next victim on Hitler's list of conquests, lay naked and lamentably ill-prepared to meet the threatened onslaught. Her army, it is true, was no match for the might of the *Wehrmacht*. It had scuttled away from the advancing tide of German militarism offering only pockets of resistance until the perimeter around Dunkirk was formed and the ferocity of the British defence enabled 350,000 Allied troops to cross the Channel to safety. But Britain possessed a number of tangible assets. Not least among these was the recently appointed Prime Minister, Winston S. Churchill.

He came to power when all appeared lost and the German's apparent invincibility made the British attempts at defiance seem absurdly puny. But Churchill possessed the remarkable ability to give the roar to the seemingly dormant British lion. With an eloquence of rare brilliance he rallied the nation and roused a fierce combative spirit.

Hitler prepared for an assault upon the south coast of England, but he failed to achieve supremacy in the air. Aircraft of Fighter Command of the RAF battled with the bombers of the *Luftwaffe*, staved off the invasion and won the Battle of Britain.

One other asset of incomparable importance was the Royal

Navy's command of the sea. Even had the *Luftwaffe* achieved domination of the Channel skies and so enabled the armada of landing barges to quit Boulogne, the Royal Navy stood guard, waiting, as so often in her history; her destroyer flotillas and cruiser squadrons mobilised and ready to disrupt the invasion attempt even before the barges ground on to English beaches.

*

In the Mediterranean theatre Britain possessed a fleet of substance, commanded by a man of outstanding courage, Admiral Sir Andrew Cunningham.

With the fall of France, Italy's dictator, eager to participate in the changing pattern of Europe, committed his nation to the gross blunder of alliance with Germany. It was not his only blunder. As well as over-estimating Germany's military power, he under-estimated the seapower of the Royal Navy. He is not alone in history in having done so. But his miscalculations of all maritime matters in the Mediterranean in stark contrast with Cunningham's sure grasp of naval strategy, revealed an abysmal ignorance which led directly to the defeat of his country, the surrender of his fleet and his own grisly death.

So eager was he to precipitate Italy into hostilities and thus harvest some of the spoils of war that he failed to observe some elementary precautions. On the day that Italy entered the war no less than 1.2 million tons of Italian merchant shipping was operating in waters outside the Mediterranean. This vast tonnage of ships, representing one-third of Italy's substantial merchant fleet, and comprising some fine ships earning foreign currency, were denied the chance of running for a home port. These ships were now committed to seek refuge in neutral harbours; many sought the sanctuary of Italian East African ports while others scuttled themselves to avoid capture. Yet more surrendered or were captured while in British ports. Mussolini, with an almost complete disregard for his merchant fleet's dispositions, lost to his country a much needed facility, for Italy's geographical position much like Great Britain's, made her dependent upon a thriving merchant fleet. Only one month's delay in declaring war would have ensured the safety of about one million tons of much needed shipping for this nation.

Nor is this all. If one considers the status of his much-vaunted navy, a blunder of almost equal proportions was perpetrated. In June 1940 Italy possessed six battleships, four of which were the modernised ships *Andrea Doria, Caio Duilio, Conte di Cavour* and the *Giulio Cesare,* and the other two were the new ships *Littorio* and *Vittorio Veneto.* But only two of these six were ready for action, and these two were not the best. It would have taken no more than a few weeks to complete the re-equipping and modernisation programme and the re-commissioning of the remaining battleships. It was a loss from which Italy never fully recovered.

But Mussolini was not the first to underrate the importance of seapower in waging war. His wartime grand strategy, if it can be so called, paid scant attention to the functions of the navy. He appeared to declare war so precipitately that operational plans had not been formulated let alone a grand strategy prepared. And this amazing, inept situation was allowed to persist throughout the duration of the Italian participation in the war, with Italy reacting to events, rarely initiating them, and allowing herself to be dominated by a stronger partner.

Account must be taken of German influence over Italian strategy. Mussolini made it clear that it was his intention of conducting 'a parallel war, not with or for Germany, but only for Italy at the side of Germany'. This declared intention appeared to have made small impact upon German military thinking; the Mediterranean at that time was regarded as unimportant to Germany. Admiral Raeder, the Commander-in-Chief of the German Navy, expounded his views on the great possibilities in this theatre to Hitler on two occasions in September 1940, but Hitler was unwilling to initiate joint strategy with the Italians at that time.

If Germany lacked interest in the Mediterranean theatre in the summer and autumn of 1940, this was not so with the British War Cabinet and the Chiefs of Staff. Italy's intervention, burdensome though it was, was not only no surprise but had long been

24

expected. Plans had been formulated with the French as early as May 1939, several months before the outbreak of World War II. This general plan had as its foundation a strong French Fleet in the Western Mediterranean, a basis completely different from that which now obtained since the surrender of France and the denial to the British of French naval support. The resultant vacuum caused a rapid review of Middle East strategy and the British Chiefs of Staff prepared a memorandum which specified the minimum requirements for the successful prosecution of the war in that theatre: the complete denial of Egypt and the Sudan to the enemy in order to safeguard the Suez Canal: the successful defence of Iraq in order to preserve oil supplies from Iraq and Persia, and of Palestine because it controlled the oil terminus at Haifa; of Aden, to control the Red Sea shipping route; and of Kenya as a second line of defence should Egypt fall.

The effective implementation of this policy made enormous demands upon the Royal Navy, for it rested upon the Navy's ability to keep open the ocean and sea routes to ensure the flow of troops and essential material to the Middle East. It was upon this rock foundation that British Mediterranean strategy was built. But for the Navy it was a burden almost too heavy to shoulder.

The Italian declaration of war immediately closed the Mediterranean as a seaway for normal shipping. Troop reinforcements, material supplies, armour and ammunition now had to be routed to the Eastern Mediterranean on the long haul round the Cape of Good Hope, straining the Navy's resources at a time when the invasion of England seemed imminent. This latter threat demanded the retention of scores of destroyers, cruiser squadrons and a host of minor vessels in Home waters to repel any seaborne invasion.[1]

British naval resources were stretched to almost unendurable limits. Admiral Sir Charles Forbes, Commander-in-Chief of the

[1] Four destroyer flotillas—based at Harwich, Humber, Sheerness and either Dover or Portsmouth—were to spearhead the attacking force, closely supported by eight cruisers. These ships—and the Home Fleet—were ordered to accept almost any risk in order to close action with a seaborne invasion force.

Home Fleet, mirrored strong opinions when he protested against the immobilisation of his destroyers and cruisers on standby anti-invasion duties, when they were sorely needed elsewhere. But the War Office decision prevailed; the ships remained on standby duty and the problem of escorting the ocean and coastal convoys became magnified.

The collapse of France worsened a situation made difficult by the successive downfall of Norway, Holland and Belgium. The fall of Norway in the spring of 1940 made a dramatic impact upon the war at sea. Germany acquired additional air bases in Norway and the passage of U-boats to their operational areas was shortened by 1,200 miles or more, which permitted them longer time on their Atlantic stations. An intensification of attacks on the convoys was awaited by the Admiralty with foreboding.

Now, within just a few weeks of this distressing situation having arisen, there came the additional burden of coping with problems arising from the fall of the Low Countries and France. The capture by the Germans of valuable airfields in these overrun countries imposed an immediate strain upon the Navy's resources. No longer did Britannia rule the waves in the Channel. British coastal convoys now became the target for regular air and E-boat attack, while Germany's coastal shipping could now shelter under the protective umbrella of escorting aircraft. Furthermore, the passage of U-boats through the Channel to the Atlantic was now greatly facilitated.

More important still was the German capture of the French Atlantic ports. The Germans saw the strategic advantage of possessing these ports as U-boat bases, and they hurriedly set in train the necessary repairs to make good the extensive damage wrought by the Allied demolitions. These Allied delaying tactics served little purpose. The first U-boat entered Lorient in July 1940. Within days Brest was opened and a little later, La Pallice. Furthermore, a long-range air reconnaissance unit was established at Lorient by the first week in August to assist in the Battle of the Atlantic. The resultant onslaught on the shipping lanes in the Atlantic brought a steep rise in the tonnage of Allied shipping sunk in the ensuing months.

The implications of Germany's redoubled efforts in the Atlantic were quite clear to the British. The need for more escorts for convoy duty assumed an even greater urgency than before. The number of destroyers, in particular, was woefully inadequate for the tasks heaped upon the Navy. At the time of the French collapse no less than sixty-six British destroyers out of a grand total of 178 were undergoing repair. The anti-invasion flotillas, as we have seen, enjoyed top priority rating and were maintained at full strength regardless of the desperate need for destroyers elsewhere.

It was against this background of collapsing Allies, of impending onslaught on Atlantic convoy routes, of imminent invasion, of severely curtailed naval resources spread thinly like a veneer over the oceans of the world, that Admiral Sir Andrew Cunningham, Commander-in-Chief Mediterranean Fleet, faced the might of the Italian Navy.

*

The Italian Navy in June 1940 consisted of six battleships, nineteen cruisers, forty-five destroyers with another thirty vessels in the 600–700 ton range, and about 120 submarines. There were also thirty torpedo boats and more than sixty anti-submarine MTBS which the Italians called Motoscarfi Anti-Sommergibili or MAS.

The four smaller battleships had been built during World War I but they had all been reconstructed and modernised during the period 1933–40. All four carried a main armament of ten 12.6 inch guns and a secondary armament of a dozen 4.7 inch or 5.3 inch guns. All had a designed speed of 27 knots.

The *Vittorio Veneto* and *Littorio*[2] were both brand new ships of a new class. They had just been completed but were not yet fully commissioned. They carried an impressive main armament of nine 15 inch guns, supported by twelve 6 inch, and were

[2] The *Littorio* suffered a chequered career including being torpedoed three times as well as being renamed *Italia* in August 1943.

capable of a top speed of 30 knots. In size and power of armament they closely resembled the *King George V* class of British battleship.

The cruiser strength of the Italian Navy rested largely upon the seven 10,000 ton ships with their 8 inch guns. These were fine looking ships, built in the early 1930s, with impressive top speeds ranging well above 30 knots.

The light cruisers, each carrying eight 6 inch guns, except the *Guissepe Garibaldi* and the *Duca degli Abruzzi* which had ten apiece, were even speedier vessels with designed speeds of up to 37 knots. All of them had been completed within the last decade.

A significant omission from the Italian Fleet was aircraft carriers.[3] But the absence of these ships did not signify an absence of supporting aircraft. The proximity of homeland air bases together with those in the Dodecanese and North Africa provided ample cover for naval operations in the Mediterranean. The size of the Italian Air Force at the time of Italy's entry into the war is variously reported, but generally thought to be approximately 2,000 aircraft of all types described as first line, with another 400–500 in reserve, including trainers and miscellaneous. These aircraft were not, of course, under the control of the navy. And herein lay the navy's trouble.

The Italian Navy did not possess its own fleet air arm and had no direct control over any aircraft—including torpedo bombers—except those aircraft actually carried aboard ships and a handful of reconnaissance aircraft. Whenever the Italian Commander-in-Chief Afloat needed air support he signalled the Italian Admiralty (*Supermarina*) who then applied to the Air Ministry (*Superaereo*). This cumbersome procedure was too slow for modern warfare and was unable to cope with rapidly changing situations afloat. Nor was the Italian Air Force well equipped with torpedo-carrying aircraft, and its massed high-level bombing

[3] The German historian Admiral Friedrich Ruge in his *Sea Warfare 1939–1945*, Cassell, claims that the Italian Navy's request for aircraft carriers had been rejected by Mussolini because of the abundance of airfields. No confirmation of this statement has been discovered, but it is a plausible claim and accords generally with Mussolini's lack of maritime knowledge.

tactics against British ships with relatively small bombs proved much less effective than the later dive-bombing techniques of the *Luftwaffe* pilots.

Nevertheless, the size of the Italian Air Force was impressive and it made the size of the British Fleet Air Arm and RAF contribution in the Mediterranean appear puny by comparison.

On paper this modern and modernised navy of speedy, well-armed vessels presented an impressive spectacle. But this is precisely the political motive of the Fascist government. It has set out to impress the world. But behind the façade the Italian Navy was seen to be lacking in a number of important features. These were only dimly suspected at the time. Suspicions grew fast after a short period of war had elapsed and units of the Italian and British navies had engaged in combat. It was not simply a question of the Italian ships having achieved their high speeds at the expense of protective armour. Although many of the Italian problems stemmed from this deficiency, there were many other factors contributing to their ineffectiveness.

While the guns and torpedo armaments of the ships were sound enough, they lacked adequate anti-aircraft protection, a common failing in all navies early in the war. Perhaps the greatest deficiency in the Italian Navy was its lack of RDF, or radar, as it was later called. This was a significant advantage possessed by the Royal Navy in encounters with the Italians: especially was this so in the night action of the Battle of Matapan where the Italian admiral was virtually blindfolded by the darkness of night.

Italian ships also sacrificed armour and design for luxurious officer accommodation and by cosseting features such as the bridges of quite small ships like destroyers being enclosed to afford shelter from the moderate Mediterranean climate. By contrast British officers and men on the bridge of Royal Navy ships were expected to endure the bitterness of North Atlantic storms and iciness of Arctic patrols; the Mediterranean climate by comparison was mild and clement. This pampering of the officers—the luxury of their accommodation, furniture and fittings, wines and food—contrasted sadly with the spartan lot of the ratings. A gulf existed between officers and men which discipline did nothing to bridge. Punishment for quite minor offences was severe. Officers gave scant attention to the welfare of their men with the result that a team spirit was lacking, and in times of stress discipline tended to break down.

The Italian Navy lacked an inherent maritime tradition which manifested itself in a number of ways, perhaps most significantly in the way it failed to pursue intensive training programmes. Night exercises were sketchy. Daytime exercises were abandoned if bad weather intervened or heavy seas were encountered. This failure to imbue a toughness in the officers and men was made evident almost every time the Italian Navy encountered the Royal Navy. Cunningham's experience in time of war and peace had taught him that war was won by defeating the enemy's mind. He had no great difficulty in inflicting this defeat upon the Italian Navy.

Perhaps the greatest weakness of the Italian Navy was the hierarchical organisation of *Supermarina,* the Navy's supreme operational command which governed conduct of all its operations at sea, with its headquarters in the Naval Ministry in Rome.

Heading this organisation was the Chief of Staff of the Navy who bore the additional responsibility of serving as Under Secretary of State for the Navy with the burden of a Ministry. He discussed all operational problems with Mussolini, the Supreme Commander of the Armed Forces, and with the Italian Supreme Command. In practice, the operational direction of *Supermarina* came under the Deputy Chief of Staff who was probably better informed on naval matters and better briefed on all facets of the naval situation than his superior who necessarily concerned himself with politics.

The Italian Navy thus suffered by being able to wield only weak influence upon the Supreme Command, which itself had a limited understanding of the strategy of naval warfare. Cunningham, and his staff, by contrast, understood their subject with crystal clarity. Cunningham summarised his intentions succinctly: 'Our object is to control the sea communications of the Mediterranean' and his fleet was set to work to achieve this major strategic concept on which all else depended.

A serious defect of the *Supermarina* organisation was its tendency to centralise the functions of command. This had the unhappy consequence that commanders of fleets or squadrons at sea, always conscious of the senior officers in the nerve centre of the efficient Operations Room in Rome, tended to wait for orders from them, or they signalled—and the Italian Navy's communications system was excellent—*Supermarina* requesting instructions.

This reliance upon *Supermarina* tended to take away from officers at sea that initiative and imaginative flair so often displayed by British officers; and often, too, the *Supermarina* officers omitted to issue instructions for fear of taking away the initiative from the officers on the spot—thus falling between two stools.

Incidents occurred when Italian commanding officers, at sea in superior strength and in favourable circumstances, were ordered by *Supermarina* to disengage, a decision dominated by the fear of sustaining losses.

Mussolini's Navy lacked one other ingredient: tradition. It had been founded in 1861 and it had no long lineage to give it a sense of confidence and pride. The Royal Navy, asserting its ancient strength through centuries of shifting maritime fortunes, had a long history of tradition to call upon and from which to draw strength. But it takes more than tradition and history to mould a fighting fleet. Constant exercising; regular routine in peace-time; the production of professional seamen who know the sea and their ships intimately; a combative spirit; these are all prime considerations for a fleet in being.

The Italian Navy lacked the combative instinct which permeated the ranks of the Royal Navy. This is exemplified by the revelation that in Italian East Africa Italy had seven old destroyers, two torpedo boats, eight new submarines and some MAS. Records reveal that no less than 590 British convoys steamed within sight of the Italian observation posts. Yet only two of these convoys were ever attacked—and in both cases the outcome was unimpressive and inconclusive. Furthermore, only one ship was sunk by all the submarines stationed in this area. The lack

31

of success of the Italian units displays an appalling lack of combative spirit.

The British Mediterranean Fleet at the time of Italy's intervention in the war was manned by men who had already survived nine months of war. Furthermore, many of the men were veterans of World War I—as, indeed, were some of their ships. The interwar years were years well spent in training and exercising. In the Mediterranean a peacetime commission lasted two and a half years with an unchanging ship's company and a regular routine: spring cruises in the Western Mediterranean; service in the Central Mediterranean in the summer; and the Eastern basin for the winter and autumn months. Exercises were a dominant feature of the curriculum. The Mediterranean Fleet enjoyed a succession of Commanders-in-Chief who trained their ships to a high degree of efficiency, and a special ingredient of the exercising over a period of many years was the emphasis upon night-fighting which for a long time had been regarded as a perilous matter to be shunned for fear of jeopardising battle squadrons by making them vulnerable to swift destroyer and motor torpedo boat attack. Admiral Lord Chatfield initiated the night-fighting exercises and his policy was pursued by his successor, Admiral Fisher, by Admiral Pound and again by Admiral Cunningham, the Commander-in-Chief at the outbreak of World War II. He had assumed command in June 1939.

Andrew Browne Cunningham entered the Royal Navy at the age of fourteen in 1897. A year later he was a midshipman aboard the cruiser *Doris,* flagship at the Cape of Good Hope where he landed with the Naval Brigade during the Boer War. On his nineteenth birthday he was promoted to Sub-Lieutenant and a year later he began a long association with destroyers when he was appointed to the destroyer *Orwell*. By the outbreak of World War I Cunningham had already been in command of his own destroyer—the *Scorpion*—for three years. He saw action in the Gallipoli campaign and earned a mention in despatches and was awarded the DSO for his services.

From the Aegean he returned home to command destroyers in the Dover Patrol and he was present at the blocking of Zeebrugge.

For his distinguished service with the Dover Patrol he was awarded a bar to his DSO together with the Belgian *Croix de Guerre*. His had been an active war from which he emerged a much decorated Commander with a reputation for his single-minded devotion to the Royal Navy.

Immediately after the war he was awarded a third DSO for his action in command of the destroyer *Seafire* in the Baltic during the campaign against the Bolsheviks and von der Goltz.

From the command of destroyer flotillas he transferred to the America and West Indies Station where he became Flag Captain and Chief Staff Officer aboard HMS *Calcutta*. But it was 1929 before he finally left small ships to take command of the new battleship *Rodney,* an experience he found irksome for it lacked the dash and verve of destroyer command. By 1934 he was back with the smaller ships as Rear Admiral Destroyers, Mediterranean, flying his flag in the light cruiser *Coventry*. He was patently destined for higher office and only three years later he was Second in Command of the Mediterranean Fleet with his flag in the *Hood*. He had, by now, completed forty years service in the Navy.

In the summer of 1939, as the clouds of war overcast the skies in Europe, Admiral Sir Andrew Browne Cunningham, popularly referred to as ABC, became Commander-in-Chief of the Mediterranean and embarked upon the most testing period of his naval career. It began with almost deceptive ease. The first year of command was not beset by the magnitude of disasters that were to be heaped upon him in the succeeding years. While the eyes of the world focused upon the convulsive events taking place in other theatres of the war, Cunningham enjoyed a period of relative tranquility. Torment and harassment by the enemy were to follow in due course. It was June 1940 when the curtain went up on the stage set by Cunningham in the Mediterranean and he began to endure his trial by ordeal.

CHAPTER 2

Cunningham
in Command

THE BRITISH MEDITERRANEAN FLEET in June 1940, just one year after Admiral Cunningham assumed command, and at the time of the Italian intervention in the war, was in jeopardy. The Admiralty, contemplating its dispositions, at one time considered withdrawing the Mediterranean Fleet from the eastern basin and concentrating all Mediterranean forces at Gibraltar, thereby abandoning Malta to the mercies of the Italian Navy and Air Force. It is a measure of the desperate straits in which the British found themselves at that time that such a drastic step was contemplated. But wiser counsels prevailed. The Fleet remained based at Alexandria.

This vital decision taken early in the war at sea in the Mediterranean led to formidable and fateful events which in turn led on to ultimate victory.

The ships which comprised the Fleet at that time were four battleships: the *Warspite, Malaya, Royal Sovereign* and *Ramilles;* one aircraft carrier, the *Eagle;* the 7th Cruiser Squadron comprising the *Orion, Neptune, Sydney, Liverpool, Gloucester;* the 3rd Cruiser Squadron comprising the *Capetown, Caledon, Calypso* and *Delhi;* there were twenty-five destroyers comprising 'D', 'H', 'I', 'J', 'K', and Tribal Class ships with the *Stuart*'s Australian flotilla of ancient 'V' and 'W' Class destroyers. There were also twelve submarines in the fleet.

Two thousand miles away at the other end of the Mediterranean, Force H under Admiral Sir John Somerville, commanded the Straits of Gibraltar. His force comprised one battle cruiser, two battleships, one aircraft carrier and eleven destroyers.

With Somerville dominating the western Straits and Cunningham guarding the eastern exit, the Royal Navy's investment of the Mediterranean, tenuous though it was during the clamorous months and years ahead, was staunch and unyielding.

At a moment of dire peril for Great Britain on what seemed to be the eve of invasion, the Admiralty saw fit to station in the Mediterranean half her complement of capital ships and thirty-three of the available destroyers, a measure of the importance attached to the Mediterranean theatre, and, incidentally, of the Home Fleet's ability to meet the threatened German invasion.

At this time, too, the British had the support of the French Fleet. At the time of the French collapse the French squadron in the Eastern Mediterranean under the command of Vice Admiral R. E. Godfroy comprised the battleship *Lorraine*, three 8 inch and one 6 inch gun cruisers and three small destroyers.

The unhappy and tragic episode at Mers el Kebir where Somerville's force opened fire on the French Atlantic Fleet and the painful though bloodless episode at Alexandria where Admiral Godfroy yielded to overwhelming force have no place in this record. The general effect of the neutralisation of the French Navy was to produce an imbalance of naval power in the Mediterranean. Whereas the combined forces of the French Fleet, the British Mediterranean Fleet and Force H substantially outweighed the strength of the Italian Navy, the scales were now counter balanced and—on paper at any rate—the Italian Fleet assumed a superiority in destroyer, submarine, light and heavy cruiser categories. In the battleship category it appeared to have a numerical superiority but in actuality it probably only achieved parity and in the aircraft carrier category it failed to match the British possession of the carrier *Eagle*. However, to outbalance possession of this obsolescent carrier, the Italians could range the massive power of about 2,000 aircraft of the *Regia Aeronautica*.

Thus, the initiative lay with the Italian Navy. Mussolini had signalled a worthless directive to the navy to assume 'the offensive at all points in the Mediterranean and outside'. Admiral Cavagnari the Naval Chief of Staff, disregarding the directive, embarked upon a more defensive strategy, except in the disposition of submarines, fifty-five of which were out on patrol in June 1940. But before the end of the month nine of these had been sunk and hurried reassessments in patrols and numbers at sea were being made. The Italian submarine arm never assumed the importance its numbers merited.

One of the prime functions of the Mediterranean Fleet in the early weeks of the war against Italy was the denial to the Italians of the Eastern Mediterranean, the Aegean, the Ionian and the Levant where the Royal Navy provided a front line of defence for the oilfields in the deserts of Iraq and Persia.

This huge area was one well-known to the Commander-in-Chief who saw service there during World War I. Indeed, the British seaman tended to know the area far better than his adversary because of the seasonal cruises operated by the Mediterranean Fleet in peacetime.

Perhaps Cunningham's main preoccupation in his capacity as Commander-in-Chief, was his concern for the defence and safety of Malta. Within hours of the Italian intervention in the war her bombers, based only thirty minutes flying time away, were beginning a bombardment of the island that was to continue for three years of almost relentless battering.

With her sister island of Gozo, Malta nestled comfortably in the Central Mediterranean barely twelve hours steaming time from the Italian Fleet base at Taranto. Malta lay almost undefended, vulnerable to assault by a resolute enemy, but she was to be spared invasion, partly because of the intervention of the Cretan episode, and instead she was to be reduced almost to rubble by aerial bombardment.

The first skirmish between opposing fleets occurred early in July 1940. The action, which arose from two important convoy operations became known as the Skirmish off Calabria to the British and of Punta Stilo to the Italians. Five troopships sailed from Naples to Benghazi with close cover provided by Admiral Campioni's force of the two battleships *Guilo Cesare* and *Conte di Cavour,* six heavy cruisers, twelve light cruisers and twenty-four destroyers. Air reconnaissance was provided from the Dodecanese and from Cyrenaica, and submarines provided remote cover.

The following day, on July 7th, 1940, Admiral Cunningham sailed from Alexandria with the three battleships *Warspite, Royal Sovereign* and *Malaya,* the carrier *Eagle,* four light cruisers and sixteen destroyers. They were to give cover to two convoys from Malta to Alexandria. The first convoy comprised three ships taking evacuees from the island; the second consisted of four ships carrying supplies.

On July 8th Cunningham's Fleet was to the south of Crete when it was subjected to a high level bombing attack by a large force of Italian bombers. One cruiser suffered slight damage.

On July 9th this force intercepted the Italian force, now returning to Taranto after safely delivering its convoy to North Africa. An inconclusive engagement ensued, firstly between the cruisers and then the battleships. The Italian cruiser *Bolzano* was hit. But events then took a more dramatic turn. At 1553, at a range of 26,000 yards, a 15 inch shell from the *Warspite* struck the leading enemy battleship with a distinctive orange-coloured flash. Admiral Campioni turned his damaged flagship, the *Cesare,* away, broke off the engagement and withdrew to the west behind a thick blanket of smoke while his destroyers launched a half-hearted torpedo attack. Cunningham's force turned away, but later resumed the chase, abandoning it only twenty-five miles off Calabria.

Torpedo bombing attacks by British aircraft and high level bombing attacks by Italian aircraft failed to score any hits despite the *Warspite* being subjected to twenty-two attacks during the passage back to base.

The failure of all the aircraft engaged to score decisive hits called for special examination by both contestants. It was the British torpedo bombers' failure to reduce the enemy's speed which ensured its escape. But there was one significant factor to emerge from this skirmish. The single hit that the *Warspite* scored achieved a result quite out of proportion to its destructive power. It was the last time Italian battleships willingly faced British battleships in combat.

But the skirmish is of importance for one other reason; it was the first in a series of steps which helped establish Cunningham's moral ascendancy over the Italians in the Mediterranean. It was an ascendancy which was never relinquished. Admiral Iachino was to be given the opportunity to seize back the ascendancy of the war at sea less than a year later during the evacuation from Crete, but he cast aside the chance. It never appeared again.

This ascendancy was lent emphasis by Captain Collins's action ten days after the Calabria clash. He commanded the Australian cruiser *Sydney*. He was in company with four British destroyers when they intercepted and sank Admiral Casardi's flagship, the cruiser *Bartolomeo Colleoni* and damaged the *Giovanni Delle Bande Nere* in a spirited action to which the Italians later gave the rather grandiose title the Battle of Cape Spada.

Time and again in the ensuing weeks and months the Royal Navy asserted her dominance at sea. Late in August the Mediterranean Fleet in the Eastern Mediterranean and Force H in the west provided cover for a Malta convoy and although Italian naval forces were at sea, the British convoys and escorts went unmolested. Yet the Italian Navy's two new battleships *Vittorio Veneto* and the *Littorio* and the modernised *Caio Duilio* and the *Andrea Doria* had now joined the fleet.

In September and October two more complex convoy operations through the Narrows were completed without intervention by the Italian Navy. Then, in late October, events in the Mediterranean theatre flared dangerously as war spread to the Balkans. It was on October 28th, 1940, that Italy presented an ultimatum to Greece which plunged the two countries into war. For a while the eyes of the world focused on this new explosive area in the Mediterranean. And it is to this location we must now turn in order to see how this stupid act of aggression by Mussolini for his personal aggrandisement led ultimately to the German attack upon the island of Crete.

*

On August 15th, 1940, the tiny Greek cruiser *Helle* lay at anchor off the mole of Tinos in the Cyclades. It was a peaceful visit.

The 2,083 ton cruiser, barely larger than a destroyer flotilla leader, presented a gay scene, the bright summer sunshine adding to the colour of the bunting and flags which decorated her overall. She—and the estimated 40,000 people ashore—were there to celebrate the Feast of the Assumption of the Virgin Mary, to the Greeks second only to Easter Sunday as a sacred day. Suddenly three torpedoes from an Italian submarine were fired at the *Helle*. Two of them missed even this stationary target exploding as they struck the quayside. But the third torpedo struck home and the cruiser sank at her anchorage.

This cowardly attack was followed just over two months later by Italy's invasion of Greece. Mussolini's ultimatum of unacceptable demands was followed almost immediately by force of arms as Italian troops crossed the border into Greece. War ensued and to the *Duce*'s chagrin his invading forces were repulsed as surely as his armies were to be repulsed in the campaigns in the Western Desert, in Eritrea and Abyssinia.

As early as the beginning of July the Governor of the Dodecanese had informed Rome that British ships and possibly British aircraft were being given supplies and refuge in Greece, since when Mussolini had been projecting an attack on that country through Albania. On October 12th he came to the decision to invade, revealing, incidentally, that it was Hitler's unexpected occupation of Rumania to safeguard the oilfield of Ploesti for the Axis, that prompted this decision. 'Hitler always presents me with a *fait accompli*. This time I am going to pay him back in his own coin. He will find out from the papers that I have occupied Greece.' He wrote to Hitler on October 22nd, the day the *Führer* was on his way to meet General Franco at Hendaye.

Hitler's decision to visit Franco in the autumn of 1940 stemmed from Germany's failure to win the Battle of Britain. He brooded disconsolately upon the failure to crush England. He viewed with dismay the consequences of his failure: in place of a war of short duration he had now become committed to a prolonged struggle with the added fear of waging war on more than one front. Great Britain, if she declined to surrender, could be left in watery isolation, even though she possessed a considerable navy—hard-pressed though it was by the U-boat menace—which formed a giant ring of armour investing Germany from North Cape via Gibraltar to Alexandria.

Hitler, unlike Churchill at this early stage of the war, could not see the defeat and humiliation that was his country's ultimate fate. Churchill saw the broad path of war stretching its serpentine route ahead towards victory with almost prescient certainty. He based much of his reasoning on three factors. Firstly, Hitler could not win the war unless he invaded and conquered the British Isles. This possibility receded further and further as each day of war passed: the opportunities which Hitler had grasped so far in his tempestuous career were as nothing compared with this one, major failure by his mighty *Wehrmacht* which had thundered across Europe, then stopped at the Channel ports as if brought to a halt by just one missing link in the chain of destiny.

Secondly, Hitler could not win the war unless he won the desperately contested Battle of the Atlantic. This possibility was always in evidence. The mounting losses of shipping in the treacherous North Atlantic brought Britain perilously close to defeat; yet, despite the burden of these losses, Churchill confidently believed that with the help of material and equipment from the USA the U-boat menace would be mastered. 'Give us the tools,' he had urged the Americans, 'and we will finish the job.'

Thirdly, Hitler could not win the war if the USA threw off the cloak of partial neutrality and entered the war alongside the British. Churchill saw clearly that the increasing involvement of the USA in the war—despite technical neutrality—would ensure, as far as anyone can ensure anything in war, ultimate victory against Germany.

Hitler was not unaware of the difficulties and problems which beset him in the autumn of 1940. If he was unable to turn westwards to conquer Britain, then he could look eastwards and southwards. And this he proceeded to do, warily and uneasily, like a fugitive glowering over his shoulder at the spectre of the USA in the far-away shadows. Covetously he focused his attention upon the broad wheatlands and the vast oilfields of the Russias.

Therein lay his country's succouring in the event of prolonged war: the food for his nation: the oil for his machines of war. But the Russian bear stood a silent and threatening sentinel from the snows of Finland in the north to the fields of Rumania in the south, ready to grapple and struggle. Her turn was to come, but now, to Hitler, it seemed that easier pickings presented themselves. The south offered a warmer invitation. The prospects were more appealing. There were three choices, all of them with their own peculiar attractions.

The first and most obvious choice, was to send an army to strengthen the Italian Army in Libya. An Axis thrust along the Egyptian coastal strip could result in the capture of the fleet base at Alexandria, the Suez Canal itself and Cairo. The East would lay invitingly at Germany's booted feet.

Hitler's second choice lay under the auspices of the Spanish dictator, General Franco. Perhaps, Hitler reasoned, the General could be bribed with the offer of Gibraltar and French Morocco to allow German troops to cross Spanish territory to attack Gibraltar and Portugal. Such a move would enable Hitler to capture the Atlantic islands—the Azores, the Canaries—and to deny Britain the use of Dakar, a factor appreciated by Admiral Raeder[1] and mentioned on more than one occasion to Hitler. This campaign[2] would also deny Britain use of the Western Mediterranean by control of Gibraltar.

It was with the object of persuading Franco to permit the use of his country for the transit of his armies that Hitler visited Hendaye in October. It has not been revealed what took place at this meeting but it is known that Franco, greedy and obstinate, made demands upon Hitler which were quite unacceptable. Franco had been impressed by the British attack upon the French Squadron at Oran, and he probably realised better than Hitler the value in war of command of the seas. Britain, he reasoned,

[1] Commander-in-Chief's report to Hitler, *Führer Naval Conferences,* September 6th, 1940.

[2] *Hitler's War Directives* by H. R. Trevor-Roper, Sidgwick & Jackson, 1964. See Directive No 18 dated November 12th, 1940.

was not as played out as Hitler would have him believe. And Germany, significantly, had not yet invaded the British Isles.

The *Führer* departed in anger, stating he would rather have three or four teeth out than go through the experience again. Operation Felix[3] was doomed before it was even fully planned.

The third choice for the Germans lay in the Balkans. In the same war directive—No 18—in which he announced preparatory measures for the Iberian campaign, Hitler directed: 'The Balkans. Commander-in-Chief Army will be prepared, if necessary, to occupy from Bulgaria the Greek mainland north of the Aegean Sea. This will enable the German Air Force to attack targets in the Eastern Mediterranean, and in particular those English air-bases which threaten the Rumanian oil fields.'[4]

Hitler's feelings on hearing of Mussolini's attack upon Greece, after his angry parting from an intransigent Franco, can be imagined. His disapproval was not lessened when, within less than three weeks, the numerically superior invaders had been thrown out of Greek territory and Italy once more became the laughing stock of Europe. Hitler determined to let Mussolini stew in his own juice—at least temporarily.

For the British, the Italian invasion brought both a lessening and a heightening of anxiety and tension. The Greek Government immediately invoked the assurance given by Neville Chamberlain in April 1939, a guarantee that Britain was bound to honour, despite her many commitments elsewhere. Apart from a few dozen aircraft, a British mission and a token force of troops, there was precious little assistance Britain could afford to give Greece.

For Admiral Cunningham there was one important strategic advantage, a prize to be snatched from under the noses of the Italian invaders. Crete, with its fine natural harbour of Suda Bay, afforded a valuable advanced fuelling base for naval operations in the Central Mediterranean. At the invitation of the Greek Government Suda Bay was occupied by British forces just three days after the Italian attack. Early in the morning of October 29th a joint Services reconnaissance party arrived in Crete and

---

[3] The German codename for the capture of Gibraltar.
[4] *Hitler's War Directives*, H. R. Trevor-Roper.

that afternoon a convoy left Alexandria for Suda Bay. It comprised two Royal Fleet Auxilliaries, two armed boarding vessels and the netlayer *Protector,* and arrived at the same time as the *Ajax* who carried aboard the 2nd Battalion Yorkshire and Lancaster Regiment. The only Italian response was a series of sporadic and ineffective air raids.

No longer was it necessary for the British to involve the Greeks by stationing tankers in Greek anchorages to refuel Cunningham's warships. The island would provide an excellent base from which to operate forces to interrupt the Italo–North Africa supply line, and even to give greater protection to Malta and shipping movements to and from that island.

Within days of occupying the island's naval base, Cunningham exploited the situation. He had for long nursed the idea of attacking the Italian Fleet with aircraft while it lay at anchor. Plans for such an attack had been prepared and the chances of its execution looked more promising for Cunningham with the arrival of reinforcements for the Mediterranean Fleet from Gibraltar. The opportunity presented itself and Operation Judgement, the Fleet Air Arm attack upon the Italian Fleet at Taranto, was put into effect as part of a series of complex moves from both ends of the Mediterranean. The story of the Fleet Air Arm raid is well documented and needs only a passing reference to the salient features here. The results led to dramatic changes in the balance of naval power in the Mediterranean.

Cunningham had hoped to execute the operation on Trafalgar Day, but conditions made this impossible so it was timed to coincide with the passage of reinforcements for the Mediterranean Fleet from Gibraltar. These additions to the Fleet included the battleship *Barham,* the cruisers *Glasgow* and *Berwick,* together with six destroyers. Admiral Somerville's Force H was to accompany this force and give cover also to the aircraft carrier *Ark Royal* who was to be detached to make a diversionary raid on Sardinia.

Cunningham's Fleet, comprising the *Warspite, Valiant, Malaya* and *Ramilles,* with the aircraft carrier *Illustrious* and screening

44

forces left Alexandria on the afternoon of November 6th to give cover to the convoys to Malta and Suda Bay.

Rear Admiral A. L. St. G. Lyster, in command of the Carrier Squadron, had trained crews from the carriers *Eagle*[5] and *Illustrious* for some weeks prior to the raid on Taranto. RAF reconnaissance aircraft from Malta provided information on the Italian Fleet movements. On November 11th photographs of the two harbours at Taranto showed five battleships at their berths and a sixth approaching the harbour. All the Italian Battle Fleet was concentrating. Now, if ever, was the chance of a lifetime for the Fleet Air Arm. It was grasped hungrily.

Lyster proceeded with the *Illustrious* and accompanying forces to the flying-off position for the attack, approximately forty miles west of Cephalonia and 170 miles from Taranto. Some of the carrier's screen, the cruisers *Orion*, Vice Admiral Pridham-Wippell's flagship, HMAS *Sydney* and the *Ajax*, together with the destroyers *Nubian* and *Mohawk* raided the Straits of Otranto and ventured into the Adriatic to interrupt the Italian lines of communications with Albania. The force encountered an enemy convoy whose escorts were put to flight and the merchant ships destroyed.

The attack on Taranto was launched by Swordfish aircraft in two waves, the first of twelve aircraft flew off at 2030. The second wave of nine aircraft took off an hour later.

At 2300 the first wave was over the target area. The weather was ideal. A full moon gave a clear night except for thin veils of cloud at 8,000 feet. Complete surprise was achieved. The defences which had been provided for the protection of the Fleet were formidable. They comprised a considerable barrage of balloons, dozens of anti-aircraft guns, well-sited anti-torpedo nets and the AA guns of the ships themselves. Despite these defences this daring and well-conducted attack was a brilliant success.

The newly commissioned battleship *Littorio*, struck by three torpedoes, sank in shallow water and was put out of action for

[5] Owing to a defect the *Eagle* failed to take part in Operation Judgement but some of her trained crews and aircraft were transferred to the *Illustrious* and thus participated in the attack.

five months: the battleship *Conti di Cavour* was struck by one torpedo and sank: the battleship *Caio Duilio* was hit forward by one torpedo and settled by the bows: the heavy cruiser *Trento* was penetrated by a bomb which failed to explode, and two destroyers were damaged by near misses.

These resounding successes were achieved at the cost of only two aircraft and their pilots and observers. Cunningham recorded that in this brief attack the aircraft 'had inflicted more damage upon the Italian Fleet than was inflicted upon the German High Sea Fleet in the daylight action of the Battle of Jutland'.[6]

The Fleet Air Arm—with slow, old-looking biplanes—had demonstrated the devastating power of aircraft over modern and modernised warships protected by shore defences. It was a victory which produced a profound effect upon the balance of naval power in the Mediterranean out of all proportion to the losses sustained.

*

The lesson of Taranto was well learned by Germany and Japan. The *Luftwaffe* was to exploit this new-found mastery in the battle for Crete and the Japanese were to demonstrate their skill in the Battle of the Gulf of Siam and at Pearl Harbour.

One immediate effect of the victory was the withdrawal of the remaining Italian battleships to Naples, thus reducing surface threats to the Malta and Aegean convoys. This enabled Cunningham to dispense with his slower battleships and before November was gone the *Ramilles* sailed westward for home and she was quickly followed by the *Malaya*.

The passing of the *Ramilles* for Gibraltar was part of another complex mass of shipping movements in the Mediterranean involving Cunningham's Mediterranean Fleet, Somerville's Force H and several convoys.

Supermarina despatched the *Vittorio Veneto* and the *Cesare*, six heavy cruisers and fourteen destroyers to seek out the British forces. Admiral Campioni, enjoying numerical superiority over

---

[6] *A Sailor's Odyssey*, Cunningham, p 286.

46

Somerville's Force H made contact with the British force and a skirmish at extreme range ensued, but the Italians broke off the action after damage to a destroyer and the failure of air support to materialise. The British rather grandly designated the engagement the Battle of Spartivento and the Italians refer to it as the Battle of Tenleda.

It was another instance of *Supermarina*'s intervening and attempting to control the admiral commanding on the spot and denying him any initiative and enterprise. This premature breaking off of the action was a lost opportunity since the advantage lay heavily with Admiral Campioni.

The repeated failures of the Italian Navy—and possibly the German Weichold's[7] representations in Rome—led to changes in command of the Italian Navy on December 10th. The Naval Chief of Staff, Admiral Cavagnari, was replaced by Admiral Riccardi.[8] Admiral Campioni vacated his position of Fleet Commander to become Deputy of Chief of Staff in place of Admiral Somigli. The new Fleet Commander was the fifty-two-year-old Admiral D'Armata Angelo Iachino, promoted from Commander of the 2nd Squadron.

Iachino had distinguished himself in his naval service and had commanded a number of ships, most of which were ill-fated and were sunk by the British during the war, including the *Zara* which he commanded in 1936, the *Fiume* (1938) and the *Pola* (1940). He had many friends in England where he served for three years—1931 to 1934—as the Naval Attaché in London. He knew the Royal Navy well and respected its power and efficiency. 'Either he acquired too much respect for his opponent, or maybe

---

[7] After Taranto, Weichold referred critically to *Supermarina*'s defensive attitude, one which 'cripples their power of decision and eventually the offensive spirit of the Italian Fleet: it invites an even stronger British offensive in Italian waters . . . a radical change in the present Italian direction of the war is essential. . . .'

Vice Admiral Eberhard Weichold was German Chief of Liaison Staff with *Supermarina*. He survived the war and died in 1960. He earns mention in C. S. Forester's book, *The Ship,* Michael Joseph, 1943, as Admiral Friske.

[8] An old friend of Cunningham's who had been entertained aboard HMS *Hood* in 1938 and kept *The Life of Nelson* on his bedside table.

he was just unlucky, but the fact remains that in his new command he achieved even less than his predecessor."[9]

The new brooms at *Supermarina* made a clean sweep and reorganised the Fleet into new units; but these new organisational plans failed to make any impression on the Mediterranean Fleet's supremacy in the Eastern and Central Mediterranean where it dominated the scene with a professional arrogance that only the German Admiral Raeder and his Naval Staff seemed to comprehend fully. But even Hitler was not as unaware of this as both Raeder and Ruge imply in their writings.

By the end of December 1940, Cunningham's Fleet could practically roam at will over his domain. On December 18th the Fleet swept into the Adriatic and the *Warspite* and the *Valiant* fired a hundred 15 inch shells into the Italian supply port of Valona in Albania. The Commander-in-Chief then took his flagship to Valetta where the thousands of wildly cheering Maltese enjoying a respite from bombing welcomed the *Warspite* as she entered Grand Harbour majestically, band playing and guard paraded. Cunningham had more than a touch of the showman in him.

*

The military situation in North Africa erupted into action in December when General Wavell launched an offensive from the entrenchment at Sidi Barani. A rapid advance developed and continued for hundreds of miles engulfing successively Bardia, Tobruk and Benghazi, until finally rumbling to a halt at El Agheila in the Sirte Desert.

As this advance began to gain momentum and the Italian forces were flushed out like game to surrender in their tens of thousands, the German High Command could no longer stand by idly and watch the disintegration of the Mediterranean situation both militarily and on the naval front where the Royal Navy's command of the sea had been demonstrated time after time.

The British could rejoice at their modest containment of the situation in the Mediterranean theatre by the end of 1940. But

[9] *Sea Warfare 1939–1945*, Admiral Ruge, p 115.

ominous moves were afoot in the Axis camp and the shadow of the swastika was soon to loom large in the Mediterranean.

*

Only a few days after the beginning of Wavell's desert offensive, Hitler took steps to buttress the crumbling fortunes of Italy whose every act seemed destined to impede the German war effort. On December 10th Hitler undertook to despatch units of the *Luftwaffe* to southern Italy to attack British shipping passing through the Narrows in the Central Mediterranean, and even in the Ionian and Aegean Seas. No action was to be taken against Greece 'for the time being' because Germany was not at war with Greece.

Hitler had promised in a letter dated November 20th to send Mussolini help from the *Luftwaffe*. Early in December he despatched the Secretary of State for Air, Field Marshal Erhard Milch, to Italy to supervise the transfer of *Fliegerkorps X* to Sicily. This combat-experienced unit from Norway was an independent force comprising all types of aircraft and supporting supply personnel and equipment.

By Christmas the unit was on the move. By January 10th ninety-six bombers and twenty-five twin-engined fighters were stationed on their Sicilian airfields. General der Flieger Hans Geisler, a one-time naval officer, took command of *Fliegerkorps X* and within a short period had no less than 400 aircraft of all types under his command.

Hitler's decision to take no action against Greece was only temporary, for he made his intentions for Greece quite clear a few days later in his War Directive No 20, dated December 13th. In this Directive he stressed that if he could not crush Britain as he had hoped by invasion, then Britain must be denied a foothold in Europe. Operation Marita sealed the fate of Greece. The German Army's targets were clearly defined: 'The first objective of the operation is the occupation of the Aegean coast and the Salonika basin. It may become necessary to pursue the attack via Larissa and the Isthmus of Corinth.' Another paragraph stated the objectives of the *Luftwaffe:* 'It will be the task of the

Air Force to give effective support in all phases to the advance of the army, to eliminate the enemy Air Force; and, as far as possible, to seize English bases in the Greek islands with airborne troops.'[10]

On January 11th, 1941, Hitler's involvement in the Mediterranean war became deeper with the issuing of War Directive No 22 which required 'that Germany should assist for reasons of strategy, politics and psychology'. The Directive went on to order the following: 'Commander-in-Chief Army will provide covering forces sufficient to render valuable service to our allies in the defence of Tripolitania.[11] Air Corps will continue to operate from Sicily. Its chief task will be to attack British naval forces and British sea communications between the Eastern and Western Mediterranean . . . The Italian Government will be requested to declare the area between Sicily and the North African coast a closed area in order to facilitate the task of the X Air Corps.'[12]

To Winston Churchill the arrival of *Fliegerkorps X* in the Mediterranean marked a period of 'evil development'. The *Luftwaffe* possessed enough bases to cover the entire Central and Eastern Mediterranean, embracing the coasts of Libya and even the Levant, and aircraft from the Dodecanese made the Suez Canal itself vulnerable and the passage of Aegean convoys more perilous.

No sooner was the *Luftwaffe* established in Sicily than its aircraft made their mark. In yet another series of complicated convoy and fleet movements throughout the Mediterranean, the aircraft carrier *Illustrious* was bombed and hit by six 1,000 lb bombs during a period of about ten minutes of concentrated bombings by three squadrons of Stuka aircraft. The carrier pulled out of line, her steering gear wrecked, badly on fire, her lifts useless and with dozens of casualties littering the decks. As she limped for Malta, escorted by the *Warspite, Valiant* and a screen of destroyers, she fought off another severe attack and reached

[10] *Hitler's War Directives*, H. R. Trevor-Roper.
[11] This force subsequently became the *Afrika Korps* commanded by General Rommel.
[12] *Hitler's War Directives*, H. R. Trevor-Roper.

harbour safely. She suffered 126 killed and 91 wounded. Six German aircraft were shot down.

During the carrier's stay in Malta attacks in strength varying from forty to eighty aircraft at a time were launched. Against this onslaught the Malta defences could muster only six Hurricanes, three Fulmars and one Gladiator. While the *Illustrious* was in harbour trying to patch up her damage sixteen German aircraft were shot down.

Cunningham and his staff meditated unhappily on this new weapon making its presence felt for the first time in the Mediterranean in most telling fashion. The efforts of the *Regia Aeronautica* with its high-level bombing were as nothing compared with the precision bombing by these diving and screaming Stuka bombers.

Within the short space of a few weeks the *Luftwaffe*—for the time being at any rate—had closed the Mediterranean to through traffic. Convoys to Malta and the Aegean would now need far more protection than could be afforded by carrier-borne fighter aircraft. Thus there became a need for more defensive measures of all kinds: shore-based fighters; more radar for warships to give early warning of the approach of aircraft, since the value of such early warning had been proved clearly; anti-aircraft defences for shore establishments and airfields; anti-aircraft guns for merchant ships and small craft, to enable them to defend themselves. Such were the needs. Alas, the resources were not there. It seemed that the *Luftwaffe* could grasp and retain mastery of the theatre by air power alone.

A few days after the escape of the *Illustrious,* the new cruiser *Southampton* was bombed and sunk, and the cruiser *Gloucester* was struck by a bomb which failed to explode. Rear Admiral Renouf was lucky. This was the second time that a flagship of his had been hit on the bridge by a defective bomb.

But better news for the Mediterranean Fleet came when the damaged *Illustrious* made good her escape from Malta to Alexandria whence she passed through the Suez Canal to the USA for repairs. She was soon replaced by the carrier *Formidable.*

Force H also contributed to bolstering up British morale after

51

the appearance of the *Luftwaffe*. Somerville's squadron comprising of the *Malaya, Renown* and the famous carrier *Ark Royal* with one cruiser and attendant destroyers made an offensive sortie into the Ligurian Sea. Aircraft dropped magnetic mines off Genoa and bombed Leghorn. The capital ships shelled Genoa at a range of 18,000 yards. The damage inflicted was small. The results in terms of morale were far reaching. In far-away Madrid General Franco was well aware of the implications of the audacious British Force which could steam unmolested into Italian waters and shell her ports and towns.

Supermarina despatched Admiral Iachino with the *Vittorio Veneto, Cesare* and *Doria*, three heavy cruisers and ten destroyers, but lack of coordination with *Supermarina* contributed to Iachino's failure to intercept Force H which escaped detection and withdrew safely. Once again the British had exhibited a dash and an enterprising use of the aircraft carrier, even in the confined waters of the Ligurian Sea.

Admiral Raeder and his staff were much concerned over Italy's failure at sea and with the unfavourable effect this had upon the Axis fortunes in the Mediterranean. Raeder could exert very little influence upon *Supermarina*, and his representative in Rome, Vice Admiral Weichold, functioned simply as an observer with no authority over the Italians.

In an effort to overcome these problems, the Germans proposed a meeting of the naval Commanders-in-Chief and their staffs to coordinate policies. *Supermarina* accepted the proposal reluctantly, for Italy and Germany were unhappy allies, each jealously guarding their secrets and wary of the designs each had upon the other. *Supermarina* felt affronted that it should have to accept a German intrusion into its affairs when it believed that it had nothing to learn from what it regarded as an inferior naval power. But Italy was in dire need of fuel oil for her ships, and Germany could help resolve this deficiency. Italy pocketed her pride and agreed to the meeting of naval chiefs.

The meeting took place in the Alpine retreat of Merano in mid-February 1941, and lasted for three days. Admiral Riccardi,

Chief of Staff of the Italian Navy acted as host to Admiral Raeder, Chief of German Naval Staff, and emphasised the limiting factor of restricted oil supplies upon his ships. The Italian Navy began the war with 1,800,000 tons of fuel oil in reserve. By the time of the Merano meeting, only 800,000 tons remained. At this rate of consumption it was calculable that by mid-summer the Italian Navy could not put to sea. *Supermarina* had already imposed a limit of 50% of the navy's needs, but in fact only one half of this amount was made available. And at times the deliveries were so low as to prove a severe limitation on operations.

Bragadin claims[13] that by the summer of 1941, despite some oil supplies from Germany, the Italian reserve was completely consumed and thereafter the navy was forced to conduct operations only as deliveries of fuel permitted.

At Merano, Raeder's Staff urged their counterparts to adopt a more aggressive attitude, but it was pointed out that *Supermarina* was subject to orders from the Italian Supreme Command who demanded prudence and the avoidance of 'exposure of the Italian battleships to undue risks, for Mussolini wanted to sit down at the peace conference with a strong navy still at his disposal'.[14]

Raeder expressed the German concern for the British consolidation in the Greek sector and urged the Italians to attack the British supply traffic from Egypt to Greece. Riccardi remarked upon the effectiveness of the British reconnaissance which largely nullified attempts at surface interception of enemy convoys.

The meeting at Merano proved substantially ineffective. About three weeks later Germany began applying more pressure on Italy. Berlin revealed the German plans for stabilising the situation in the Balkans and insisted that the Italian Navy acted promptly to intercept British traffic to Greece. The Italian Supreme Command, accepting political direction, instructed *Supermarina* to increase naval activity. An attempt was made

[13] *The Italian Navy in World War II* by Commander M. Bragadin, US Naval Institute, Annapolis, 1957, p 82.

[14] *The Italian Navy in World War II*, Commander Bragadin, p 83.

to do this, even though it was against *Supermarina*'s better judgement.

The number of submarines in Cretan waters was increased. A special explosive motor boat assault on Suda Bay was initiated and plans were laid for a surface force to undertake a strike to the east. For by now, early in March 1941, the British activity in Greek and Cretan waters was substantial. An army was being transported to Greece from Egypt, and associated with this operation were all the accompanying naval movements.

It was this increased naval activity which brought home to Cunningham the fact that the major problem in the Mediterranean was one of aerial supremacy. On March 11th he wrote to the First Sea Lord: 'There seems to be some bad misunderstanding of our Air Force out here. I feel the Chiefs of Staff are badly misinformed about the number of fighter squadrons available. Longmore is absolutely stretched to the limit.' He went on to report that in Cyrenaica the Germans and Italians outnumbered the British fighters by 200 to 30, while in Malta the situation was even more desperate with only eight Hurricanes serviceable. This letter was evidence of anxiety which had persisted for some weeks. When he had been created a Knight Grand Cross of the Bath in January, Cunningham had commented sourly, 'I would sooner have had three squadrons of Hurricanes.' He was to wish this more fervently in the weeks ahead.

CHAPTER 3

Balkan Entanglements

THE TRANSPORTATION OF the British Army to Greece and its subsequent nourishment there lasted a total of seven weeks. It started on March 4th, 1941, when the first convoy from Alexandria departed, until April 24th when the situation ashore in Greece reached disaster proportions. The transportation operation was then reversed and there began another melancholy evacuation of British troops by sea. The Greek episode thus falls quite readily and simply into two distinct phases: the seven week build-up period, designated Operation Lustre, followed by the brief evacuation period from April 25th until April 29th, designated Operation Demon.

The whole of Operation Lustre was effected smoothly despite the magnitude of the task and the fact that the port facilities at Alexandria were subjected to considerable strain and confusion. Nearly all commercial shipping was brought to a standstill as the military and naval needs took precedence. No less than 58,000 British and Imperial troops complete with their military paraphernalia, mechanical transport and full equipment, and plethora of stores, were transported from Alexandria to the Piraeus. This port of Athens was virtually the only one in the country of any consequence and the only one through which the thousands of troops and their mountain of stores could pass.

The passage to the Piraeus from the Egyptian ports was a distance of about 600 miles. It was not a specially hazardous sea route. Italian submarines could be expected to straddle the route and aircraft could always be expected to put in an appearance. But with a few isolated exceptions, Italian submarine commanders never menaced Allied shipping seriously, even though their dispositions set them astride the British sea lanes.

55

Ever since the Italian invasion of Greece British convoys had been run regularly between Egypt and Greece and all told 58,364 personnel were safely transported, 11,000 of these being carried in cruisers.

The provision of adequate screen for these various convoys posed a problem for the Naval Staff at Alexandria. On average, three destroyers accompanied the more important convoys while AA cruisers gave further protection in the more dangerous zones. Further, other cruisers were disposed so as to give cover in the Aegean, and, for the greater part of the period, major units of the Battle Fleet were maintained at sea to the west of Crete.

For the first six days of Operation Lustre sailings of convoys from Alexandria were made at a rate of more than one every day, and thereafter until the operation ceased on April 21st a convoy sailed practically every other day.

During this period three notable events intervened and deserve our attention: two of them of merely passing interest but meriting a tiny place in the giant jigsaw of Mediterranean events leading up to the Greek and Cretan campaigns.

The first of these was the passage of a vital convoy, code-named MC 9, from Alexandria to Malta. The convoy comprised four storeships which were given powerful cover by the Battle Fleet, accompanied by the newly arrived armoured carrier *Formidable* which had replaced the *Illustrious*. This operation also entailed the use of the 3rd and 7th Cruiser Squadrons. The whole complicated operation was effected smoothly and without loss.

The second tiny event to intrude into the narrative, merits inclusion because it spotlights a sector of naval activity in which the Italian Navy gave a pioneering lead, and in which its exploits were executed with much courage and personal bravery. One such exploit was the attack upon the fleet base at Suda Bay on March 26th by explosive motor boats.

On the previous day two Italian destroyers, the *Crispi* and the *Sella,* each transported three explosive boats from the island of Stampalia in the Dodecanese, close to the entrance of Suda Bay. These explosive boats were very small motor boats fitted

56

with heavy charges in the bows. They were piloted by one man wearing a frogman's rubber suit. The pilot approached the enemy harbour or anchorage, then aimed the boat at the target, locked the rudder and, when about a hundred yards away, jumped overboard. Such was the method employed at Suda Bay. The six explosive boats were launched, they traversed the seven or eight miles across the Bay, penetrated the defences by surmounting the triple boom and net barrage protecting the anchorage and scored hits on two important targets. One of these was the tanker *Pericles*. She was hit and holed amidships then she settled, but the bulk of her valuable cargo was salved.

The second target was the 8,250 ton heavy cruiser *York*. She was built in 1930 and mounted six 8 inch guns and was capable of a speed of 32 knots. The explosion severely damaged her, causing flooding to her engine room and boiler rooms. She was robbed of all power for pumping, lighting and the working of her turrets. To prevent her sinking she was beached, and she subsequently served as an AA battery even while sitting on the bottom. But during the aerial bombardment of Crete in the next few weeks she was bombed and became a total loss, a fact which led the Germans to lay claim to having sunk her, a claim justly and hotly disputed by the Italians.

All six of the pilots were rescued after the attack, including the commander of the attacking squad, Lieutenant Faggioni. Cunningham, lamenting the loss of his only 8 inch gun cruiser, bore the adversity with characteristic composure.

The third episode which intervened in Operation Lustre, stemmed directly from the intense activity of British naval forces in the Aegean and Cretan waters in particular. As we have seen the Italians were finally impelled by the Germans to send surface forces to seek out the weakened and depleted British Battle Fleet. *Supermarina,* with tame conformity but resigned uneasiness, despatched a battle fleet and in this lone offensive foray fought and lost the Battle of Matapan.

It is not necessary to relate the story of this battle which is well known and which has been fully described in a number of accounts. For the British it was a fortuitous victory, coming as it

57

did at a juncture in the Royal Navy's fortunes which was singularly devoid of successes: at a time, in fact, when the nation's fortunes were at a particularly low ebb. The victory shone amid the stresses and strains of that time.

But just before the battle, changes in flag command and other promotional changes occurred in the Eastern Mediterranean. A new appointment was that of Rear Admiral Irvine G. Glennie, until recently Captain of the *Hood*. He became RA(D), the Rear Admiral in command of the Mediterranean Fleet destroyers. Rear Admiral Elliott in charge ashore at Alexandria, was relieved by Acting Rear Admiral G. H. Cresswell, an experienced destroyer man. Vice Admiral Lyster returned home to become Fifth Sea Lord. Captain D. W. Boyd assumed command of the aircraft carriers with the acting rank of Rear Admiral and hoisted his flag in the *Formidable*. At this time, too, Cunningham lost his Chief of Staff, Rear Admiral A. Willis, who was relieved by Captain J. H. Edelston. All these officers were to be put to the test in the ensuing weeks and months of strenuous hardships and perils ahead. However, fortune favoured them with a victory early in their command: a victory off Cape Matapan.

*

On March 19th the Italian Naval Staff received a situation report from Vice Admiral Weichold which he based on a faulty claim that German torpedo bombers three days earlier had hit the *Warspite* and *Barham,* leaving the *Valiant* as the only seaworthy battleship in the Mediterranean Fleet. 'Thus, the situation in the Mediterranean is at the moment more favourable for the Italian Fleet than ever before. . . . The German Naval Staff considers that the appearance of Italian units in the area south of Crete will seriously interfere with British shipping, and may even lead to the complete interruption of the transport of troops, especially as these transports are at the moment inadequately protected.'

The Italian Historical Division have since revealed that both Admiral Iachino and *Supermarina* were firm in their belief of the unreliability of the *Luftwaffe* claim. Italian reconnaissance flights had failed to confirm the reports of damage. Nevertheless, Iachino reluctantly took a battle fleet to sea after repeated and insistent calls for improved reconnaissance facilities. He finally secured assurances of massive and extensive aerial support in the form of reconnaissance and bomber missions and fighter escort for the sortie, both from the Italian Air Force and from *Fliegerkorps X.* The sortie was conceived as a cruiser raid by six heavy cruisers, two light cruisers and fourteen destroyers, supported by the admiral's flagship, *Vittorio Veneto.*

Cunningham was aware of Iachino's heavy cruiser movements within hours of their leaving harbour. Suspecting a battle force in support he ordered his Mediterranean Fleet to depart from harbour after dusk, thereby allowing Italian reconnaissance aircraft to report all quiet at Alexandria.

Cunningham himself took part in an elaborate ploy to bluff the Japanese consul in Alexandria who it was known reported any British fleet movements he observed. The consul spent most afternoons on the golf course. Cunningham went ashore as if to play golf, complete with an overnight suitcase, knowing full well that it would be deduced that the fleet was staying in harbour overnight. The plot worked. Cunningham hurriedly returned aboard after dark and the fleet sailed at 1900.

The resulting night action, which cost the British one torpedo aircraft and its crew of three cost the Italian Navy three fine, modern heavy cruisers, two destroyers and a damaged battleship. Cunningham lamented the escape of the Italian battleship, but the battle had an immeasurable effect upon the maritime scene in the Eastern Mediterranean.

The Italian Navy's acceptance of British supremacy at sea in the Mediterranean was now complete. It was never to be challenged again. Even during the agony of the Cretan evacuation, when Cunningham's resources were stretched to the utmost limit, the Italian Navy resolutely refused to risk another rough handling such as it experienced at Matapan. It is true to say that what little success was achieved by the British during the naval operations off Greece and Crete was made possible by the devastating broadsides of the battleships during the night action of the Battle of Matapan.

*

On April 2nd, with the resumption of convoys to Greece, convoy ANF 24 suffered loss when the ss *Devis* was struck during a high-level bombing attack which killed seven men and injured another fourteen.

This same convoy was attacked the next day by nine dive bombers and the ammunition ship *Northern Prince,* 10,917 tons, was hit and set on fire with a great pall of yellow smoke billowing aloft. Later she blew up and sank. She had several thousand tons of powder aboard for Greek ordnance factories and her loss was a serious blow.

Apart from the hazards from the air, this convoy had endured the perils of the sea, battling through high winds and high seas. When it arrived at the Piraeus on April 4th it encountered a scene of confusion and congestion. 'The creaking machinery of the Greek docks organisation, working beyond the limit of its capacity, had shown signs of breaking down. Now, there were not enough stevedores, lorries, railway trucks or cranes to handle such an influx of transports all laden to their maximum . . .' And three days later it was reported, 'Every berth alongside every quay was occupied by ships off-loading and out in Phalerum Bay other merchantmen lay at anchor waiting their turn to berth.'[1]

As soon as the Greek military authority realised that the *Northern Prince* and her valuable cargo had been lost they ordered that priority be given to the off-loading of the 350 tons of TNT stored in the *Clan Fraser* whose ill-fortune we will follow in a later chapter.

*

Thus Operation Lustre came to its end. It had been conducted smoothly and with little fuss or bother. From March 22nd to April 18th, twenty-five vessels had been sunk, eighteen of them while in Greek ports and only seven while in convoy.

[1] *Greek Tragedy '41* by A. Heckstall-Smith and Vice Admiral Baillie-Grohman, Anthony Blond, 1961.

In following the conduct of this Operation we have overtaken the more dramatic events taking place ashore and in order to appreciate the naval situation it is to these military developments that we must now turn our attention.

CHAPTER 4

Defeat in Greece

ON APRIL 6TH the Germans launched an attack in the Balkans. It began with a three hour aerial bombardment of the undefended city of Belgrade and a simultaneous invasion of Greek soil. On the following day the *Luftwaffe* bombed the port of Athens—the Piraeus—and created widespread devastation. Almost from the outset the Greek and British troops began to fall back in the face of strong and determined attacks by the Germans and within days of the start of the campaign Hitler was beginning to reap his victories. On April 13th Belgrade was occupied. The German 12th Army, advancing from Bulgaria, entered Macedonia and separated Yugoslavia from Greece. On the 17th Yugoslavia capitulated and three days later the Greek armies on the Albanian front surrendered, exposing the British left flank. The British retreated from their untenable position at Thermopylae and headed south. The retreat to the sea had begun. Two days later—on the 24th—the Greek Government surrendered to the Germans and the evacuation of British forces from Greece began.

Thus, it can be seen that even while Operation Lustre was still in progress, the more melancholy business of withdrawal, retreat and eventual evacuation of British troops was already being enacted. The disastrous turn of military events ashore was not altogether unexpected.

Months before, when the decision to send British troops to Greece was finally taken, Cunningham prudently started to plan to bring them all out again. Nor was he alone in contemplating evacuation. It had also engaged the attention of the other Middle East Commanders-in-Chief. Furthermore, the Australian and New Zealand governments had sought some assurances from the British Government on this matter, because of the high proportion of Dominion troops among the British forces in Greece.

Cunningham was told specifically by the First Sea Lord in a personal signal on March 24th that, when agreeing to the use of New Zealand and Australian troops, the governments had asked that adequate arrangements be made in advance to withdraw the troops in case of necessity. A pessimistic, defeatist attitude which one might deplore; but an eminently sensible precaution in view of the British war record so far.

Cunningham gave his guarantee that everything possible would be done to withdraw the Dominion troops with the British. It was unfortunate, therefore, that the percentage of Australian and New Zealand troops subsequently left ashore in Crete on the completion of the Balkan affair was greater than that of the British troops.

Preparations for the evacuation—code named Operation Demon—were already well in hand. An impressive collection of warships and merchantmen had been assembled: four cruisers, three AA cruisers, twenty destroyers, two of the three *Glen* ships, the assault ship HMS *Ulster Prince*, five escort vessels, six A lighters, the Royal Fleet Auxilliary *Brambleleaf*, and a number of merchant ships made up the fleet of rescue vessels.

The overall responsibility for these ships at sea devolved upon Vice Admiral Light Forces (VALF), Vice Admiral H. D. Pridham-Wippell, second in command of the Mediterranean Fleet. His had been an enviably distinguished naval career. When the Italians entered the war he was the Rear Admiral 1st Battle Squadron in the Mediterranean, flying his flag in the *Royal Sovereign* and later the *Malaya*. In the former he took part in the Battle of Calabria and had often run the gauntlet of the *Regia Aeronautica* in the Narrows and defied the threat of the Italian Fleet.

Pridham-Wippell had the distinction of being the first British commander of a naval squadron to sweep through the enemy-held Straits of Otranto and forage north into the Adriatic with his 7th Cruiser Squadron, a diversionary raid which helped distract the enemy's attention from the primary task of neutralising the Italian Fleet at Taranto.

A few months later he led his cruiser squadron into the Battle of Matapan, in one phase of which he came under fire from the 15 inch guns of the *Vittorio Veneto*. It is ironical that he was awarded the Italian Silver Medal for Military Valour for his World War I conduct in command of a destroyer in the Adriatic. For his gallantry and distinguished service in the withdrawal of troops from Greece he was appointed a Knight Commander of the Order of the Bath.

Pridham-Wippell would have been the first to acknowledge the valuable help and strenuous efforts of Rear Admiral H. T. Baillie-Grohman and Rear Admiral G. H. Cresswell.

Baillie-Grohman bore the title Flag Officer Attached Middle East and carried the responsibility for organising the naval interests ashore in Greece throughout the evacuation. Cresswell, until recently Captain (D) of the 4th Destroyer Flotilla, was appointed Rear Admiral Alexandria and became responsible for the provision of the necessary troopships for Operation Demon and for the organisation of the northbound convoys, ensuring their arrival at the right time and place in the Aegean.

Baillie-Grohman recalls his appointment when Cunningham sent for him. 'It was a meeting of old friends as much as a meeting between the Commander-in-Chief of the Mediterranean Fleet and one of his junior flag officers, for before the war when Cunningham had been Rear Admiral Destroyers in Malta, B-G as he was generally known, had commanded one of the crack flotillas. And until five months ago . . . he had commanded the *Ramilles* in Cunningham's Fleet.'[1] The Commander-in-Chief is reported as saying 'I sent for you because I had a signal from Turle[2] early this morning saying that the situation in Greece is deteriorating. He thinks we shall probably have to pull out within six weeks. I want you to fly to Athens as soon as possible to size up the situation for yourself so that if we do have to bring the

---

[1] *Greek Tragedy '41*, Heckstall-Smith and Baillie-Grohman.
[2] Naval Attaché in Athens and the first officer of any Service to warn of an evacuation.

army out, you can organise and take charge of the shore arrangements.' The date was April 13th, Easter Sunday.

It was a daunting prospect. The sheer magnitude of evacuating approximately 58,000 troops from inhospitable shores, across mile upon mile of placid seas under skies dominated by the *Luftwaffe,* to far distant Alexandria, or Port Said, at least 600 miles away, was a frightening thought. The reality was no less comforting.

The plan was discussed in outline with the C-in-C's Staff. Soon Baillie-Grohman found cause for some comfort. Force Z which consisted of three assault ships, the *Glengyle, Glenroy* and *Glenearn* with supporting transport and supply ships together with eighteen new tank landing craft, was even now arriving in the Mediterranean. It had been intended to recapture the Italian island of Rhodes in an Operation codenamed Mandibles. But Mandibles was shelved at the last minute much to Churchill's annoyance. The disappointment felt by Layforce, the commando detachment aboard the *Glen* ships, and all the naval personnel concerned in the operation, was short-lived. No sooner did Mandibles die than Demon was born. Baillie-Grohman wasted no time in acquiring the vessels of Force Z for his Greek evacuation: the TLCs—now renamed A lighters for security reasons— were to proceed to Suda Bay immediately.

These gawky, unhandy vessels, square bowed and lacking any semblance of graceful style, became the mainspring of the Greek and Crete evacuations. Without them, thousands of British troops would have been condemned to languish for years in prisoner-of-war camps. Five of these craft, the first of eighteen to be built, had been shipped to Egypt in sections, bolted to the decks of merchant ships. They were riveted together in the Suez Canal Company's yards at Port Tewfik. Some carried no AA weapons and those that did only managed Lewis machineguns. Another unattractive feature of these vessels was the deafening roar developed by their twin 500 horse-power petrol driven motors.

This 1st Flotilla was commanded by Lieutenant-Commander P. Hutton, a resourceful and enterprising officer who was awarded a DSC for his gallantry.

The *Glen* ships which were ordered to sail for Suda Bay to act as a reserve force, ready for any emergency, were a valuable windfall. They had been requisitioned by the Admiralty at the outbreak of war from their owners, the Glen Line. Eight fast 10,000 ton cargo liners had been ordered, capable of 18 knots. The first off the stocks was the *Glenearn*. After she and the *Glenroy* had completed their second voyages in October 1939, they were taken over, stripped of their considerable refrigerator capacity and converted to wartime use. The following month the *Breconshire*,[3] having completed her maiden voyage, suffered a similar fate. The *Glengyle* was requisitioned while still on the stocks at Caledon, Dundee.

The three *Glen* ships endured yet another conversion to fit them for their combined operations function. It was a conversion which proved ideal. Baillie-Grohman was fortunate, indeed, in having these fine vessels at his disposal for the Greek evacuation.

Baillie-Grohman arrived in Athens on April 17th. He was confronted by a scene of indescribable devastation in the Piraeus. The perplexing and contradictory task thrust upon him was clouded with the uncertainty of defeat. Defeat hung over the port like a pall of smoke.

The devastation was the result of a severe air raid on the port by the *Luftwaffe* during the night of April 6th–7th. The Piraeus was the only port of any consequence in Greece, apart from Kalamata in Morea, with quays fit for large vessels. On Sunday the 6th, the day that Germany declared war on Greece, the harbour was congested to the point of chaos.

Baillie-Grohman attributes the breakdown in administration to the failure to appoint a British Naval Officer in Charge in the first instance. As it was, the Captain of the Port, Captain Scarpetis, did his best to cope but his efforts were unavailing: his order to all ships to clear the harbour swiftly came too late: but he failed to order the removal of the ammunition ship *Clan Fraser* to a berth of greater safety. Since Friday morning she had

---

[3] This ship became the most famous of the Glen Line ships for her part in the gallant efforts to sustain Malta, finally succumbing to a torpedo and then a mine when being towed into the harbour at the end of March 1942.

been the cause of muddle and confusion. By late Sunday evening all the decks and between decks of the ship had been cleared of the motor vehicles and their stores: her cargo of explosives had been partially removed; much of this had simply been unloaded into lighters still secured alongside, and the Greek tugmen went home for the night at sundown. Furthermore, 250 tons of TNT still remained aboard in No 3 hold.

At 2035 that Sunday evening the air raid alarm sounded for the fifth time. The gang of stevedores left the *Clan Fraser* for shelter ashore. Another ammunition ship, the *Goalpara*, lay alongside near the Sea Transport Office. The *City of Roubaix* with a cargo of ammunition for Turkey and the *Clan Cumming* lay alongside near the Custom House. Outside the harbour, lying at anchor in the Bay in the calm of a fine evening were some of the escort vessels of Convoy ANF 24, the cruisers *Perth*, *Calcutta* and *Coventry* and some destroyers.

Aboard the *Clan Fraser* the crew prepared for the air raid. Lights were blacked out, fire hoses run out, the gun's crew manned the 12 pounder and soldiers who had sailed aboard as gunners prepared the Hotchkiss machineguns.

The first wave of bombers arrived at 2100 and mines were seen to parachute into the harbour. The mine-laying aircraft were quickly followed by the main wave of bombers.

It was soon after 2200 when the *Clan Fraser* was hit. Three bombs struck home. The first exploded on the foredeck. The second burst into the engine room killing the chief engineer and some crew. The third exploded aft. Simultaneously, violent explosions erupted in the sheds and buildings on the quay alongside the ship. The resulting blast wrecked the bridge and upperworks, showering debris over the ship and wounding the master. Worse still, so great was the blast that it lifted *Clan Fraser* bodily, snapped her mooring wires and she drifted gently several yards from the quayside, still with her lighters secured alongside.

The *Clan Fraser* was not alone in her agony. Other ships in the harbour were sharing a similar fate. They too had been reduced to blazing infernos. The *City of Roubaix* and the *Goalpara* were both afire, their cargoes of ammunition in imminent danger of exploding. The *Clan Cumming,* undamaged so far, but berthed close to the *City of Roubaix,* was doomed.

When Rear Admiral Turle in Athens heard the news of the *Clan Fraser*'s ordeal he hurried from the Legation in Athens to the Piraeus with Commander Buckler, RNR, to survey a scene of utter devastation and confusion.

Turle called for tugs to tow the blazing vessels from the harbour for therein lay the only hope of avoiding complete wreckage of the harbour and its installations. But the port authorities had forbidden any shipping movements owing to the presence of magnetic mines: a sunken ship in the fairway would block the harbour. Thus the harbour was at a standstill. And by this decision to stop shipping movements the port was condemned to destruction.

It was at midnight that the Master of the *Clan Fraser,* Captain Giles, and those still alive aboard the ship managed to scramble ashore along a mooring rope which had been secured. The ship's sides were now glowing red with heat. By now, even had movement in the harbour been permitted, the *Clan Fraser* was incapable of being towed, for no line could be secured aboard her.

Undeterred by this, Turle decided to minimise what was now becoming inevitable, the explosion of the ship's remaining 250 tons of TNT. He determined to salvage the two lighters still alongside with their 50 tons of TNT.

Buckler himself took one of the Sea Transport tugs and braving the mine menace threaded a way through the harbour waters, now lit by blazing merchantmen, now obscured by drifting smoke and dust, under the very stern of the *Clan Fraser.* Before a line could be made fast aboard the lighters, the ammunition ship blew up with a mighty explosion. In one eruption the Piraeus suffered enormous damage. The explosion reverberated as far as the capital. The two lighters, engulfed in the explosion, erupted almost simultaneously, wrecking the tug and killing the gallant Commander Buckler and his brave crew.

Blazing debris hurled abroad by the detonation ignited buildings and near-by small craft. The violence of the blast reduced sheds to rubble and red hot plates of steel flung about the quayside added to the devastation. Fire and smoke and dust engulfed the area.

Devastating though the explosion was, it was not the end of the night's destruction. Even while the fires wrought by the *Clan Fraser*'s destruction still raged, another violent explosion convulsed the harbour. The *Goalpara,* secured alongside No 3 berth blew up. Near-by buildings, including the Sea Transport Office building, were demolished in the blast. Seven miles away from the fiercely burning dockland, the city of Athens rocked to the explosion of the *Goalpara,* and the noise of bomb-bursts was heard throughout the night.

Minutes later, at about 0300 another giant explosion rent the night when the third merchantman with a cargo of explosives blew up, reducing even more dock buildings to rubble. The wreck of the *City of Roubaix* settled by the quayside. Alongside her, damaged by the blast, the *Clan Cumming* began to blaze. It was hours before she was towed clear of the wreckage of the *City of Roubaix;* but these efforts were ill-rewarded, for after temporary repairs some days later she was mined and sank in the Gulf of Athens.

Daylight brought respite from the bombs. But the port was a shambles. Eleven ships totalling more than 40,000 tons were lost. Damage to the dockland area and port installations was enormous. The Piraeus ceased to function as a port for ten days while it was closed to all shipping, and it never recovered sufficiently for it to operate efficiently during the rest of the Greek campaign.

It was against this background of devastation that Baillie-Grohman arrived ten days later, to find the port still failing to function. Telecommunications had been disrupted. Seven of the twelve berths were still out of commission. The port's administration had collapsed. Twenty merchantmen were brought to a standstill outside the harbour, unable to take aboard water and coal. The Greek pilots, like the stevedores and dockyard workers, stunned and frightened by the intensity of the bombing and explosions, had fled the port. The Piraeus was virtually at a halt.

From this welter of chaos and confusion Baillie-Grohman fashioned a sense of order and semblance of stability. By astute diplomacy he gradually encouraged the Greek authorities to relinquish control of their shipping in local waters and, in time, the conduct of all local naval affairs. A general HQ was set up in the Hotel Acropole in Athens where the military HQ was already established. Into this HQ the Rear Admiral gathered around him his Divisional Sea Transport Office and Naval Control Service Office. From here, too, he despatched 'combined naval and military parties to reconnoitre all suitable beaches and landing places in Euboea, the Gulf of Corinth, the south and east coast between Khalkis and the Corinth Canal, and the south and east coasts of the Morea between the Corinth Canal and Kalamata'.[4] Further, a signal station manned by naval ratings was set up in Phalerum Bay to establish contact with Greek ships and a communications system installed.

At one time many of these duties had fallen upon the British Naval Attaché. Now that Turle found himself relieved of these responsibilities he was able to concentrate his energies upon his diplomatic duties, which assumed greater and greater importance as the tide of war flooded the country and flowed nearer and nearer to the capital.

Baillie-Grohman was fortunate in having the services of Commander K. Mitchell. To him was given the responsibility of chartering and equipping caiques, motor boats and other small local craft. His Greek and British military aides scoured the harbours, coastal villages, inlets and island to haggle with, and to persuade and impel reluctant owners of small craft to help rescue the retreating British Army. These craft were essential for embarking troops from beaches and shallow ports and ferrying them out to the waiting destroyers and cruisers.

To get the troops from the approach roads on to the beaches and aboard the ferries, Baillie-Grohman needed officers and men such as those in Egypt idly awaiting assignment since the cancellation of Operation Mandibles. These men were trained in the use of landing craft, familiar with getting men on to beaches—not so dissimilar from getting men off beaches. But the twelve

4 *Greek Tragedy '41*, Heckstall-Smith and Baillie-Grohman.

officers, twenty-four petty officers and leading seamen, seventy-two seamen and six signalmen requested by Baillie-Grohman came not from the disbanded Mandibles contingent, but from the bombed HMS *York* in Suda Bay. Nor was the full complement despatched. Of the middle category requested—the twenty-four petty officers and leading seamen—Baillie-Grohman only got one petty officer and seven leading seamen.

In the midst of all this administrative activity, more practical steps were being taken to clear the congested harbour and the devastated quayside and dock zone and to reinstate the port facilities of the Piraeus in an effort to get the port functioning again. And the minesweepers *Salvia, Hyacinth* and *Muroto* swept the channels to allow shipping movement within the harbour and through the anchorage outside the Bay.

*

While Baillie-Grohman was engaged in these multifarious duties other equally dramatic events were unfolding. On April 18th, the day after he arrived in Athens Baillie-Grohman attended a conference with General Wilson and Air Vice Marshal D'Albiac. At this meeting he learned that there had been a marked deterioration in the military situation and that General Papagos, the Greek Commander-in-Chief, had informed General Wilson that 'if it was possible, he would like the British forces to be withdrawn as soon as practicable'.

This request for withdrawal received a cabled reply from Winston Churchill the following day stating that there was to be no question of withdrawal of British troops unless the Greek King and his Government requested it.

At this same meeting on the 18th it was decided that the earliest date of D 1 for Operation Demon was likely to be Monday, April 28th. But on April 21st it was learned in Athens that the German invaders had reached Yannino the previous evening and that the Greek Army in the Epirus had capitulated without informing the Greek Government and without reference to General Papagos. The British authorities were not warned of the impending disaster. This action put the ANZAC Corps under threat and General Wil-

72

son decided that evacuation must start as soon as possible, probably the night of April 24th–25th. After this sombre meeting Baillie-Grohman took the precaution of asking for certain shipping to be held in readiness at Suda Bay.

On this same Friday—18th—large numbers of the British colony in Greece fled the country in two Greek ships which sailed at night seeking darkness to escape the hordes of German aircraft which enjoyed virtually undisputed air supremacy.[5]

On this day, too, the Greek Prime Minister, Koryzis, shot himself only twenty-four hours after an emergency cabinet meeting called by the King, possibly in the hope of expiating his policy of appeasement.

At this time the military events were moving with frightening speed and changing like a kaleidoscope as the German *blitzkrieg* advanced almost unchecked. Measures and counter measures conflicted. Precautions proved fruitless. Action ordered became outdated before implementation. Confusion engendered more confusion, which spread like the ripples on a pond from the battle front in Greece to Alexandria itself. Contributing to the chaos were the air attacks which were executed with an intensity which stunned the senses. In the forty-eight hours of April 21st and 22nd the *Luftwaffe* concentrated mass attacks upon shipping and it was reported that twenty-three vessels including two hospital ships and the Greek destroyer *Hydra* were sunk by bomb attacks.

Such was the perplexing and contradictory state of affairs, that muddle and confusion in Egypt almost damned Operation Demon right from the outset. At one stage an Operation Lustre convoy—for the transportation of the Army and its stores to Greece—was at sea heading for that country, and yet trailing astern by only twenty-four hours an Operation Demon convoy was putting to sea to embark the retreating British troops.

Baillie-Grohman's chief staff officer ashore in Alexandria, Commander R. D. Hughes, arranged in concert with Cunningham's staff and a small inter-services committee in Cairo that 'no preparatory action for Operation Demon was to be taken unless

[5] By April 21st the RAF fighter force had been reduced to eighteen Hurricanes.

demanded by GHQ Middle East'. It was also clearly understood that the navy needed four days' notice to get the ships to the beaches of Greece. This notice was needed in order to allow the navy to continue with its mass of routine duties such as suc- couring the army in the Western Desert, discharging stores to the troops in besieged Tobruk, escorting convoys throughout the whole of the Eastern Mediterranean, and for victualling, fuelling and ammunitioning. It was to participate in one of these Western Desert sorties that the *Glengyle* set out from Alexandria to land a raiding party at Bardia on April 19th. A little further along the coast, the A lighters were being put to good use, being blooded at Tobruk.

It was for these reasons that the navy could not stand by idly awaiting a call for immediate assistance in Greece. She needed just four days to marshal her resources.

Captain A. L. Poland, a veteran of the Battle of Jutland in the battlecruiser *New Zealand,* of the Dogger Bank and the Heligoland Bight actions, and much-decorated for gallantry in the present war, was the Senior Naval Officer Inshore Squadron. Under his command came all the small craft operating on the supply run to Tobruk. With commendable enterprise he sailed the A lighters to Suda before GHQ Middle East asked for them, an action which elicited a protest from the army garrison com- mander in Tobruk.

On April 20th Baillie-Grohman outlined his plan for the em- barkation of a maximum of 56,000 troops during a five-day pe- riod from April 28th. It was proposed that no less than twenty-one embarkation points be used for lifting the troops. Most of the ships engaged in this operation were to sail direct to Egypt while others were to be employed operating a ferry service between the embarkation points and the island of Crete.

In the event, the advanced date of the evacuation resulted in a greater use of Crete as a staging post and in a severe reduction in the number of embarkation points. These were: Kalamata in the south-west of the Morea; Rafina and Port Raftis, east of Athens; Megara, west of Athens; Nauplia, Myli and Tolon at the head of the Gulf of Nauplion; and Monemvasia in the south-east.

Baillie-Grohman instructed that rescue ships reach their embarkation points one hour after dark and leave by 0300 the following day in order to gain maximum advantage from darkness and to minimise the number of air attacks. He had already had attention drawn by the Air Officer Commanding 'to the precarious state to which his fighter strength was being reduced'.

At a meeting in Cairo late on the afternoon of the 21st it was decided that D 1 for Operation Demon would be April 28th and it would rate topmost priority. Furthermore, the three *Glen* ships and the A lighters were now to be officially released to Suda Bay. The order also specified: 'special tractors, workshop lorries, 4.5 inch and AA guns were to be withdrawn from Greece.' This absurd order was clearly incapable of execution: such weighty items would be impossible to embark from open beaches into lighters. Cunningham displayed a better appreciation of the situation three days later when he signalled the Mediterranean Fleet: 'The object of the operation is to embark men, if possible with arms; but no material must be allowed to take precedence to men.'

From his HQ in Suda Bay, Pridham-Wippell was to see that the navy shepherded the right ships to the right beachheads and provided the necessary warships to give cover to the operations. He had available a substantial number of vessels. The major units were the cruisers *Orion,* Pridham-Wippell's flagship, *Ajax, Phoebe* and the Australian *Perth,* the three AA cruisers *Calcutta, Coventry* and *Carlisle,* twenty destroyers, three sloops, two of the *Glen* ships—the *Glenearn* and the *Glengyle*—and fourteen troopships or transports.

Such was the muddle now that on the afternoon of April 21st —the day that the decision was taken to start the evacuation one week later on the 28th—the last Operation Lustre convoy, AN 29, left Alexandria and twenty-four hours later, Rear Admiral Cresswell despatched the first Operation Demon convoy to Suda Bay to be held there in readiness. This convoy, AG 13, comprised the three *Glen* ships and the assault ship HMS *Ulster Prince,* which was loaded with a thousand troops for Crete. But the

Glenroy ran aground while leaving Alexandria and she took no further part in the operation. Sensibly, her beach parties and six of her small landing craft were transferred to the *Thurland Castle*. This convoy was escorted by the *Calcutta*, the *Phoebe* and the two destroyers *Stuart* and *Voyager*.

On this day, too, Captain J. A. V. Morse, flew into Suda Bay to take up his duties as Naval Officer-in-Charge, another last minute appointment typical of so many changes in command made during moments of stress in battle which more often add to the confusion rather than alleviate it. The choice of Morse as NOIC was a specially fortunate one. He performed sterling work and Cunningham later praised his efforts during the Crete evacuation: his 'stout-hearted vigour and counsel had been of the greatest value throughout.'[6]

On this same day, the 22nd, just three hours after the Demon convoy had left Alexandria, Cresswell received a signal indicating that D 1 might now be April 24th. Three hours later still—at 1900—this information was confirmed. Cresswell now had to cancel many complex arrangements in his sailing schedules including instructing the transport *Delane* to stop embarking AA guns for Crete immediately and prepare to sail in convoy for Suda Bay within hours. This convoy, ANF 29, escorted by the *Coventry* and the destroyers *Wryneck, Diamond* and *Griffin,* comprised the transports *Pennland, Thurland Castle* and the *Delane*.

The next day, the 23rd, the shipping movements got into their stride and two more convoys were despatched: AG 14 comprising the *Costra Rica, City of London, Dilwara, Salween, Khedive Ismail* and the ill-fated *Slamat,* escorted by the *Carlisle, Kandahar* and *Kingston.*

This was quickly followed by convoy AG 15 which included the *Ionia, Corinthia, Itria* and *Comliebank,* escorted by the destroyers *Kimberley* and *Vampire,* and the sloop *Auckland.* Thus, squadrons of warships with an armada of transports confided to their care threaded their way northward on their rescue mission. The navy, with the merchantmen as companions in misfortune,

[6] *A Sailor's Odyssey*, Cunningham, p 387.

set out yet again amid lurking dangers from Italian submarines beneath them and German aircraft aloft to endeavour to extricate another British Expeditionary Force. And like Gallipoli, Norway and Dunkirk, it was to be another painful experience.

CHAPTER 5

Retreat to Suda Bay

THE NIGHT OF Thursday, April 24th was D 1 for Operation Demon. At midnight on that date the naval dispositions were as
follows:[1]

At Nauplia embarking troops:

Cruiser	*Phoebe*
Destroyers	*Stuart*[2] (D 10) and *Voyager*[2]
Corvette	*Hyacinth*
Assault Ships	*Ulster Prince* and *Glenearn*

At Raftis embarking troops:

AA Cruiser	*Calcutta*
Cruiser	*Perth*[2]
Assault Ship	*Glengyle*

On Passage:

(*a*) This was the last Lustre convoy AN 29 arriving in the Aegean
April 25th.

Sloop	*Grimsby*
Destroyers	*Vendetta*[2] and *Waterhen*[2]
Transports	*Themani, Zealand, Kirkland, Araybank* and *Rumo*. None of these merchantmen actually took part in the evacuation from Greece.

(*b*) This was the fast ANF 29 convoy arriving in the Aegean April
25th.

AA Cruiser	*Coventry*
Destroyers	*Wryneck, Diamond* and *Griffin*
Transports	*Pennland* and *Thurland Castle*

[1] This information is based upon Vice Admiral Pridham-Wippell's *Report* to
the Commander-in-Chief Mediterranean Fleet May 5th, 1941, published as a
Supplement to the *London Gazette,* May 19th, 1948, but corrected and added to
in the light of later knowledge.

[2] Ships of the RAN.

(c) Vice Admiral Light Forces arriving Suda Bay April 25th at 1800.

Cruiser   *Orion* (VALF)

Destroyers   *Decoy, Hasty, Havock* and *Defender*

(d) Arriving Suda Bay early on April 26th.

Destroyers   *Isis, Hero, Hereward* and *Hotspur*

Fleet oiler   *Brambleleaf*

(e) Arriving Suda Bay April 26th at 0400

Destroyer   *Nubian*

(f) Convoy AG 14 arriving in the Aegean on April 26th at 0700.

AA Cruiser   *Carlisle*

Destroyers   *Kandahar* and *Kingston*

Transports   *Costa Rica, City of London, Dilwara, Salween, Slamat* and *Khedive Ismail*

(g) Arriving Suda Bay on April 26th at 1700

Sloop   *Flamingo*

(h) Convoy AG 15 arriving at Suda Bay on April 27th at 1300.

Destroyers   *Kimberley* and *Vampire*[3]

Sloop   *Auckland*

Transports   *Itria, Corinthia, Ionia, Comliebank, Belray* and *Elonora Maersk*. The last two ships did not take part in the evacuations from Greece.

In his *Report* to the C-in-C, Pridham-Wippell omitted reference to the indomitable little A lighters. Like their larger consorts they too were ready when the need came, on their proper station in good time. It will be recalled that Captain Poland sailed the 1st Flotilla under the command of Lieutenant-Commander Hutton with Lieutenant B. W. Waters as his Number One, from Tobruk to Suda Bay where four of them arrived on April 21st. The A 5 had been detached to sail to Nauplia independently. They made a strange sight. The Mark I variety of A lighter was about 160 feet long and upwards of 350 tons. They were incredibly uncomfortable craft. 'Two officers snatched what sleep they could in an alcove above the engine room, with the ship's galley smelling greasily a couple of yards opposite their bunks. In these craft

[3] Ship of the RAN.

twelve ratings lived in a claustrophobic space measuring twelve by fifteen feet.'[4]

On the day after their arrival they experienced their first Aegean air raids. Two of the craft were secured alongside the beached cruiser *York*. Strenuous efforts had been made to salvage this ship even to the extent of flying out a team of specialists from England. Two divers were over the side working below on her hull when some Ju 88 bombers carried out a high-level attack on the shipping in Suda Bay. Two merchant ships were sunk, two of the A lighters fuelling alongside the damaged tanker *Pericles* (one of the human torpedo targets of a month before), were shaken by blast. One large bomb exploding near the *York* only fifty feet from the A 16 commanded by Mr E. J. Boissel, Bos'n, RN, lifted the craft bodily from the water resulting in damage to a port engine bearing. The explosion killed the two divers and further damaged the cruiser which over the weeks was gradually to be reduced to a wreck.

Two of these valiant small craft arrived off Megara at 1700 on the 23rd: they were the A 1 commanded by Sub-Lieutenant D. Peters, RNVR, and the A 19 commanded by Mr Cooper, Skipper RNR. Both were attacked by dive bombers and the A 1's Fiat machinegun was blasted from its mounting by a near miss. Altogether some thirty bombs were aimed at Peters's craft before she found refuge under a cliff face. A 19 was also near missed by eight bombs all of which exploded close astern.

Meanwhile, further east along the coast, the A 6 underwent a baptism by bombing and machinegunning near Raftis but managed to escape serious damage.

The A 1 tucked away under the cliffs, was singled out for special Stuka attention in the evening. She was repeatedly struck by bombs and settled in two fathoms of water where she remained at rest until blown up by a naval demolition party.

A 5's experiences at Nauplia were equally spectacular. In his account Lambton Burn quotes an interview with a survivor who described his experiences about a year later.[5]

[4] *Down Ramps!* by Lambton Burn, Carroll & Nicholson, 1947.
[5] *Down Ramps!*, Lambton Burn.

Aboard A 5 I was ordered to Nauplia. . . . We beached in the forenoon of April 24th and were told by the Colonel in charge that he thought the evacuation would start that night. At 1630 a Lieutenant-Commander Clark arrived by truck from Athens to set up shop as principal beachmaster. An hour later a Greek ammo[6] ship previously bombed blew up in Nauplia Bay and that helped to give the scene an authentic atmosphere. . . . Stukas were already busy so we weighed anchor and hid the ship in a small cove until dark then proceeded to Nauplia Pier and then made three trips to different ships, each time loaded with nine hundred troops.

Hutton's luckless flotilla was being whittled away from his command. One failed to leave Alexandria because of mechanical troubles. One remained in Suda Bay because of a bearing damage. One lay wrecked and awash near Megara. Only three of his original six remained afloat. They were to suffer infinite privations and render invaluable service to the British, Australian and New Zealand troops during the ensuing nights. But only one was to survive this Greek episode.

As the cruisers and destroyers and the merchantmen confided to their care closed on the embarkation points, the army ashore was executing a rearguard action to cover the retreat of tens of thousands of troops now beginning to assemble at the embarkation points to patiently await rescue.

*

On April 24th, the first full day of the evacuation, naval activity abounded and it is difficult to present a coherent account of the day because of constantly changing scenes amid the eruptions of war at sea and on land.

Baillie-Grohman prudently decided to extricate his HQ from Athens where the dominance of the *Luftwaffe* cut across all normal activities in the city. Myli was chosen as the new site. A w/T set and a new set of cypher books were despatched to the new HQ, but on the very first night of the evacuation there was a complete breakdown of communication with Baillie-Grohman's HQ.

[6] This ship was the *Nicolaos Georgios*.

On this day, too, the King of Greece and some members of the Greek Government left Athens by Sunderland flying boat for Crete. Other civilians, notably the British colony and members of the legation staff had been leaving the capital for some days, boarding whatever Greek steamers were available in the Piraeus. But the scarcity of ships, the difficulties of obtaining water and fuel and the understandable reluctance of the Greek steamer captains to subject their vessels and themselves to the peril of the *Luftwaffe* made this operation lengthy and tiresome.

On this Thursday, the 24th, the sudden appearance of the large Greek yacht *Hellas* in the Piraeus harbour was a rare stroke of fortune. She was speedy and capacious, capable of taking on 1,900 passengers and steaming away at 18 knots. She was immediately requisitioned and instructed to sail after dark, embarking her passengers as late as possible, a routine precaution adopted for these evacuations so as to ensure that no ship was caught partially loaded in daylight and bombed while still alongside. About 500 of the British community, mostly Maltese and Cypriot, began to board the *Hellas* well before darkness. The walking wounded and the nursing staff from the Australian hospital ashore were instructed to board the *Hellas*.

At about 1800—with the sun still well above the horizon—Ju 88s appeared and the expected bombing attack developed. Contrary to instructions the *Hellas* had taken aboard hundreds of her passengers. At about 1900 the yacht was dive-bombed. Two bombs struck her and others exploded near by on the quayside. Within a few minutes the graceful lines of the yacht were obscured by smother and smoke: her expensively appointed cabins and apartments burst into flames which spread rapidly and soon enveloped the ship from stem to stern. The jetty alongside her blazed and the single gangway was destroyed.[7] Thus the yacht became a blazing trap for the wounded and for those stowed between decks. She became a funeral pyre for untold hundreds of people. Colonel Renton reports that fire hoses were not rigged aboard the ship, nor on the jetty until more than an hour after the ship

[7] Colonel Renton who was aboard at the time and was one of the very few lucky survivors revealed that there was only one gangway to the jetty.

was struck. A few passengers from up top managed to jump overboard and were rescued by small craft which approached the yacht. But the survivors were precious few.

It was also on this first day that the assault ship *Glenearn* was bombed and damaged. She was on passage northwards from Suda for the first night's pick-up at Nauplia when two Heinkel bombers selected her as their target. The first bomber dropped four bombs close astern of the ship. The second aircraft was hotly attacked by Captain Waller's destroyer *Stuart* and the *Voyager* but it pressed home the attack. The *Glenearn* was hit on the fo'c'sle, the explosion starting a fire in her paint store, blasting her capstan, destroying the port anchor and cable gear and carrying away a part of her side plating. The ship continued on her way to Nauplia but it took an hour to extinguish the fires.

In the meantime the *Ulster Prince,* escorted by the *Voyager* and the *Hyacinth* was sent on ahead. All the ships arrived safely. The night was moonless and dark when the force entered the Sound approaching the harbour but stars brightened the sky. The sea was calm and phosphorescent. The gentle breeze blew the smoke still rising from the smouldering hulk of the *Nicolaos Georgios* across the Bay towards the land. Within minutes of anchoring with her remaining anchor, the *Glenearn*'s commanding officer, Captain L. B. Hill, got away the landing craft. In the darkness, one was rammed and sunk by the *Hyacinth.*

The commanding officer of the *Ulster Prince,* Captain F. A. Bond, RNR, took his ship into the harbour with the aid of the Sea Transport Officer at Nauplia, Lieutenant-Commander Carr, RNR, who took out to Bond an old chart with a plan of the harbour. He also carried orders from the principal beachmaster, Lieutenant-Commander Clark, to take the *Ulster Prince* alongside the central jetty. In doing so she grounded only a few hundred feet from the jetty. All attempts to dislodge her including towing by the *Hyacinth* and pushing by the A 5 were unavailing. Matters worsened when the *Hyacinth* fouled a tow wire with her propellers. But worse still followed when the *Ulster Prince* swung round to block the harbour entrance making it impossible for the destroyers *Stuart* and *Voyager* to berth both on this night and the ensuing nights.

Thus it was upon the A 5, the *Glenearn*'s landing craft and the collection of Greek caiques that the success of the night's operation now depended. These small craft laboured hard and well as they plied back and forth until 6,685 men had been ferried aboard the waiting ships. The congestion aboard the *Glenearn* became alarming as 5,100 evacuees were crammed aboard, including two German prisoners and thirty cot cases of wounded.

The *Voyager* embarked 340, including 160 Australian, New Zealand and British nurses brought out to her by the caique *Agios Georgios,* one of whom owed her life to Ordinary Seaman C. J. Webb of the destroyer who jumped overboard to rescue her when she fell between the two ships now rolling in the rising swell.

Shortly before 0400 all the ships except the *Ulster Prince* had cleared the harbour and were heading down the Sound. A 5 made desperate efforts to help Bond refloat his 3,791 ton vessel, but all attempts were futile. Bond had lightened ship by pumping all water and spare fuel overboard, cast overboard ammunition, rafts and heavy gear of all sorts, but when all this failed he called for volunteers among the crew to remain aboard to man the guns, and sent the rest ashore. But these attempts to save the *Ulster Prince* came to nought. With daylight on the 25th there came the German bombers and by evening she had been reduced to a wreck, on fire for her whole length. She became a total loss. Not only had the British lost the valuable troop-carrying capacity, but the wreck now blocked the harbour and denied access to ships larger than destroyers.

At 0800 on the 25th the ships retiring from Nauplia made rendezvous with the Raftis convoy and the combined forces steamed for Suda.

*

The evacuation from Raftis on the Thursday night of 24th–25th went more smoothly than that at Nauplia. The *Calcutta* and the *Glengyle* threaded their way through the darkness into the port and let slip anchors. Their boats immediately set out for the beach and the lift-off started. In the next few hours with scarcely a glimmer of light to work by, 5,750 troops were embarked in the *Calcutta* and the *Glengyle*. The cruiser *Perth* was in company but took no part in the actual embarkation of troops.

The three ships met the Nauplia squadron at 0800 and set course for Suda Bay which they reached safely in the afternoon after an ineffectual bombing attack at midday. The total number of troops evacuated by Pridham-Wippell's ships on the first night was 12,435.

*

Friday, April 25th was another day of intense naval activity. Baillie-Grohman, having now restored communications, had signalled Pridham-Wippell his embarkation programme for the remainder of the evacuation period:

25th–26th April	5,000	Megara
26th–27th	27,000	Unspecified areas
27th–28th	Nil	No embarkations
28th–29th	4,000	Githion and Monemvasia
29th–30th	4,000	Kalamata, Githion and Monemvasia

Convoys and their escorts, and Pridham-Wippell's own squadron, were at sea or in Suda Bay on the afternoon of April 25th. He retained the *Defender* with his flagship but detached the other three destroyers, the *Decoy, Hasty* and *Havock,* to Nauplia to discover the fate of the *Ulster Prince,* and to investigate the situation there.

The force despatched to operate that night's Megara evacuation was convoy ANF 29, comprising the *Pennland,* the *Thurland Castle* (with *Glenroy*'s landing craft aboard), the *Coventry, Wryneck, Diamond* and *Griffin.* This force was in the Aegean, *en route* to its destination. In order to give additional support to this important convoy, Pridham-Wippell despatched the *Waterhen* and *Vendetta* from Suda Bay where they were anchored with convoy AN 29, having arrived there on the 24th and having suffered heavy bombing attacks.

Convoy AG 14, on this afternoon, was in the Kaso Strait bound for Suda Bay and under air attack. AG 15 was still to the south of Crete and heading northwards. The naval oil tanker, *Brambleleaf*, urgently needed in Suda now that no fuel remained there, in company with the four destroyers *Isis, Hero, Hotspur* and *Hereward* was nearing her destination. Her estimated time of arrival was early on the morning of the 26th.

The destroyers *Waterhen* and *Vendetta* were speeding to catch up with the Megara force having left Suda at 1430 on the 25th. About four hours later they came upon one of the Megara squadron, the *Pennland*, crippled by a dive-bombing attack, with the *Griffin* standing by. The convoy had been attacked at about 1400 off the island of San Georgio. The *Pennland*, at 16,082 tons the largest of the transports employed in the operation, was hit on the fo'c'sle and her bridge, compasses and steering were wrecked. But greater damage was caused by a near miss which started some plates forward and flood water poured in.

Captain W. P. Carne aboard the *Coventry* ordered Lieutenant-Commander J. Lee-Barber in the *Griffin* to stand by while the rest of the force proceeded to its destination.

The *Pennland*'s crew struggled to strengthen the forward bulkhead to contain the flood water while Captain van Dulken turned his ship back towards Crete. But another attack developed in the evening and a large bomb penetrated the starboard boat deck and exploded in the engine room. The weakened forward bulkhead gave way and the transport started to settle. She was abandoned and the *Griffin* rescued the survivors and set course for Suda.

In the meantime, the two Australian destroyers, advised that they could render no help, carried on towards Megara.

When Pridham-Wippell heard of the loss of the *Pennland* he diverted the *Decoy, Hasty* and *Havock* from Nauplia to Megara to take aboard all those troops which might have boarded the *Pennland*.

The *Waterhen* and the *Vendetta* safely reached Megara at 2200 to find the *Thurland Castle, Coventry* and *Wryneck* already at anchor opposite the beach and their attendant boats, seven caiques and the lighter A 19 commanded by Skipper Cooper, RNR, already embarking troops from the beaches.

Lieutenant-Commander Hutton was appointed temporary beachmaster at Megara in the absence of Lieutenant-Commander Willmott whose strenuous efforts to muster the necessary caiques for the evacuation ended ironically with his being stranded in a broken down caique on his way from Raftis. Hutton coped manfully with the constant changes thrust upon him: the loss of the biggest transport, *Pennland*, necessitated re-planning the night's work: a second change became necessary by the substitution of the three destroyers sent by Pridham-Wippell; throughout the dark, busy night Hutton supervised a motley fleet of small craft to ferry troops from the beaches and an inadequate jetty to the waiting ships: ships' whalers and a skiff were used, as was a small caique with Able Seaman Pike from the *York* put aboard to dissuade the Greek skipper from deserting. Another caique was commanded by Lieutenant Trevor, RNVR, a wounded survivor from the yacht *Hellas,* and yet another was crewed by sappers rescued from the Piraeus. The *Coventry* had her two motor boats, a motor cutter and a whaler operating. Communications between all these vessels and the need to direct them to beaches where the concentration of troops was greatest, made the task onerous.

Serious trouble came when A 19 loaded with about 800 men fouled one of her propellers and was reduced to walking pace on one engine. Sometime later—at about 0200—this lone engine broke down beyond repair. The troops were rescued but the A 19 became a complete loss.

At about 0230 Hutton collected his beach parties and boarded the *Coventry*. In his subsequent *Report* he wrote: 'Immediately I arrived on board I asked the Captain to detail a destroyer to sink A 19. The signal was apparently not understood, and, I regret to say that she was not sunk. It is to be hoped, however, that the enemy dive-bombers will carry this out before they discover she has been abandoned . . . It is a cause of very great regret to me that some 300 men and the Army embarkation staff were left ashore . . . Had A 19 continued to run for one more hour the operation could have been comfortably completed.'

Lieutenant-Commander Rhoades, commanding the *Vendetta*, asked the *Coventry* if he could remain to attempt the rescue of a group of 250 wounded reported to be left ashore but permission was not granted and a hasty withdrawal was made by these two ships to rejoin the remainder of the force now heading southwards through the Gulf of Athens.

The total evacuated from Megara that night was about 5,900. Pridham-Wippell gave the figure of 1,300 for those taken aboard the destroyers *Decoy*, *Hasty* and *Havock* and 4,600 for those aboard the *Thurland Castle*, *Coventry*, *Wryneck*, *Diamond* and *Griffin*. But neither the *Diamond* nor the *Griffin* took part in this night's evacuation. He evidently confused them with the two Australian destroyers, *Waterhen* and *Vendetta*, to whom he made no reference in his *Report*, but who, in fact, rescued about 420 officers and men including many wounded.

The passage to Suda Bay was punctuated by three heavy but ineffectual dive-bombing attacks. Rhoades reported that the troops aboard the *Vendetta* 'maintained a battery of Bren guns on the fo'c'sle and quarterdeck and appeared to enjoy the air raids, as they said it was the first time they had seen some decent opposition to German aircraft since the beginning of the withdrawal'.[8]

But no bombs struck home and Suda Bay was reached safely at 1800 on the 26th. But a melancholy postscript is needed to complete the story of Hutton's contribution to this Greek episode. On arrival at Suda he boarded the A 15, commanded by Mr Dennis, Bos'n, RN, and set course for Monemvasia with the intention of assisting the A 5. But this was the last ever heard of the A 15. She failed to reach Monemvasia and was presumed lost at sea with all hands, believed sunk by aircraft only fifteen miles from her destination.

[8] Quoted in *Royal Australian Navy 1939–1942*, Series 2, Navy, Vol 1, Canberra, Australian War Memorial, 1957, by G. Hermon Gill, p 323.

CHAPTER 6

Triumph and Tragedy

VICE ADMIRAL PRIDHAM-WIPPELL'S responsibilities assumed frightening proportions during the hours of daylight and darkness on Saturday, April 26th and during the early hours of Sunday. A mass of shipping movements of bewildering complexity called for unending decisions during this week-end of fluctuating fortunes.

The Saturday started happily enough for him at 0300 with the arrival in Suda Bay of the oiler *Brambleleaf* and her destroyer escort. They were quickly followed by the lone destroyer *Nubian* who had sailed independently from Alexandria. These fine destroyers brought a welcome strengthening of the forces under Pridham-Wippell's command.

A few hours later convoy AG 14—comprising six large transports in the care of the *Carlisle, Kandahar* and *Kingston*—arrived safely in the Aegean and awaited destination instructions for the night of Saturday–Sunday, the 26th–27th. Convoy AG 15, another collection of transports escorted by the *Kimberley, Vampire* and *Auckland,* had passed through the Kaso Straits safely and steamed west along the north coast of Crete to reach Suda Bay early on Saturday afternoon, but without the *Vampire* who had been detached earlier in the day to assist a merchant ship, the *Scottish Prince,* 4,917 tons, which had been bombed, brought to a standstill and abandoned by her crew forty miles ENE of Suda. The *Vampire* located the crippled steamer at 1730 and relieved the destroyer *Hasty* who had been standing by and had managed to get some of the merchant seamen back aboard their ship. At 1930 the trawler *Grimsby* also arrived to assist. Soon the merchantman managed to raise steam and got under way. With the trawler leading and the destroyer screening, the *Scottish Prince* was brought to Suda Bay at 0610 on Sunday.

Pridham-Wippell's cruiser squadron had been at sea throughout the night of Friday–Saturday giving general cover to the night's operations. On the forenoon of Saturday 26th his force gave close cover to the concentration north of Crete of all the ships allocated to that night's evacuation. Just how hard-pressed were the warships at this time is exemplified by the four *Brambleleaf* escorts. They had arrived at Suda Bay at about 0400 that morning and had immediately oiled and then rested for one hour before setting off again at 1000. On their way to the concentration zone just before midday they passed the southbound Megara convoy of the night before with the *Coventry* and her destroyers blazing away in defiance repelling one of the heavy attacks they experienced that day. The destroyers joined Pridham-Wippell soon after midday.

Other ships were also hard-pressed. Both the *Calcutta* and the *Glenearn*—minus her anchor gear and a chunk of her fo'c'sle—had barely had time to discharge their troops before cleaning up and getting under way again. These were desperately gruelling and tiring days for the men of the Navy who toiled strenuously without much respite and little reward.

At the concentration zone, the assembling ships formed up into convoys and set off for their destinations. Pridham-Wippell's intentions for the night of Saturday–Sunday were:

Rafina	*Glengyle, Nubian, Decoy, Hasty*
Raftis	*Salween, Carlisle, Kandahar, Kingston*
Nauplia	*Slamat, Khedive Ismail, Calcutta, Isis, Hotspur*
Tolon	*Glenearn, Diamond, Griffin, Havock*
Kalamata	*Dilwara, City of London, Costa Rica, Phoebe, Defender, Flamingo, Hero, Hereward*

The destroyer *Nubian* was instructed, in addition, to embark 600 men reported to be awaiting rescue at Port St Nikolo on Zea Island and then to return to Rafina to help the *Glengyle*.

In response to a signal from Baillie-Grohman, Pridham-Wippell despatched the destroyer *Havock* to call at Myli, where

Baillie-Grohman had his HQ, on the opposite shore of the gulf to Nauplia, to embark important personnel. Baillie-Grohman had no way of knowing whether his signals were being received because of a failure in communications. Baillie-Grohman and his staff had only reached the new HQ at Myli at 0530 on the 26th. But the military situation was deteriorating rapidly, and it took a further sudden plunge towards disaster in the early forenoon when the Germans made a leapfrogging movement by dropping parachute troops ahead of their vanguard to capture the Corinth Canal. 'This necessitated a further alteration of plan, as it was then evident that the only place from which the rearguard could be withdrawn with reasonable safety was from embarkation points in the area to the east of Athens.'[1]

But Baillie-Grohman was bedevilled by communications problems contributed to by the almost continual presence of enemy aircraft overhead. He prudently dispersed his W/T sets among the near-by olive groves. Unknown to him, his signals were, in fact, being received by Pridham-Wippell who was initiating the necessary action.

By sunset on Saturday the party of important personnel assembling at Myli had reached sizeable proportions. They made their way down to the pier hopefully to await rescue. It was an impressive sight. The party included the General Officer Commanding, General Sir Henry Maitland Wilson and his staff, Major-General T. G. G. Heywood and other members of the British Military Mission, Rear Admiral C. E. Turle, Naval Attaché and his staff, Prince Peter of Greece, the Greek Minister of the Interior and other ministers, including Admiral Sakellariou, ex-Vice Premier. In addition there was Baillie-Grohman himself, his staff and liaison officers.

But we must leave this party of important refugees while they wait impatiently for a destroyer which none of them knew would materialise, and retrace our steps to follow more closely the fortunes of the mass of shipping heading away from its concentration zone towards the embarkation points in Greece.

[1] *Greek Tragedy '41,* Heckstall-Smith and Baillie-Grohman.

*

Although most of the groups of ships reached their destinations without incident, misfortune befell the convoys destined for Nauplia and Tolon which had far-reaching effects upon the over-all evacuation programme.

This group, the *Glenearn*, *Khedive Ismail*, and the *Slamat*, escorted by the *Calcutta*, *Diamond*, *Griffin*, *Hotspur*, *Isis* and *Havock*, had made a good 14 knots through a calm sea under clear skies, unmolested until 1640 when a series of air attacks by eight aircraft were repulsed without loss. Nearly two hours later another dive-bombing attack developed and one pilot, pressing home his attack with courage in the face of a barrage of AA fire, released a single large bomb which fell very close alongside the *Glenearn*. The explosion stove in the strong hull of the ship and erupted a column of water which deluged those on the bridge. The sea water flooded into the engine room, crippling the main engines and dynamos and bringing the ship to a standstill with a list to port. Captain Hill signalled the extent of the damage to his ship to the Senior Officer of the escort, Captain Lees in the *Calcutta*. The latter ordered Lieutenant Letts in the *Griffin* to tow the disabled ship back to Suda. It was an unenviable assignment: close to enemy airfields with still two hours of daylight to go, with a 9,869 ton crippled ship like a giant sheet anchor trailing astern as a handicap.

All ships engaged in the Greek evacuation were conscious of the need to keep clear of the coastal regions in daylight. Baillie-Grohman had pointed this out and Pridham-Wippell commented in his subsequent *Report:* 'It will be noticed that nearly all losses from aircraft were sustained in the region of the parallel 37 degrees north, which was approximately the range of the dive-bombers. . . . Throughout there was no fighter support for ships at sea to the northward of 37 degrees north. The RAF in Crete did what they could for convoys south of this latitude, but the protection was slender by reason of the small number of aircraft available.'

Despite these lurking dangers the *Griffin* and her cumbersome

94

tow survived the remainder of daylight and safely reached Kissamo Bay near Cape Spada in Crete.

The damage suffered by the *Glenearn* was relatively unimportant. It was her absence from the beach at Nauplia, and graver still, the absence of her landing craft which gave rise to so much concern, for the *Glen* ships and their shallow-draught craft had proved to be the most valuable vessels for the evacuation. Ironically, these assault craft were performing precisely the opposite tasks to those intended by their designers and planners. Fortunately, soon after she had been disabled the *Glenearn's* small craft were lowered and sent down the coast to Monemvasia where they were put to good use.

During the afternoon of the 26th, Pridham-Wippell received a signal from Baillie-Grohman asking for a *Glen* ship to go to Nauplia instead of Tolon, but no sooner was an effort being made to comply with this request than the situation changed dramatically with the crippling of the *Glenearn*. As soon as Pridham-Wippell received Lees's signal reporting the damage he decided to withdraw his own flagship and accompanying ships from their patrolling station and remedy the situation himself. He took the *Orion, Perth* and *Stuart* and sped for Nauplia.

Meanwhile, Lees in the *Calcutta,* with the two transports *Slamat* and *Khedive Ismail* together with the *Hotspur* and *Isis* had arrived at Nauplia where the still burning *Ulster Prince* smoked like a spectre of doom foreshadowing the toils and struggles of the night. The wreck lay close to the quay, a hazard to shipping and effectively blocking the fairway and denying access to the quay.

Nor did the picture at near-by Tolon look any rosier. The original force of ships was largely dispersed and it is fortunate that only a small number of troops were assembled for rescue. The *Glenearn* and the *Griffin* were now lumbering south to Crete. The *Havock* was instructed to collect Baillie-Grohman and his considerable party of senior officers from Myli. Only the *Diamond* of the original ships destined for Tolon remained available and she was instructed to patrol outside in the bay to give anti-submarine cover to the Nauplia force now at anchor. The lighter

A 5 was the only craft embarking men from Tolon and she carried 400 out to the *Isis* and later a second load to the *Stuart*.

At Nauplia the assembly of small craft for ferrying comprised the life-boats from the transports, pulling-whalers, motor boats and cutters from the warships and two Greek caiques commanded by British officers, the *Dolphin* and the *Agios Georgios*.

This small force struggled as well as it could in the deteriorating weather conditions, giving rise to a choppy sea and increasing wind which made broaching to in the surf difficult to combat especially when dealing with troops unaccustomed to boats and in darkness off unknown beaches. One of the *Calcutta*'s boats capsized and her motor boat fouled her propellers. The evacuation proceeded, albeit at a lumbering pace. It seemed, at times, a daunting task and the mass of soldiers undiminishing.

Half an hour before midnight Pridham-Wippell's force appeared out of the gloom. He detached the redoubtable Waller in the *Stuart* to Tolon and took the *Orion* and the *Perth* to Nauplia. The report he received was disquieting. To improve the situation he ordered the *Hotspur,* now with 500 troops aboard, to relieve the *Diamond* out in the Bay on anti-submarine patrol, which so far had no troops aboard. But because of a mechanical failure the *Hotspur* had to raise anchor by hand, reminiscent of the days of old, piping all seamen to the fo'c'sle, rigging the capstan bars and delaying her departure by an hour.

This delay resulted in the *Diamond* being unable to take any troops aboard during the night. But more poignant and distressing was the waste of the transport *Khedive Ismail*. She had accommodation for thousands of troops but because of the dearth of small craft for ferrying the troops from shore to ship she embarked none. Her brave errand to Nauplia went unrewarded. Worse still, while the empty transport finally weighed anchor and sailed for the Bay, thousands of troops, variously estimated at between 2,500 and 6,000, were abandoned ashore.

At Tolon, the indomitable A 5 struggled, it seemed, alone and disconsolate in the face of many ordeals. When Waller arrived with the *Stuart* at about 2315 he found the A 5 waiting offshore with 600 troops packed aboard. These men were immediately transferred to the destroyer and Waller signalled Pridham-Wippell requesting a cruiser at Tolon to embark a large number of men still ashore. He sent A 5 back inshore to load up again and to await the arrival of a cruiser. The *Perth* arrived at 0140 and embarked 300 men from the lighter.

In the meantime Waller hastened off to Nauplia, transferred his 600 men to the *Orion* and sped back to Tolon, anchored inshore of the *Perth* and these two Australian ships put their own boats into use in ferrying more troops aboard. These two ships stayed until 0430, dangerously late, at which time the beachmaster told Captain Sir Philip Bowyer-Smith, of the *Perth,* that there were less than a lighter load ashore and that the Germans, advancing from their Corinth Canal parachute drop, were only seven or eight miles away. Bowyer-Smith told the beachmaster to embark the remaining troops in the A 5 and to work down the coast away from the advancing Germans. The A 5 duly took aboard a full load of no less than 600 men, but the previous estimate of men ashore was wrong for at least as many were still left ashore when the lighter sailed. She eventually reached Monemvasia safely twenty-four hours later.

At 0700 the *Perth* and *Stuart* joined VALF about fifty miles south-east of Nauplia and the force sped for Suda Bay where it arrived without incident later that afternoon. Between them, the ships brought nearly 2,000 men to safety.

While these ships were speeding on their way south, matters ashore in Nauplia were building up to a dramatic and tragic finale. By 0300—the deadline set by Baillie-Grohman for ships to depart from their anchorages—the Dutch vessel *Slamat* was still at anchor and making no preparations for departure. By 0330 two signals from Lees in the *Calcutta* ordering the master, Captain Lundinga, to sail went unacknowledged. It has been suggested that because Lundinga and his crew were Dutch they failed to understand the signals; some suggest it was the Nelson touch; yet others, probably far closer to the truth, believe that some Australians already aboard the 11,636 tons transport prevailed upon the Captain to delay longer to embark hundreds of their friends still ashore. After all, he might have reasoned, his ship could accommodate thousands more and it may well have gone against the grain for this mariner to think he was wasting his ship by quitting the anchorage with it mainly empty. And in a fit of misplaced pity he waited patiently for the troops to come aboard. But this is mere conjecture. Whatever the reason—and now we shall never know the truth—the Dutchman remained obdurately at anchor until an officer from the *Diamond* clambered aboard the *Slamat* and gave the Master a direct order to weigh anchor. It was well after 0400 on Sunday morning, considerably over an hour late, before the ship was got under way.

As the convoy assembled and sailed south into the Gulf of Nauplia the sky to the east was already brightening. Officers aboard the warships viewed this with profound uneasiness. But before we focus our attention upon the progress and plight of this convoy we must briefly chronicle the other events of the night of Saturday–Sunday, April 26th–27th.

*

The destroyer *Havock,* it will be recalled, had been instructed to embark Baillie-Grohman and his considerable party of important personnel from Myli. On their arrival at the pier it was evident that no destroyer awaited the party, but a Sunderland flying boat rode to her small anchor. General Wilson and fifty-five other important persons were embarked upon the aircraft which eventually flew off at 0630 on Sunday for Suda. Included in this party was Baillie-Grohman's Chief of Staff, Commander Fearn, sent to give a detailed account to Cairo of the situation in Greece. Baillie-Grohman remained behind intent upon reaching Monemvasia fifty-six miles away, by daylight. The patience of the remainder of the party was rewarded when Lieutenant-Commander Watkins carefully conned the *Havock* through the unknown waters of the bay and entered the tiny harbour of Myli and Baillie-Grohman and his party climbed aboard.

On the way south to Monemvasia, just before dawn on the 27th, *Havock* came upon the flotilla of landing craft which Captain Hill of *Glenearn* amid the stresses of handling his battered ship had lowered overboard and thoughtfully instructed

Lieutenant-Commander Best, RNR, to proceed to Monemvasia for use two nights hence.

Best was signalled to come alongside the destroyer and was astonished when a Rear Admiral clambered down the ladder into his landing craft. Baillie-Grohman, accompanied by Brigadier Galloway and a number of others, set off for Monemvasia and at daybreak the strange flotilla beached on a sandy cove four miles north of the embarkation point. The landing craft were scattered at half-mile intervals along the coast and were camouflaged to avoid detection from the air. The Rear Admiral and his miniscule command hid themselves and gave in to the physical exhaustion which now overwhelmed them.

The *Havock* and the Sunderland flying boat with their hundreds of refugees both reached Suda Bay safely without further incident.

*

As we know from Pridham-Wippell's intentions there were other embarkations that night of Saturday–Sunday, April 26th–27th; at Port Raftis, Rafina and Kalamata. At Raftis the wind had strengthened to Force 6 and conditions for embarkation were almost intolerable. This was especially upsetting for Lieutenant-Commander N. Willmott, the principal beachmaster for Operation Demon who planned the evacuation with meticulous detail. He guided and impelled the activities with energy and zeal. Yet his plans were bedevilled by an infinite variety of problems and misfortunes. He bore all these adversities with composure.

It was 2130 on Saturday night when the *Carlisle* led the *Salween* with only a sketch map of the port into the pitch dark anchorage of Raftis followed by the *Kandahar* and *Kingston*.

The lighter A 6, three large caiques under the command of Lieutenant-Commander T. K. Garrard, sundry smaller caiques —almost unmanageable in the sea conditions—and small boats from the warships, all displayed seamanship of a high order in ferrying the patient troops out to the anchored ships in the Bay. No less than 4,750 men were embarked.

At near-by Rafina the conditions were no better and the heavy swell created problems for the *Glengyle* which protracted the proceedings. By 0300 the *Glengyle* had recovered the last of her landing craft which in a period of two hours completed a total of no less than forty-six trips and rescued a total of 3,500 troops.

The *Glengyle* joined the Raftis group—the *Salween, Carlisle, Kandahar, Kingston* and now the *Nubian*—at 0330 and the convoy set course for Suda Bay which was reached safely without loss.

The *Nubian* had been sent on a fruitless errand during the night to Port St Nikolo on Zea Island to pick up a reported 600 New Zealanders. She collected only three, another 450 having been collected earlier in the night by the A 6 which had then transferred them to the *Salween* at Raftis.

Despite the large number of troops embarked on the night of Saturday–Sunday, it was reported that at least another 4,000 had been left in the neighbourhood of Raftis, but before pursuing their fate, there was still more activity on this Saturday night—at Kalamata.

*

Kalamata lies at the head of the wide Gulf of Kalamata. The force that Pridham-Wippell had assigned to this embarkation point comprised the 11,100 ton British Steam Navigation Company's *Dilwara,* the antiquated Ellerman passenger ship, *City of London,* 9,000 tons and the thirty-year-old Royal Netherlands steamship *Costa Rica* of 8,700 tons. These ships were escorted by the *Phoebe, Defender, Hereward* and *Hero.* Even while they were heading north-west from Suda, events ashore in Greece were reaching disaster proportions for the British in the Peloponnese.

British troops in their thousands retreating from the Germans headed for the port of Kalamata by any means at their disposal hoping for escape by sea. By Saturday evening a force numbering some 15,000 had marshalled in the neighbourhood of the port. Morale had reached its nadir. Many thousands of the troops no longer bore arms. A pall of defeat overhung the area like a leaden mantle. The only glimmer of brightness to penetrate the gloom was the hope of rescue by the Navy.

It is a pity that such confidence and trust in the invincibility of the Navy was missing in more senior army officers in the Kalamata area; despite naval plans, made known to the military authorities ashore in Kalamata, for the embarkation of troops on the Saturday night, one Brigadier was reported as believing there would be no embarkation that night and he failed to marshal his troops with the result that thousands of dispirited men were denied rescue. Other army commanders with less jaundiced views paraded their men ready for embarkation.

The destroyers *Hero* and *Hereward* were the first to arrive at Kalamata, having been sent on ahead of the convoy by Captain G. Grantham of the *Phoebe*. Lieutenant-Commander Biggs of the *Hero* groped his way into the unlit and deceptive harbour entrance. He subsequently reported: 'The quay was practically deserted and great difficulty was experienced in finding anyone to berth the ships. It appeared that no information had been received about embarkation as the telegraph system was out of action and the army w/t set had failed to receive any signals during the day.'[2]

The two destroyers finally secured alongside with the aid of searchlights and, despite the lack of help, did so as smoothly as if they were in their familiar berths in Alexandria. The time was only 2100. Within minutes 400 RAF personnel and 150 troops had congregated ready for embarking. But time had been wasted rigging harbour lights and making preparations ashore for marshalling the troops into some semblance of order, preparations which should rightly have been performed before the arrival of the warships. Biggs considers that with better prior arrangements the destroyers could each have made another ferrying trip to the anchored transports outside the harbour, thus rescuing another 3,000 troops.

By 0300 on the Sunday morning the night's haul totalled

---

[2] This does not alter the fact that the Senior Military Officer ashore had been informed by the beachmaster Captain Clark-Hall, RN, of the night's intentions several hours before the arrival of the destroyers.

101

8,650 troops, including 250 aboard the *Defender* who had also had time to load a number of large packing cases containing the priceless Yugoslav crown jewels.

Despite the large number of men rescued it was a saddening experience for the navy to depart with the *Phoebe, Hereward* and *Hero* empty knowing that there were probably 7,000 or more troops still left ashore with a forlorn hope of rescue. The convoy assembled and finally departed at 0340 and headed down the Gulf of Kalamata to the Ionian Sea and thence through the Antikithera Channel into the Aegean. There we must leave this force for a moment while we revert to the Nauplia convoy which we left early on the morning of Sunday, April 27th having been delayed by the misplaced compassion of Captain Lundinga aboard the Dutch transport *Slamat*.

*

When daylight came on Sunday morning the convoy—*Slamat* with an estimated 500 troops aboard, the empty *Khedive Ismail*, the *Calcutta* with nearly 1,000 troops and the destroyers *Isis, Hotspur* and *Diamond*—was still in the Gulf of Nauplia, well to the north of latitude 37° N regarded by Pridham-Wippell as the danger zone.

It was about 0700 when the attacks began. It was a clear, bright day with a fresh wind which whipped the sea into a short swell. Ju 87 dive-bombers put in an appearance and immediately singled out the largest ship, the *Slamat*, as their target. Captain Lees in the *Calcutta*, took station between the two transports to afford them both maximum protection while the three destroyers concentrated ahead of this formation to create a barrage of AA gunfire through which the Stukas must dive. The pilots dived through this apparently fearlessly and pressed home their attacks despite the added shell fire from the *Calcutta*.

Within minutes the *Slamat* was convulsed by two direct hits, the forward one engulfing the bridge in a sheet of flame, disabling the ship, destroying the wheelhouse and killing Captain Lundinga. The time was 0715: the position 37° 01′ N 23° 10′ E. The *Slamat* took charge, narrowly missed colliding with the

Calcutta, turned head into wind and fanned the flames from the fo'c'sle aft through the length of the ship which soon became a funeral pyre.

The *Diamond,* who had collected no troops during the night, was ordered to remain with the ship to rescue survivors while the rest of the convoy proceeded. Some Stukas flew over the burning wreck to spray it with their machineguns and cannons and subjecting the *Diamond* to sporadic dive-bombing attacks, but the main attack continued to be launched against the *Khedive Ismail* who emerged miraculously from the mass of near misses which threw up pillars of water so closely together that they appeared like a huge water barrier. No bombs struck her nor her escorts. The final wave of aircraft—Ju 88s—their bombs expended, departed at about 0900.

It was at this time that the destroyers *Wryneck, Vendetta* and *Waterhen* closed the convoy at high speed from the south, having been sent from Suda Bay by Pridham-Wippell to relieve the *Isis* and *Hotspur* to allow them to press on at speed to Suda to unload their cargo of troops.

Meanwhile, at 0815, Lieutenant-Commander P. A. Cartwright, commanding the *Diamond,* had signalled asking for support in picking up survivors, and reported that he was being constantly dive-bombed.

At 0910 when the three relief destroyers joined him, Lees in the *Calcutta* despatched Commander R. D. H. Lane in the *Wryneck* to assist the *Diamond.*

The *Wryneck* reached the *Diamond* at about 1000 by which time the latter had collected about 500 soldiers and crew from the still burning *Slamat.* The *Wryneck* picked up about another fifty from boats and rafts then the *Diamond* despatched the blazing Dutchman with a torpedo and the two destroyers headed for Suda Bay at speed.

At 1025 a signal was received from the *Wryneck* asking for fighter protection. This was the last heard of both these destroyers until a mere handful of survivors were clutched from the sea later and related their mournful tale of disaster.

It was soon after noon on the Sunday when the blow was

struck. A Messerschmitt swooped down almost unobserved and raked the upperworks of the *Diamond* with machinegun and cannon fire. Almost immediately a Ju 88 dived low and released a stick of bombs. One grazed the port side and its detonation on the water stove in the destroyer's hull. The forward messdecks, crowded with Australians snatched once from the clutches of the advancing Germans and then from a blazing transport, became a scene of carnage. A second bomb crashed through into the engine room, demolished the after mast and funnel, flung soldiers overboard and opened up the ship to the sea. Flood water poured aboard and the *Diamond* began to settle fast by the stern. Within moments another bomb was seen to fall from an aircraft and explode on the destroyer's torpedoes.

The *Wryneck,* in company with the *Diamond,* was attacked simultaneously and the pattern of the attack upon her closely resembled that made upon the *Diamond*. Firstly there came a raking of the decks with machinegun and cannon fire, killing and wounding many of the guns' crews in exposed positions. Secondly, there came the bombing attacks. The first bomb burst near the ship and was followed almost immediately by another explosion close alongside. The destroyer heeled over to port. The stokers' messdeck forward was shattered and the casualties among the soldiers and the ship's company were heavy. The *Wryneck,* like her consort, was also struck in the engine room and she was brought to a standstill, clearly doomed. She filled with water rapidly while the ship was abandoned. In fifteen minutes the destruction was complete. Both destroyers had gone. The Gulf of Nauplia became a scene littered with the grisly flotsam of war at sea.[3]

Nothing of this tragedy was known to Pridham-Wippell. Neither of the two destroyers had got away signals telling of their agonies. Nor was there any reason to suppose that these two ships were in such peril. Pridham-Wippell in his flagship *Orion* with the returning Nauplia convoy was not far from the scene of

[3] For detailed reports from Stoker Petty Officer H. T. Davis senior survivor from the *Diamond* and Mr Waldron, Warrant Engineer of the *Wryneck,* see the excellent account in *Greek Tragedy '41.*

destruction of his two destroyers, but he was not to know this. He had, instead, the heartening sight of welcoming the cruiser *Ajax* steaming to join his command at 0730 that Sunday morning. Four hours later the Vice Admiral and his cruisers reached Suda Bay and began discharging their troops.

No sooner had the newly arrived *Ajax* reached Suda Bay than she was despatched with the destroyers *Kingston, Kimberley* and *Havock* soon after noon for Raftis for that night's evacuation.

Such was the overcrowding of Suda Bay that Pridham-Wippell was compelled to take action to clear the threatening congestion. A large convoy was formed to clear the area. The troopships from the previous night's embarkation were ordered not to enter Suda Bay but to concentrate at a point north of the island on the early afternoon of Sunday to form convoy GA 14. It comprised the following: *Glengyle, Salween, Khedive Ismail, Dilwara, City of London* and *Costa Rica*. As close escort Pridham-Wippell provided the *Coventry, Calcutta, Flamingo, Stuart, Vendetta, Waterhen* and *Vampire*. The convoy formed up in a position about twenty miles north of Maleme aerodrome. The Senior Air Officer, Crete, was asked to provide fighter cover while the convoy formed and escorts were exchanged.

Sporadic air attacks were launched against the converging convoys during the forenoon and early afternoon. It was at about 1500 when an attack by three dive-bombers was directed at the ancient *Costa Rica* and a 1,000 lb bomb burst close alongside. The explosion caused a vertical split in the hull abreast the engine room. With typical Dutch stubbornness the vessel refused to sink for over an hour, allowing enough time for the destroyers *Defender, Hereward* and *Hero* to secure alongside and take off all the troops and the ship's company.

Additional protection for convoy GA 14 was afforded by a covering force with orders to patrol to the north-west during the night of Sunday, April 27th. It comprised the *Perth, Phoebe, Decoy, Hasty, Nubian, Hereward, Hero* and *Defender*.[4]

Just how hard-worked these light forces were at this time is

[4] Pridham-Wippell also quotes the *Wryneck*, but as we have seen, she had already been sunk.

demonstrated by this timetable: nearly all these ships had arrived at Suda Bay at about 1900, they discharged what troops they had collected the previous night, refuelled, then at 2030—just ninety minutes after arrival—many of them sailed again to escort the convoy. At 2300 the remaining destroyers, having landed their troops and the *Costa Rica* survivors and refuelled, also sailed to join the escorts.

The convoy sailed throughout the rest of Sunday afternoon without undue incident, then darkness cloaked their movements and brought respite from the attention of the *Luftwaffe*. Alexandria was reached safely without further loss and tens of thousands of British troops found sanctuary in Egypt.

Another safe arrival in Alexandria was HMS *Glenearn*. As already related, she had been towed to Kissamo Bay near Cape Spada by the *Griffin*. The latter took off 150 of the assault ship's company leaving ninety aboard. The *Grimsby* came round from Suda Bay to prepare to tow the disabled ship to Alexandria which was accomplished despite an air attack off Gavdos Island which proved abortive.

*

We must now revert, for a moment, to the *Diamond* and *Wryneck* sinkings. When the *Phoebe* with her destroyers reached Suda Bay at 1900 and made ready for her hasty departure, she realised that the *Diamond* was not among the ships entering harbour. Anxiety for her safety mounted. From 1922 till 1955 she was called repeatedly but there was no response. In his subsequent *Report* Pridham-Wippell recorded: 'As *Diamond* had last been heard of with *Wryneck* during the forenoon, *Phoebe* and *Calcutta* were asked whether *Wryneck* had been seen going away with GA 14 since I did not wish to ask *Wryneck* herself to break W/T silence. Their replies at 2235 and 2245 gave no definite indication. I therefore despatched *Griffin* to the position of the sinking of the *Slamat* to investigate.'

The first news which confirmed that tragedy must have befallen the destroyers came in a signal from the *Griffin* at 0230 on Sunday. She reported having come upon one of *Wryneck*'s rafts.

The *Griffin* continued her search but the numbers of survivors was distressingly small. Only one officer, forty-one ratings and eight soldiers survived the loss of the *Slamat,* the *Diamond* and the *Wryneck.* A total of 263 officers and men were missing from the two destroyers, all of the *Slamat*'s ship's company was lost and an estimated 500 troops. It was a heavy toll to pay for the Dutchman's refusal to obey orders.

Before we close this chapter on the sombre events of Saturday and Sunday the scales should be balanced by recording that the total number of troops rescued on the night of April 26th–27th was 21,400.

Thus, in the three nights of unflagging toil, the Navy had harvested nearly 40,000 soldiers. It was not an insignificant total. The hazards had been measureless. Nor were they ended, for the evacuation was to continue for several more nights.

CHAPTER 7

The Kalamata Episode

EMBARKATION ON THE NIGHT of Sunday–Monday, April 27th–28th was from Port Raftis and Rafina, both of which had been used the previous night. As we have already seen the newly arrived cruiser *Ajax* with the three destroyers *Kingston, Kimberley* and *Havock* were despatched from Suda Bay soon after noon on Sunday to arrive off Raftis at 2200 that night. The object of this, the final evacuation north of the Corinth Canal, was to embark an estimated 3,000 troops forming the British rearguard, plus beach parties.

At Port Raftis three Greek caiques had loaded up with New Zealand and Australian troops and hopefully awaited the arrival of the warships. These vessels were the fifteen ton caique *Evangellistria,* commandeered and commanded by Lieutenant-Commander N. Willmott, the principal beachmaster, the *Agios Dimitrios,* commanded by Sub-Lieutenant R. B. McAusland, RNR, and the *Agios Minas,* commanded by Lieutenant-Commander T. K. Garrard. The lighter A 6 which had hidden in a bay on the south side of Zea Island emerged at dusk and sailed for Rafina where she beached herself in readiness for embarking. She was quickly followed by the welcome arrival of the *Ajax* and her destroyers. As soon as the warships anchored the fully laden caiques proceeded alongside to discharge their cargoes and the night's ferry service began.

As soon as Captain E. D. B. McCarthy of the *Ajax* heard from Willmott of 800 troops remaining at Rafina some miles farther north along the coast, he ordered the *Havock* to rescue them. The *Havock* was accompanied by McAusland's caique. They located the troops which had held the Germans at bay a mere quarter of a mile from the beach. The caique and the de-

109

stroyer collected all the troops safely and returned to Port Raftis.

There, the embarkation was proceeding apace. When Willmott had embarked Brigadier Puttick and satisfied himself that no other British troops remained ashore, he informed McCarthy and the *Ajax* and her destroyers departed with a total of 4,640 troops[1] at 0330 on Monday 28th.

When this force safely reached Suda Bay later on the Monday, preparations were already well advanced for that night's evacuation which it was intended would be the final one. Barely had the *Ajax* and her destroyers discharged their troops than they were off again as part of the force destined for Monemvasia. The destroyers *Hotspur, Griffin* and *Isis* were to accompany them to rescue 4,000 troops of the 6th New Zealand Brigade and their Commander, General B. Freyberg. Baillie-Grohman, it will be recalled, was also there.

A smaller operation was to be launched to rescue troops from Kasali Bay on Kithera Island. A tiny, mixed force of ships were assembled to effect the rescue. They were the sloop *Auckland,* the two corvettes *Salvia* and *Hyacinth* and they were to be assisted by one of the landing craft from the *Glenroy* for ferrying duties. This craft was taken to Kithera by the *Ajax* on her way to Monemvasia and was to be towed back to Suda Bay after the operation by one of the corvettes. The embarkation was well executed and this little force collected sixty soldiers, 700 RAF personnel and sixty Greeks.

The Monemvasia ships were late in arriving. They had been delayed by a fruitless submarine search in the course of which a flare was sighted and the *Havock* sped off to investigate. She found two bedraggled Australian airmen in a rubber dinghy, survivors of the *Perth*'s Walrus aircraft shot down earlier that morning by a Ju 88. The delay caused Baillie-Grohman some anxiety. He himself had arrived with the landing craft soon after 2130 and met General Freyberg. As the bay was large and the evacuation beaches hidden from seaward by the island of Monemvasia, Baillie-Grohman sent his signal officer Lieutenant-Commander

[1] The official figures quote: *Ajax* 2,500; *Kingston* 640; *Kimberley* 700; and *Havock* 800.

110

Robertson in an LCA beyond the island to meet whatever ships might be approaching and guide them into the anchorage. Robertson soon met the destroyers and by the time the first one, the *Isis,* had come close inshore the troops were aboard the *Glenearn*'s LCAS and ready to embark. The *Griffin* soon followed and then the *Havock.* The *Hotspur* remained to seaward on anti-submarine patrol.

Baillie-Grohman commented on the smoothness of the night's operation in his *Report.* 'The whole embarkation,' he recorded, 'was remarkably well carried out from five different points. The Army organisation in rear of the beaches and the discipline of the troops were magnificent, especially considering that they had been fighting a rearguard action for some weeks from Salonika almost to Cape Matapan. *Ajax* and the destroyers all closed well in to the jetties and the organisation for embarking the troops in the ships was excellent.'

It was intended that the LCAS should be destroyed on completion of the embarkation. But the warships were being silhouetted by the fires ashore of blazing army equipment and transport. 'The Commanding Officer of *Ajax,*' Baillie-Grohman reported, 'decided he could not wait to complete the destruction. The lights on shore had been bright for some time, and with the danger of submarines, I considered he was correct to leave at once. One submarine had been depth charged on the way to the beaches.[2] One or two LCAS were destroyed by the destroyer *Hotspur* but four or five were left afloat.'

The total number of troops embarked at Monemvasia on Monday night, April 28th–29th was 4,320.

Baillie-Grohman and Freyberg were the last to leave the beach and to board the *Ajax,* having seen the 6th New Zealand Brigade safely embarked. The warships weighed anchor and headed away from the inhospitable shore. Baillie-Grohman believed, with much justification and not a little relief, that he had accomplished his mission and that Operation Demon had been successfully completed. In the circumstances, with w/T communications

[2] According to post-war evidence no German or Italian submarines were in the area at this time.

111

sporadic and unreliable, he can be excused for not knowing that the evacuation from Kalamata was not only incomplete, it was floundering.

*

The situation at Kalamata on the departure of HM ships, it will be remembered, was confused. Because of the failure to ensure the proper marshalling of the troops, the rescuing ships departed leaving probably 7,000 more troops ashore, while hordes of refugees—Palestinians, Yugoslavs and Cypriots—were converging on the port. By the Sunday evening this figure was estimated at 10,000. And close on the heels of these refugees and troops came the Germans.

Nearly all day Sunday the *Luftwaffe* carried out an intensive bombardment of Kalamata which added to the confusion and chaos and made more difficult the problem of safeguarding the troops ashore while waiting for the Navy to return. So rapid was the German advance that the spearhead of their attack, comprising a motorised force of about 300 men and two 60 pounder guns, penetrated into the heart of the town on Monday evening. A counter attack drove them back a few hours later, but the Germans had captured Captain Clark-Hall and his staff.

This was a serious blow because Clark-Hall was the only naval officer in Kalamata and his knowledge of embarking troops during the evacuation from France a year ago would have helped immensely. His absence added to an already confused and complicated situation.

In Suda Bay, Pridham-Wippell believed that about 7,000 troops awaited rescue from Kalamata where the mole and the quay would facilitate a speedy embarkation. Accordingly he despatched a considerable force of HM ships with the expectation that the total force ashore could be lifted in the one night's operation. This force which was designated Force B was under the command of Captain Sir Philip Bowyer-Smith, a Royal Navy officer commanding the Australian cruiser *Perth*.

This ship, in company with the cruiser *Phoebe* and the destroyers *Decoy* and *Hasty* left Suda Bay at 2130 on the 27th to give cover to convoy GA 14. This convoy proceeded through the Kithera Channel, then southwards towards Gavdos Island before the two cruisers and two destroyers turned about and headed north-westerly for Kalamata. The intention was that these ships and those about to join the force would embark troops, then sail direct for Alexandria.

Soon after midnight four more destroyers sailed from Suda Bay, the *Nubian, Hero, Hereward* and *Defender*. They joined Bowyer-Smith in the Mediterranean in a position sixty miles south-west of Gavdos Island at 0800 on the 28th.

Meanwhile, Pridham-Wippell learned that there were possibly 1,500 Yugoslav refugees at Kalamata hoping for rescue, so he reinforced Force B by despatching three more destroyers, the *Kandahar, Kingston* and *Kimberley*. Force B now comprised two cruisers and nine destroyers, a not inconsiderable portion of the Mediterranean Fleet.

At 1930 on Monday, April 28th when in a position about twenty miles south-west of Kalamata, Bowyer-Smith detached Commander Biggs's destroyer *Hero* from Force B to proceed ahead, to enter the harbour and to establish contact with those ashore. As the *Hero* approached, fires were seen to be burning, firing was heard ashore and tracer bullet patterns seen.

At 2045 Biggs had conned his destroyer to within only three miles of the shore when a signal was received from the break-water. It read 'Bosche in town'.[3] Biggs anchored his destroyer close to the beach east of the town and signalled Bowyer-Smith at 2100: 'Harbour occupied by Germans. British troops to south-east of town.' This signal was received by Bowyer-Smith ten minutes later at 2110 when Force B was approaching at 16 knots and was still about ten miles from Kalamata, sufficiently close to see the tracery of incendiary bullets, the glow of fires and hear 'big explosions'.

In his *Report* a few days later Bowyer-Smith wrote: 'As soon

[3] *Greek Tragedy '41* records this signal as 'Bosch in harbour' and goes on to suggest the word should be 'Bombs', a reference to four bombs seen to fall into the harbour but not explode during the day, but this explanation is difficult to accept.

113

as I saw these explosions I realised that during embarkation Force B would be in an extremely hazardous tactical position in the event of attack from seaward. Ships would be silhouetted against explosions and fires on shore, would be embayed and unable to scatter, and there was no covering force in the offing. Taranto was only twelve hours' steaming away and with the information the enemy obviously had, such an attack was far from improbable.'

It is evident that Bowyer-Smith had made a rapid appreciation of the situation and had quickly decided to abandon the operation. The factors which led him to this course of action are numerous, as he indicated in his report. He was influenced by the belief that enemy submarines were in the vicinity. He was more strongly influenced by the threat of surface attack from seaward. He was apprehensive in case the secrecy of the operation had been disclosed. He considered that the time at his disposal was insufficient to embark the estimated numbers from open beaches without the aid of landing craft. He was influenced, too, by the enormity of possible failure: 'The forces under my command,' he reported, 'constituted a substantial part of the light forces of the Mediterranean Fleet whose loss would be in the nature of a calamity, particularly in view of recent cruiser losses.'

Bowyer-Smith considered the choices open to him: firstly, to withdraw the whole force; secondly, to commit the whole force to the embarkation; thirdly, to withdraw the cruisers and leave the destroyers. Weighing all these thoughts carefully, he concluded that 'either all must stay or all must go. Reluctantly I decided that the number that could be got away did not warrant the substantial risk to an important force'.

Accordingly, at 2129 Bowyer-Smith, who had made a cautious approach to within six miles of Kalamata, now reversed course and increased speed to 29 knots to get clear of the embarkation area. Bowyer-Smith ordered the *Hero* to rejoin the Force.

Meanwhile, events ashore in Kalamata were taking a more favourable turn. Biggs ordered his First Lieutenant, Lieutenant-Commander R. F. G. Elsworth, to land and entrusted him with the task of contacting Brigadier Parrington, the Senior Military Officer ashore. He was hampered by the fact that there were no organised beach parties ashore owing to the capture of Clark-Hall, and by the general confusion, not unexpected in a town besieged by a determined attacker on the one hand and a dispirited and disorganised defender on the other hand.

By 2125 Elsworth reported the beach safe for embarking and Biggs made a signal, timed 2125, to Bowyer-Smith: 'Troops collecting on beach east of town. All firing ceased in town. Consider evacuation possible from beach. Brigadier is reporting.'

When Bowyer-Smith received this encouraging signal Force B was already retiring from the scene at speed and was then about twenty miles from Kalamata. Two more signals amplifying the information already given were soon made by Biggs. The first timed at 2134, was received by *Perth* at 2203. It reported: 'Germans in town. Some of our forces attacking. Remainder collecting at beach south-east of town. Officers and signalmen have been landed there, made contact with Senior Officer. Am sending boats. No air raids night previously.'

The second amplifying signal was timed at 2154 and was received by Bowyer-Smith at 2217: 'Germans have only light craft artillery. Consider a certain number of men can be evacuated from beach two miles south of town.' Biggs also asked for *Perth*'s position so he could leave the beach and close the cruiser to report the situation fully.

But these amplifying signals failed to induce a change of mind in Bowyer-Smith. His report states: 'But the decision had been made by then and they did not in any event alter the arguments on which I had based it.'

Meanwhile, back in Suda Bay Pridham-Wippell was watching events with great interest, handicapped though he was by the time lag between signal despatch and interception at Suda. Pridham-Wippell was under the impression that *Perth* and Force B were still in the vicinity of the embarkation beach organising the rescue, guided by *Hero*'s signals. Pridham-Wippell subsequently reported: 'At 2250 I instructed *Perth* to use his discretion but to make no promises for the following night, unless he heard from me. I impressed on him that he was to sail at the time ordered. However,' and here one can trace a hint of condemnation in the *Report,* 'at 2315/28th I received *Perth*'s 2231/28th that the town was occupied by Germans, that he had abandoned the operation and was steering 175 degrees, 29 knots, with the whole of his force in company except *Hero.*'

When Pridham-Wippell received this signal announcing the abandonment of the operation three-quarters of an hour before midnight, Force B was then some sixty miles from Kalamata, heading south and having passed the point of no return.

Meanwhile, in Kalamata, the *Hero* laboured bravely and alone, handicapped by lack of information and instructions. Boats were lowered and began the wearisome ferrying of troops from the open beach. Biggs, in concert with a military staff officer who had warned that the harbour might be mined, decided to keep clear of it and to work from the beaches, instructing the troops ashore to assemble there in readiness for lifting off.

The mining report was a case of unfortunate exaggeration common in wartime. A senior RAF officer, Arthur S. Gould Lee, was in Kalamata on the morning of the 28th and reported:[4] 'I watched a salvo of four bombs drop in a line in the harbour, just where the destroyers had previously berthed (the previous night) and as there were no explosions I assumed they had been given delay action fuses.' He reported the incident to Brigadier Parrington's staff officers. 'I warned them about the possible delay action bombs near the quays and suggested that if destroyers came they should berth on the inside of the mole.' This report gained stature as the day of disaster progressed. To the navy the report became a warning of the harbour being mined. But while restricting the *Hero*'s movement in the harbour it seemed to have carried little weight in Bowyer-Smith's deliberations.

At about 2200, hardly before he had got his own rescue operation under way, Biggs received the recall signal and quite wrongly he concluded: 'That the Commanding Officer must be in possession of some information of which I did not know, or that he had encountered enemy surface forces.'

[4] *Special Duties* by Arthur S. Gould Lee, Sampson Low, 1946.

Accordingly, Biggs decided to close the *Perth* to report fully. He recalled his boats and sailed at 2250. But twenty-five minutes later he intercepted Bowyer-Smith's signal to Pridham-Wippell in which the *Perth*'s course and speed were given. Biggs realised he could not close the *Perth,* so he sensibly returned to Kalamata to do what he could alone. The destroyer anchored again just before midnight and resumed the slow business of bringing off the troops.

At 0110 on the Tuesday morning Biggs's lonely command was relieved by the arrival of the destroyers *Kandahar* (Senior Officer) *Kingston* and *Kimberley,* all of whom anchored about 200 yards from the shore. However, less than one and a half hours later, at 0230, the destroyers weighed anchor and departed. The number of troops embarked were miserably low: *Kandahar* 126, *Hero* 134, *Kingston* 39, *Kimberley* 33: a total 332. The small force sped for Suda Bay and arrived without mishap at 0800 on Tuesday 29th.

Bowyer-Smith's decision to abandon the Kalamata evacuation was described as 'unfortunate' by Cunningham.[5] He seems to have been overly concerned with the possible intervention by Italian surface craft though the evidence for such a foray is scanty. On the contrary, the safe assumption would have been that Italian cruiser and destroyer forces would not intervene in another night action, especially as they must now know from their experience at Matapan that the British possessed radar. Fear of attack by motor torpedo boats or submarines would have had more credence, but these craft rated no mention in Bowyer-Smith's report.

It is surprising that no attempt appears to have been made to seek further information from Commander Biggs whose destroyer lay at anchor close to the shore and whose First Lieutenant had the advantage of being in close contact with the admittedly confused situation. If Biggs's signals lacked answers to many vital questions Bowyer-Smith sought no means to elicit the necessary missing information to arm himself with all available facts. He sent Biggs only one signal, abandoning the operation, and that

[5] *A Sailor's Odyssey,* Cunningham, p 356.

was not despatched until twenty-three minutes after he had already altered course away. It was an unhappy decision with unhappy consequences for those troops left ashore.

*

The end of the evacuation from Greece, the end of Operation Demon, had now been virtually reached with only mopping up to be done. Yet still the light forces of the Mediterranean Fleet were called upon to exert themselves. For example, no sooner had Biggs brought the *Hero* back to Suda Bay after his exhausting experience sneaking in and out of Kalamata during the night than his ship was ordered back to pick up any stragglers.

General Wilson, the General Officer Commanding British Troops in Greece, gave it as his opinion to Pridham-Wippell, and this was confirmed by Parrington's opinion expressed to Biggs, that the Kalamata troops would be forced to surrender on the Tuesday morning. These forecasts proved accurate. The surrender took place at 0530. Thus only stragglers were available for embarkation on the night of Tuesday–Wednesday 29th–30th, when the *Hero* with the *Isis* (Senior Officer) and the *Kimberley* rescued sixteen officers and seventeen other ranks.

The same destroyers repeated the operation the following night and picked up another 202 troops in isolated parties.

On this night, too, another embarkation took place at Milos Island. The destroyers *Hotspur* and *Havock* rescued 700 British and Palestinian troops from the island in an uneventful operation from which the destroyers proceeded via the Kaso Strait direct to Port Said.

While these last two nights' operations were being executed the Naval Officer-in-Charge at Suda Bay was engaged in a complicated evolution which was handled with skill and celerity. He was entrusted with the task of sailing another convoy—GA 15. It comprised six of the transports with a close escort and covering force of cruisers and destroyers with 10,931 persons aboard for evacuation to Alexandria.

The convoy sailed at 1100 on Tuesday, April 29th from Suda Bay via the Kaso Strait. It had been organised and assembled

118

with outstanding skill. Of the troops aboard 5,000 had only arrived in Suda Bay from Greece at 0730 that morning in a variety of ships. These men had to be re-distributed, destroyers refuelled and a further 5,000 troops taken aboard, all in a brief, bewildering three hours.

Pridham-Wippell in the *Orion* sailed from Suda Bay at 1300 and made rendezvous with Bowyer-Smith's Force B at 1400 north of Suda and set course for the Kaso Strait to give cover to the convoy.

Meanwhile, in Alexandria, the First Battle Squadron with Rear Admiral Rawlings in the *Barham*, with the *Valiant, Formidable* and escorting destroyers prepared for sea. They left at 1500 to rendezvous with Pridham-Wippell at 0600 the next day. This was accomplished about eighty miles south of the Kaso Strait. Rawlings relieved Pridham-Wippell who detached his exhausted ships and sped for Alexandria, leaving the *Perth, Phoebe* and *Nubian* to join the First Battle Squadron.

At about this time, too, Rawlings was joined by the destroyers *Ilex* from Alexandria and *Juno* and *Jaguar* from Malta. The convoy hove into sight at 0700 on Wednesday, April 30th and Rawlings remained in close touch with it for the next twelve hours, then at 1900 he detached the *Perth* and *Nubian* to join the close escort and to see convoy GA 15 safely into Alexandria where it arrived the following forenoon.

When he detached the *Perth*, Rawlings took the First Battle Squadron back towards Crete to give distant support to the destroyers *Hotspur* and *Havock*, returning from Milos Island with their 700 refugees, and to the *Isis, Kimberley* and *Hero*, speeding south from their final visit to Kalamata. Nothing interfered with this general withdrawal to Egypt and by Saturday, May 3rd, the Battle Squadron and all other units were safely in harbour recuperating from the exertions and hazards of Operation Demon.

Thus ended the retreat from Greece. 'This melancholy operation,' as Cunningham referred to it in his *Despatch*, 'threw a very severe strain on both men and material of the Mediterranean Fleet: a strain which was most nobly shouldered in the face of heavy air attack.'

The total number of personnel evacuated from Greece is officially quoted at 50,672. The figure is undoubtedly wrong, but it is accepted by the Admiralty as the nearest approximation to the truth.

The figures are those compiled by Pridham-Wippell whose source was the individual ships themselves. They made their returns to him. Even here discrepancies arose, but in such insignificant detail as to warrant dismissal. Figures quoted by beachmasters and by Baillie-Grohman were, of necessity, only approximations.

G. Hermon Gill, the Australian naval historian, who incidentally wrongly quotes Pridham-Wippell's total as 50,662, related the story of another four officers and 128 Australian troops who escaped from the island of Chios in the Aegean near the Turkish coast in a Danube tug under the command of Lieutenant-Commander Wells, RNVR. They were taken to Turkey, collected another eighteen men and transferred to a Greek yacht, reaching Famagusta in Cyprus safely some days later.

It is a measure of the difficulties and endeavours of the warships engaged in the evacuation to record that about 36,000 of the total embarked were brought off in small craft from open beaches in darkness, a procedure of agonising slowness, made depressingly more so by the final fumbling climb up scrambling nets and unfamiliar gangways. Ships' companies of cruisers and destroyers wearied by weeks of working at full pressure found time and energy, as is the British seamen's custom, to comfort the rescued soldiers with modest but genuine hospitality. This did not go unnoticed.

Theodore Stephanides[6] who had borne the burden of tending wounded in a long, fatiguing retreat was rescued by the Australian cruiser *Perth*. He recorded: 'What struck me most when we set foot on the barge was the *efficiency* of everything. We seemed to have been translated to another world where everything was more civilised, trimmer, cleaner, better run, and even the officers' uniforms were neat. Orders were given in a calm, matter-of-fact

[6] Stephanides, born of Greek and English parents in India, was attached to the RAMC in Greece. See his book *Climax in Crete,* Faber & Faber, 1946.

manner, there was brightly polished machinery around us and a bell which clanged to the engine room with a very reassuring sound. Everybody relaxed almost instantaneously; I saw wounded men clapping sailors and even officers on the back and shaking them enthusiastically by the hand . . . to show their gratitude and delight for the rescue. And once more the unanimous refrain was on everybody's lips "Thank God for the Navy".'

*

Thus ended the evacuation from Greece. Cunningham later wrote: 'I feel that the episode is one to which the Royal Navy and Merchant Navy can look back with pride.'[7] But no sooner had it been completed than the main act in this Aegean drama came to be enacted. The Royal Navy and the *Luftwaffe* contested for supremacy and struggled for the prize of Crete. It is on that island that we must now focus our attention and follow the fortunes of the Mediterranean Fleet.

[7] *A Sailor's Odyssey*, Cunningham, p 357.

CHAPTER 8

Assault on the Island

THE ANCIENT ISLAND to which the British Army and the Mediterranean Fleet retired lay like a giant basking crocodile in the early summer sunshine, lapped by the warm waters of the Aegean. Crete is an untidy island. It is approximately 170 miles long and thirty-six miles wide at its widest point. But it is nipped into two waists, one seven miles across and the other nearly twenty. The island is a complex of gashed ravines that scar the mountainsides which themselves are spattered with rocky outcrops and rise to rugged and inhospitable peaks, reaching a height of 8,000 feet. The mountains run like a crippled backbone from the White Mountains in the west which are among the highest in the island. They stretch for fifty miles before merging with the Central Ida Massif which extends until it joins the Lasethe Mountains in the eastern half of the island.

Around the coastal plains uneven slopes are covered in scrub bushes and grass, with here and there little terraces of cultivation. Olive groves and cypresses abound, but there are always displays of flowers softening the harshness of the terrain, masses of little white irises and big daisies. Others provide luxuriant colour, oleander, tamarisk, poppies and flowering thistles. Dawn over Crete is enchanting and watching the day unfold over the island one appreciates the attraction of the Greek legends and the many islands beloved by Byron and Rupert Brooke.

But the sailors and soldiers saw little poetry in the island. They saw only temporary salvation from the ferocity of the enemy and this sufficed for the moment. Churchill, possibly more in hope than anything else, had viewed the island differently. He had visualised it as being capable of being fortified and armed into a

123

fortress to such an extent that it would become a second Scapa Flow. His vision was poetic in its conception. It bore small relation to reality. He first expressed his views on this subject in the autumn of 1940. 'One salient strategic fact leaped out upon us— CRETE! The Italians must not have it. We must get in first— and at once.'[1]

The Prime Minister cabled to Anthony Eden then in Khartoum with General Smuts: 'We here are all convinced an effort should be made to establish ourselves in Crete and that risks should be run for this valuable prize.' Later on the same day, October 29th, 1940, he telegraphed Eden again: 'It seems of prime importance to hold the best airfield possible and a naval fuelling base at Suda Bay. Successful defence of Crete is invaluable aid to defence of Egypt. Loss of Crete to the Italians would be a grievous aggravation of all Mediterranean difficulties. So great a prize is worth the risk, and almost equal to a successful offensive in Libya. Pray after an examination of whole problem with Wavell and Smuts, do not hesitate to make proposals for action on a large scale at expense of other sectors, and ask for any further aid you require from here including aircraft and anti-aircraft batteries. We are studying how to meet your needs.'[2]

A few days later on November 3rd he was again urging upon Eden: 'Establishment of fuelling base and airfield in Crete to be steadily developed into permanent war fortresses (is) indispensable.' And later in the same message: 'I am trying to send substantial bomber and fighter reinforcements to Crete and Greece, flying from England, with stores by cruiser . . . Trust you will grasp situation firmly, abandoning negative and passive policies and seizing opportunity which has come into our hands. "Safety First" is the road to ruin in war, even if you had the safety, which you have not.'[3] On this day too he remarked in a letter to General Ismay, his personal staff officer, that he would like to see Suda Bay a second Scapa. Doubtless he had in mind his own efforts,

[1] *The Second World War,* Vol II, *Their Finest Hour* by Winston S. Churchill, Cassell, 1949, p 472.
[2] *Ibid,* p 472.
[3] *Ibid,* p 476.

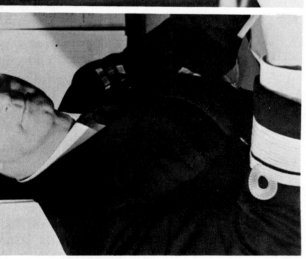

1. Admiral Sir Andrew Cunningham, Commander-in-Chief of the Mediterranean Fleet. He dominated the naval scene like an Olympian.

2. Rear Admiral I. G. S. Glennie was Rear Admiral Destroyers with his flag in the light cruiser *Dido*.

3. Rear Admiral H. B. Rawlings survived the bombing of two of his flagships, the battleship *Warspite* and the cruiser *Orion*.

4. The assault ship *Glenearn*, one of the three Glen Line ships, who gave invaluable service in the Greek and Cretan campaign.

5. The Italian destroyer *Sagittario* which gallantly defended the Maleme invasion convoy.

6. Lieutenant Fulgosi of the *Sagittario* and Commander Mimbelli of the *Lupo*, the commanders of the escorts of the Maleme and Heraklion convoys; both fought bravely against overwhelming British naval forces. With the help of the *Luftwaffe* Mimbelli, right, extricated his force almost intact. Fulgosi's convoy was destroyed.

7. Lieutenant Colonel Dinort commanded squadrons of the Stuka dive-bombers which played such a large part in the *Luftwaffe*'s victories.

8. Major Walter Enneccerus led the attack on the carrier *Formidable*, crippling her and damaging the destroyer *Nubian*.

9. General Wolfram Freiherr von Richthoven, commander of *Fliegerkorps VIII*, marshalled over 700 aircraft to defeat the Mediterranean Fleet in the battles off Crete.

10. A Junkers 87 Stuka dive-bomber of the type which caused such devastation amongst the British naval forces.

11. Suda Bay after a *Luftwaffe* attack leaving tankers ablaze with the disabled cruiser *York* discernible in the centre.

12. The battleship *Warspite* under air attack on May 22nd. In the bottom picture she is struck on the starboard 4-inch gun battery. The *Valiant*, also seen in the picture, was damaged later in the afternoon.

13. HM cruiser *Fiji*, bombed and sunk on the day the *Luftwaffe* unleashed its attack upon the Mediterranean Fleet, was reduced to firing practise shells.

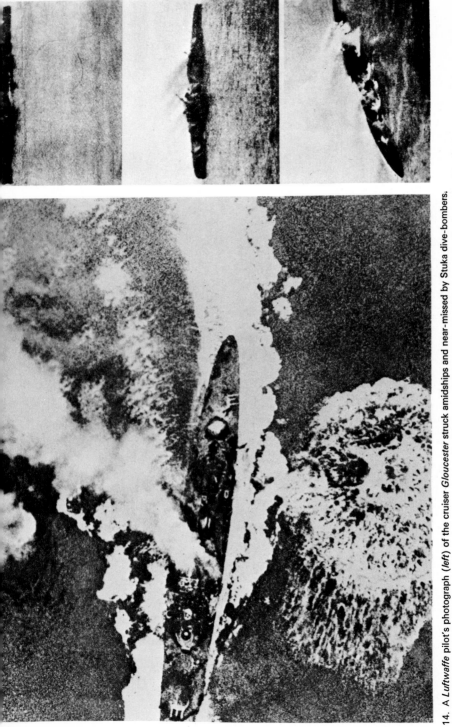

14. A *Luftwaffe* pilot's photograph (*left*) of the cruiser *Gloucester* struck amidships and near-missed by Stuka dive-bombers.

15. A sequence of photographs from a German pilot's film of the sinking of the *Gloucester* during the intensive air attacks of May 22nd 1941.

16. Captain H. M. L. Waller RAN of the *Stuart* with Lieutenant-Commander R. Rhoades on the *Vendetta's* bridge.

17. Captain Sir Philip Bowyer-Smith and officers on the bridge of his cruiser HMAS *Perth*.

18. The Australian destroyer *Nizam* returns to Alexandria crowded with troops from Crete.

19. The destroyer *Kipling* crowded with survivors from Mountbatten's *Kelly* and the *Kashmir* is welcomed into Alexandria by the cheers of the Fleet.

20. The destroyer *Kimberley* emerged undamaged from the weeks of sea-time, evacuations and air assaults. More than 50 per cent of all British destroyers were sunk or damaged during the Crete campaign.

21. Admiral Rawlings's flagship, the cruiser *Orion*, severely damaged in the flight from Heraklion, suffered 262 killed and 300 wounded.

22. HM destroyer *Nubian* preparing to leave harbour to escort a convoy from Suda Bay. She survived the campaign despite having her stern blown off in the same air attack that crippled the carrier *Formidable*

23. Yeoman of Signals, the commanding officer of the destroyer *Hotspur*, Lieutenant-Commander Cecil P. F. Brown, Lieutenant C. G. Forsberg, Lieutenant L. P. Tillie and Lieutenant Hugh Hodgkinson: 'How we all came to be smiling so cheerfully . . . I do not know – perhaps the sheer joy of still actually being alive.'

as First Lord of the Admiralty, before World War I in establishing the great naval base in the Orkneys.

On November 7th Churchill was still tormenting all concerned with his preoccupation with the island of Crete: 'Every effort should be made to rush arms and equipment to enable a reserve division of Greeks to be formed in Crete . . . to lose Crete because we had not sufficient bulk of forces there would be a crime.'[4] Less than a month later he returned to the subject with further exhortations: addressing Lord Ismay, he asked: 'Exactly what have we got and done at Suda Bay (Crete)—ie troops, AA guns, coast defence guns, lights, wireless, RDF nets, mines, preparation of aerodromes, etc? I hope to be assured that many hundreds of Cretans are working at strengthening defences and lengthening and improving the aerodromes.'[5]

But all these persistent, compelling exhortations brought little or no response. The island did not become a fortress. No arms arrived to equip the Cretans. The reserve Cretan Division was not formed. No inhabitants were employed in the urgent task of improving the airfields. Hundreds of troops languished on the island and became imbued with the same languor that the afternoon sunshine induced among the local citizenry. Crete slumbered as she had for centuries.

Wavell, understandably, had greater, more compelling campaigns upon his hands. The Western Desert offensive of December had gained a stunning success, but he was also encumbered by the mounting of the expedition to Greece, and the undertaking to campaign in East Africa. His preoccupation with these larger concepts relegated Crete and its fortification to just another obscure Mediterranean island of mild academic interest only. Exactly how disinterested he and his staff were in the island is reflected in the appointment of no less than six commanders to the island in a period of five months—from November 1940 until April 1941. None of these officers saw their task in terms of the whole island. Their primary function appears to have been to set up an administrative system and the defence of Suda Bay.

[4] *The Second World War*, Vol II, Winston S. Churchill, p 478.
[5] *Ibid*, p 485.

But the months passed, and when April arrived no more time was available to implement Churchill's intentions.

By that time, too, even Churchill's list of priorities relegated Crete to the lowest division. The Commanders-in-Chief in Cairo, oppressed by extreme anxieties on all sides sought guidance from Churchill for a ruling on priorities. He set down on paper: 'Libya counts first, evacuation of troops from Greece second. Tobruk shipping, unless indispensable to victory, must be fitted in as convenient. Iraq can be ignored and Crete worked up later.'[6]

It was a far cry from the original conception of Suda Bay being the amphibious citadel of which all Crete was the fortress. The island became at best a minor garrison, at worst a mere dumping ground. Suda Bay never became anything remotely approaching a second Scapa. If both the naval and military authorities had failed to fortify the island, the RAF story is equally uninspiring.

Lord Tedder in his memoirs[7] is often at pains to emphasise—to the point of tedium—the view that it was not the RAF that let down the Army and Navy in Greece and Crete; one such reference quotes his wartime journal: 'I am quite sure,' he recorded with prescience, 'the Army will say we lost Crete because the RAF let them down. Actually we have been put out of commission because the Army have lost all our bases for us and without bases one cannot do much. I have been trying for the past three weeks to rub it into Wavell and Cunningham that this war is one for air bases.' Tedder at the time was deputy to Air Marshal Longmore who was Air Officer Commanding-in-Chief Middle East. He has nothing to say about the RAF preparations in Crete during the six-month period intended for intensive fortification. Until April 17th, 1941—just five weeks before the German paratroops descended upon the island—the Officer Commanding the Royal Air Force in Crete was a Flight-Lieutenant. The only aircraft, comprising the fighter defence of Suda Bay, consisted of a squadron of the Fleet Air Arm which was now stationed on the primitive airfield at Maleme. The squadron consisted of a mixed collection of Brewsters, Fulmars and Gladiators. Most of the available

[6] *The Second World War*, Vol III, Winston S. Churchill, p 201.
[7] *Without Prejudice*, by Lord Tedder, Cassell, 1966.

aircraft were, of course, in Greece, but even if these had been made available for Crete where would they have been housed? How would they have been sheltered and protected and defended on the ground? How could they all have operated from the rudimentary facilities of the airfield: and how would they have been maintained without technical staff and ground staff? The apology that the Army lost all the bases and thus denied the RAF the opportunity of operating is not as watertight as at first appears. Even when the RAF possessed the bases such as those in Crete before the invasion, it still lacked the necessary aircraft to operate from them and thus stand at least a fighting chance of dominating the air.

The lack of British fighter and bomber aircraft in the Middle East theatre was lamentable. The wastage rate of Hurricane fighters and Blenheim bombers just about balanced the flow of supply. Tomahawk fighters, recently arrived, were afflicted with many teething troubles which kept them grounded. At one stage Longmore had for the whole of his sprawling command only ninety bombers and forty-three single-engined fighters. Just a few days before the evacuation from Greece Longmore told Air Marshal Portal, Chief of the Air Staff in London that the stock of Hurricanes available to Air Commodore D'Albiac, who was commanding the air forces in Greece, was less than a dozen and might well be less by the time the telegram went off. Six more Hurricanes were going to Crete at D'Albiac's disposal but no more could be sent without denuding the RAF's slender fighter forces now defending Tobruk and the Western Desert.

Tedder probably put his finger firmly on the nub of the Royal Air Force's Middle East problems when he wrote in his memoirs: 'I noted in my journal that the disaster in Greece was traceable to the Keep it on the island policy of Beaverbrook and Company, which stopped material from coming out to the Middle East months earlier.'[8]

Time and time again Tedder refers to the absence of suitable aircraft, of the low numbers of aircraft available and of the un-

8 *Without Prejudice*, by Lord Tedder.

serviceability of others. The flow of replacements from Britain was woefully inadequate to meet even the basic needs of the Middle East Command. Combat losses were serious, both in terms of aircraft and pilots and air crews. More than 200 aircraft and 150 air crew were lost in Greece. After the fall of Greece Longmore thought that there was a reasonable chance of keeping Suda Bay usable by the Navy if one Hurricane squadron was employed there, but it would be at the estimated cost of 100% reserve pilots at a replacement rate of 100% per month. At this time he had at his disposal twenty-one serviceable Hurricanes to defend the British position in the Western Desert. To cover the Suez Canal and Alexandria he had another fourteen. In the pipeline, within seven days, were another nineteen and farther away another thirty, twenty-three of which were at Takoradi. It was a sombre reflection on Britain's ill-preparedness for war in the Mediterranean.

Admiral Cunningham, disparagingly called 'the Old Man of the Sea' by Tedder in his journal, was often critical of the lack of air support which was a feature of so many operations undertaken by his Fleet. On May 15th Tedder wrote Cunningham a long message after re-examining the whole problem of cooperation between the Air Force and the Navy in the Mediterranean and in particular the provision of the reconnaissance aircraft that Cunningham needed for the impending operations in Crete. He wrote to Cunningham: 'The position is, of course, that you are having to operate in waters quite literally surrounded by enemy air bases from which shore-based aircraft are operating. That in itself cuts out the employment of Sunderlands which have the range necessary for this role. The only bases we have from which to operate are those in the Western Desert, a precarious base in Malta . . . and the still more precarious one at Heraklion.'[9]

Cunningham, to Tedder's annoyance, disagreed that the problem was insoluble, and pointed out that these same difficulties at home were solved by Coastal Command, an argument which Tedder declined to accept. Cunningham's reply continued: 'It isn't

[9] *Without Prejudice,* Lord Tedder, p 96.

only a question of the Crete operation, but we must have steady and reliable reconnaissance every day over the Ionian Sea. I quite realise that your resources are meagre, but that seems to me only one more reason for pressing the Air Ministry to face up to facts and realise that the air situation out here calls for drastic measures.'

There the matter rested, unhappily for the Navy which was now committed to operate in an area three-quarters ringed by enemy air bases amply stocked with a large fleet of modern aircraft including fighters, bombers, torpedo carriers and reconnaissance planes. The RAF was unable to provide any fighter cover from Egypt whatsoever. Its only contribution would be raids by bombers on enemy airfields, raids which proved miserably ineffective, as is evidenced by the ferocity and magnitude of the ensuing attacks on the Navy.

The absence of the RAF found expression and some relief on the warships' mess decks by paraphrasing a well-known lament:

Roll out the Nelson, *the* Rodney, *the* Hood,
Since the whole bloody Air Force is no bloody good.

It is also recorded that one able seaman was heard to remark as he blew up his lifebelt, 'This is all the ruddy air support I'm going to get this trip.'

*

We have looked briefly at the meagre resources of the RAF and have seen how the Navy was now committed to preventing a seaborne invasion of Crete without any appreciable air support. We are not concerned here with the preparedness or otherwise of the Army ashore. But the appointment of the commander of the Army in Crete deserves mention. This doubtful honour was accorded General B. C. Freyberg of New Zealand, described in so many reports as 'a soldier's soldier'. He must have been one of the Army's most decorated officers. He won a VC as commanding officer of the Hood Battalion of the Royal Naval Division in World War I for most conspicuous bravery in an exploit during which he was wounded four times. He won the DSO, like Cunningham, no less than three times, was mentioned in despatches seven times and was wounded nine times. Churchill related with relish the occasion he made the General strip to count the twenty-seven scars on his body.

He was no stranger to the Aegean. In April 1915 he and fellow officers of the Royal Naval Division had carried the body of Sub-Lieutenant Rupert Brooke to his grave under the olive trees on the island of Skyros on the eve of the assault upon Gallipoli. He distinguished himself in the Dardanelles, arriving back in England with a severe stomach wound. While he was to suffer no further personal wounds in Crete he was to suffer the chagrin of inheriting the forlorn situation on the island. It was he who discovered the inefficiencies, the lack of preparation for attack, the gaps in the defences, the absence of a headquarters staff, the motley collection of troops, the depressingly deceptive picture given by the figures. There were probably 30,000 British and Imperial troops on the island; but they were gunners without guns, drivers without vehicles, signallers without equipment; mixed indiscriminately in transit areas awaiting shipment to Egypt. From this ramshackle command Freyberg had to fashion a fighting force to combat the *élite* of the German Army. The wonder is that in the event it was only by a razor's edge that he failed.

While General Freyberg was sorting out the fragmentary remnants of his inheritance into some semblance of order, while Cunningham and Tedder squabbled over the distribution of the handful of aircraft available for the Cretan campaign and Wavell lamented he was 'at his wit's end for aircraft' the Germans planned with methodical precision the air invasion of the island. Their plans for the seaborne support of the initial air assault were less precise.

*

Admiral Karlgeorg Schüster was designated Admiral South-East with overall command of the Axis naval aspects of the Crete campaign. He had two Chiefs of Staff, the German Captain Heye and the Italian Count Pecori Giraldi.

Schüster was a fifty-four-year-old admiral with thirty-six years

130

service in the German Navy. Within weeks of the outbreak of war he became Chief of Staff for commercial and economic warfare on Field Marshal Keitel's Supreme Command of the Armed Forces (OKW—*Oberkommando der Wehrmacht*). He was later promoted Admiral West and then Commanding Admiral France. In March 1941 he was appointed Chief of the Naval Command Group South, and soon became charged with the task of supporting the air invasion of Crete with naval forces. But he was an admiral with virtually no fleet. Gone were the days of grandeur of the High Seas Fleet and the glory of Jutland. Schüster's command was a collection of ramshackle Greek steamers and minor Italian warships.

Schüster's task was to ensure the safe arrival in Crete of the heavier guns and equipment needed by the paratroops. In order to achieve this two convoys comprising caiques and local small steamers escorted by Italian destroyers were to be formed. The first convoy was destined for Maleme where it was planned to beach on May 21st, and the second was planned to arrive at Heraklion twenty-four hours later. But both were to be intercepted by Cunningham's forces and their fates will be considered later.

In preparation for these shipping movements Schüster occupied the island of Milos, eighty miles north of Suda Bay, as a naval base assembly point for the convoys. All told sixty-three small vessels were marshalled for the two invasion attempts together with another seven merchant ships intended as a follow up to Suda Bay as soon as the harbour was in German hands. To protect these convoys Pecori Giraldi provided two destroyers, twelve torpedo boats, a number of speed boats and some minesweepers. The whole operation was also promised continuous air support.

It was not intended to use the Italian Fleet in support of these operations, a fact which was unknown to the British. And for the duration of the campaign the mere existence of the Italian Fleet exerted a latent threat which demanded the presence of a British battle fleet in Cretan waters.

For the British the prevention of a seaborne invasion of the island of Crete was paramount. This became Phase 1 of the naval aspect of the Battle for Crete.

It was well known that the German intentions were to mount a massive air invasion, and it was realised that this would entail supporting sea forces to transport the heavier reinforcements that the initial assault forces would need: heavy guns, vehicles and tanks. Cunningham's staff needed no great intelligence to appreciate that the German targets would be Canea, Retimo and Heraklion, while two other sites, Kissamo Bay and Sitia in the eastern end of the island were regarded as possibilities. To counter these suspected approaches, Cunningham could marshal a formidable force. Let us now consider his strength.

THE BRITISH MEDITERRANEAN FLEET MAY 1941

Commander-in-Chief Admiral Sir Andrew B. Cunningham

Battleships	*Warspite* Captain D. B. Fisher
	Valiant Captain C. E. Morgan
	Queen Elizabeth Captain C. B. Barry
	Barham Captain G. C. Cooke
Aircraft Carrier	*Formidable* Captain A. W. Le T. Bisset
Cruisers	*Orion* Captain G. R. B. Back
	Dido Captain H. W. U. McCall
	Gloucester Captain H. A. Rowley
	Fiji Captain P. B. R. W. William-Powlett
	Ajax Captain E. D. B. McCarthy
	Perth Captain Sir P. W. Bowyer-Smith
	Naiad Captain M. H. A. Kelsey
	Phoebe Captain G. Grantham
AA Cruisers	*Coventry* Captain W. P. Carne
	Calcutta Captain D. M. Lees
	Carlisle Captain T. C. Hampton
Destroyers	*Napier* Captain S. H. T. Arliss
	Nizam Lieutenant-Commander M. J. Clark
	Kelly Captain The Lord Louis Mountbatten
	Kandahar Commander W. G. A. Robson
	Kingston Lieutenant-Commander P. Somerville
	Kipling Commander A. St Clair-Ford
	Kashmir Commander H. A. King

132

Kelvin Commander J. H. Allison

Kimberley Lieutenant-Commander J. S. M. Richardson

Juno Commander St J. R. J. Tyrwhitt

Janus Commander J. A. W. Tothill

Jervis Captain P. J. Mack

Jackal Lieutenant-Commander R. Mc. P. Jonas

Jaguar Lieutenant-Commander J. F. W. Hine

Nubian Commander R. W. Ravenhill

Isis Commander C. S. B. Swinley

Imperial Lieutenant-Commander C. A. de Kitcat

Ilex Captain H. St L. Nicholson

Hero Commander H. W. Biggs

Hotspur Lieutenant-Commander C. P. F. Brown

Hereward Lieutenant-Commander W. J. Munn

Hasty Lieutenant-Commander L. R. K. Tyrwhitt

Havock Lieutenant G. R. G. Watkins

Griffin Lieutenant K. R. C. Letts

Greyhound Commander W. R. Marshall-A'Deane

Decoy Commander E. G. McGregor

Defender Lieutenant-Commander G. L. Farnfield

Stuart Captain H. M. L. Waller, RAN

Voyager Commander J. C. Morrow, RAN

Vendetta Lieutenant-Commander R. Rhoades, RAN

Sloops	*Auckland* Commander J. G. Hewitt
	Flamingo Commander J. H. Huntley
Minelayer	*Abdiel* Captain The Hon. E. Pleydell-Bouverie
Assault Ships	*Glenroy* Captain Sir James Paget Bt
	Glengyle Commander C. H. Petrie
	Glenearn Captain L. B. Hill
Oiler	*Brambleleaf* Captain R. T. Duthie

133

In order to meet the impending assault upon the island of Crete Cunningham disposed his Fleet in a number of complex moves:

1. FORCE A. 1st Battle Squadron under the command of Vice Admiral Pridham-Wippell with his flag in the *Queen Elizabeth,* the *Barham* and five destroyers was to take up a position to the westward of Crete to interpose itself between the British light forces operating off Crete and the Italian Fleet.

2. FORCE B, comprising the cruisers *Gloucester* and *Fiji* was to patrol to the north-west of the island with instructions to intercept and sink any enemy forces and to give support to Force D.

3. FORCE C. Rear Admiral Destroyers, RAD, Rear Admiral Glennie with his flag in the cruiser *Dido* and the destroyers *Kandahar, Nubian, Kingston, Juno* and the AA cruiser *Coventry,* was ordered to be at hand to deal with the expected landing at Heraklion and to cover the Sitia possibility as well.

4. FORCE D, comprising the cruisers *Naiad* and *Phoebe,* supported by two destroyers was ordered to protect the coast from invasion in the area to the west of Retimo.

5. RESERVE FORCE at Alexandria comprised the battleships *Warspite* and *Valiant,* the carrier *Formidable* and the cruisers *Orion* and *Ajax* together with all the available remaining destroyers.

6. HM Submarine *Rorqual* was to patrol in the vicinity of Lemnos.

7. A Flotilla of MTBs based at Suda Bay was to act as a high-speed emergency service.

8. HM Minelayer *Abdiel* was to lay a minefield between Cephalonia and Levkas in an endeavour to interrupt enemy shipping and communications through the Corinth Canal.

9. Air Reconnaissance was arranged but was expected to be wholly inadequate.

Cunningham directed that this phase of the Cretan battle was to be controlled by himself and his staff at Alexandria, but he made it clear to sea-going senior officers engaged in the operation that they were expected to take independent action as the situation warranted to intercept and destroy any enemy forces reported.

Cunningham instructed that all forces were to retire from their sweeps and concentrate north of Crete at dawn, but this was subsequently altered in the face of increasing aerial attacks and ships were instructed to retire to the south of the island by daylight.

Despite the availability of the carrier *Formidable,* which on the face of it looked impressive, the prospects of air support were lamentably poor. In fact, only four serviceable aircraft remained aboard the carrier, with no reserve of machines or flying crews, and it was not until May 25th that the *Formidable* was able to provide any fighter protection for the fleet. The reduction to four aircraft was due to operational losses and normal combat wear-and-tear during the recent fleet bombardment of Tripoli and Operation Tiger.

This latter operation was a determined attempt to strengthen the British forces in Egypt where plenty of trained troops lacked weapons and equipment. There were enough troops, for instance, for six armoured regiments, but barely sufficient armour to equip two regiments. In order to effect this replenishment a convoy was passed through the Mediterranean. It comprised five large merchant ships, and among the important reinforcements were 300 new tanks and 180 motorised guns.

The passage of this convoy took from May 4th to May 9th. Powerful escort was provided in case of a sortie by the Italian Fleet. Force H from Gibraltar provided three battleships, one carrier, plus cruisers and destroyers. Escort was given as far as the Sicilian Narrows where the Mediterranean Fleet then assumed responsibility.

The convoy was located by Italian reconnaissance aircraft on the morning of May 8th in the Bone area, and the Mediterranean Fleet was also sighted in the Central Mediterranean. Commander Bragadin,[10] the Italian historian, reported: 'Locating the British forces at this late date made it impossible for the Italian Fleet, for the usual reasons of time and distance, to intercept them before they would arrive in the Sicilian Channel. Consequently orders were given for night patrols by destroyers and MTBs. These

10 *The Italian Navy in World War II,* M. Bragadin, US Naval Institute, 1957.

units were to be supported west of Trapani by two cruiser divisions. Meanwhile, the Italo–German air forces went into action and damaged the British battleship *Renown*.[11] The high seas prevented the Italian destroyers from carrying out any sneak attacks, but during the night repeated explosions from the minefield area were heard in Pantellaria. In the morning much wreckage was observed and there were clear indications of ships having been sunk.'

In fact, one ship, the *Empire Song*, 12,656 tons, was struck by a mine on May 8th and subsequently sank, taking with her a quarter of the total load of tanks. A second ship was also mined but reached her destination safely.

Bragadin continued: 'The next morning, eight bombers with thirty-seven fighter escorts and thirteen Stukas were sent to attack the British units, but the bombers never located their targets and though the Stukas found and attacked the target, they scored no hits. Finally, on the morning of the 10th, an enemy cruiser and four destroyers were sighted north of Tunisia, proceeding westward at high speed. They had escorted the convoy as far as Malta and now, having passed unobserved through the Sicilian Channel during the night, were on their way back to Gibraltar. Twenty-one Italian planes went out to attack the convoy which was now off Crete but they did not succeed in locating it.'

The German historian, Admiral Ruge, with cool disdain recorded: 'Throughout the operation the Italian Fleet remained in harbour.'[12] Bragadin attempted to justify the Italian actions, but without conviction. He then revealed with dismay that 'the information received in those days from the air reconnaissance service was so confused that *Supermarina* did not have the least idea that a British battleship, the *Queen Elizabeth,* had made the passage eastward with the convoy . . . the despatch of the *Queen Elizabeth* with all urgency to Alexandria, gave the British a nucleus of four battleships ready to oppose strongly any action whatsoever by the two Italian battleships.'

The number of sorties flown by the *Formidable* aircraft during

---

[11] She was, of course, a battlecruiser.
[12] *Sea Warfare 1939–1945*, Admiral Ruge, Koehler, 1954, p 151.

this operation drastically reduced the numbers available for service later in the month. The story of the few shore-based fighter aircraft in Crete is no less happy. They were being reduced rapidly by enemy air action and could not give the fleet any assistance. By mid-May the number of serviceable RAF aircraft on Cretan airfields had been slashed to seven. It was evident that during the forthcoming operational sweeps around Crete, the fleet would be compelled to operate close to enemy bases without any fighter protection whatsoever while exposed to a scale of air attack expected to exceed anything yet experienced afloat.

Before the German conquest of Greece, it had been possible to operate a token force of RAF and Fleet Air Arm fighters from Cretan airfields which afforded some protection to shipping at a time when it was rarely needed. Now that the Navy was to be subjected to the overwhelming superiority of the *Luftwaffe* operating from many bases in Greece and neighbouring islands, the decision was taken, albeit reluctantly, to withdraw RAF fighters from Crete. To submit them to inevitable destruction could not be justified, especially in view of the dangerous depletion of Middle East air forces as a whole. This was a decision which Cunningham was compelled to subscribe to even though it was a decision which was tantamount to denying shore-based fighter cover to British warships operating to the north of Crete. The aircraft were withdrawn from Crete on May 19th.

Efforts by bombers of the RAF based in Malta and North Africa to attack the German airfields made little or no impression on the enemy efforts for the strength of the British bomber force was scarcely better than the seriously depleted fighter strength.

Thus, the warships of Cunningham's fleet were now to be committed to try to prevent a seaborne invasion of Crete without any air protection save their own guns, the speed and manœuvrability of their ships and the ability of the commanding officers to con their ships out of danger. It was a grim prospect.

The naval sweeps ordered by Cunningham were put into effect on May 14th and for the next few days there were only a number of relatively minor incidents, as if to give a foretaste of things to come. Force A, Pridham-Wippell's squadron, gave substantial covering strength to a southbound convoy, ASF 31, as it steamed out of the Kaso Strait. This convoy comprised the Dutch *Nieuw Zeeland*, 11,069 tons, and the merchantman *Lossiemouth*, 5,627 tons, which suffered from engine room defects which at one time allowed her to steam at nothing less than 11 knots.

The convoy had one narrow escape as it steamed south for Egypt. The *Dido*, who was Senior Officer, Escort, had on board Greek bullion to the value of about £7,000,000 which she had embarked at Suda Bay. The Australian destroyers *Stuart* and *Vendetta* also provided close escort. The *Lossiemouth* had aboard 2,000 non-combatant troops. Just before daylight on May 15th at the northern end of the Kaso Strait the *Lossiemouth* broke down, first on one engine and then the other.

Captain H. W. U. McCall commanding officer of the *Dido* sent the *Nieuw Zeeland* ahead with the *Stuart*. At 0624 the merchantman signalled that she would be ready in fifteen minutes. McCall replied 'If you are not ready then I will come alongside, disembark troops and sink ship.' The signal acted like a catalyst. In ten minutes both engines were functioning adequately. At 1145 a flight of five Italian bombers from Rhodes attacked the convoy. The bombers concentrated on the *Lossiemouth* who at one time was straddled by bomb bursts, but managed to emerge unscathed. Shortly afterwards Pridham-Wippell's Force A appeared on the scene and the convoy proceeded safely to Alexandria.

The following day Force A took up its patrolling position to the west of Crete to guard the approaches to Southern Greece, Crete and the Aegean Sea. Force B and Force D steamed to their positions north-west of Crete to guard the approaches to the island from Greece, and Force C entered the Kaso Strait to assume its patrolling position. On May 17th and 18th two dive-bombing attacks were carried out upon the hospital ship *Aba*. The second of these was driven off by some of the ships of Force C which appeared on the scene to give protection. In the course of this action the AA cruiser *Coventry* was swept by machinegun fire and there were nine casualties. In one of the gun director towers Petty Officer A. E. Sephton displayed extreme gallantry.

After being mortally wounded he stayed at his post directing the guns till he died. He was awarded the Victoria Cross posthumously.

On this same day there was an intensive series of air attacks on Suda Bay in the course of which the beached *York* and the *Salvia* were damaged and suffered some casualties.

The various Forces carried out their respective sweeps but intensive searches revealed no enemy invasion attempts. By the 18th, refuelling needs necessitated changes and arrangements were made to relieve the Forces at sea. A complete re-distribution was made as follows:

(*a*) FORCE A 1. Rear Admiral H. B. Rawlings
Battleships *Warspite,* flagship, and *Valiant*
Cruiser *Ajax*
Destroyers *Napier, Kimberley, Janus, Isis, Hereward, Decoy, Hero* and *Griffin*

(*b*) Force A 1 was to relieve Force A which was to return to Alexandria. But Force A was to release the destroyers *Hotspur* and *Imperial* who were to transfer to Force A 1.

(*c*) Rear Admiral E. L. S. King in the *Naiad* with *Perth* and the destroyers of Force C—*Kandahar, Nubian, Kingston* and *Juno*—was to return to Alexandria, refuel his ships and sail again immediately on May 19th.

(*d*) Rear Admiral Destroyers, Rear Admiral I. G. S. Glennie, in the *Dido* was also to return to Alexandria, and like King was to leave again early the following morning in company with the cruiser *Orion* and the destroyers *Hasty* and *Greyhound*. This force was later to be joined by the *Ajax* and the two destroyers *Hero* and *Hereward* all three of whom would be released from Force A 1.

(*e*) Finally, the two cruisers *Gloucester* and *Fiji* whose fuel supplies were running low were to return to Alexandria, refuel and depart promptly to give some cruiser strength to the Battle Squadron—Force A 1.

Hardly had all these precautions been taken and the refuelled ships resumed their patrolling stations by the night of May 19th than the overdue assault by the Germans upon the island of Crete was launched. At 0800 on May 20th Captain Morse, the

Naval Officer-in-Charge, Suda Bay, looked out from his HQ to the wireless station at Canea and to the hills beyond where lay Maleme. He watched heavy German bombing south of Canea and over towards Maleme, followed by a vicious machinegunning attack.

Then at 0900 he watched a sight never seen before as the cumbrous Ju 52 transport aircraft of the *Luftwaffe* discharged their cargoes of parachute troops to the south and west of Canea. He also identified concentrations of troop carriers and gliders making for Maleme. He was witnessing the first airborne invasion in history.

The Germans were launched upon an historic airborne enterprise. They had marshalled an impressive air armada. It was planned that nearly 23,000 German troops would engage in Crete within three or four days. They would be transported by a fleet of 500 troop-carriers, the Ju 52, from *Fliegerkorps IX* together with scores of gliders. The preliminary softening-up of the island's defences and reconnoitring aircraft was to be provided by *Fliegerkorps VIII* under the command of General Wolfram Freiherr von Richthoven. He had under his command a formidable force comprising bombers, dive-bombers, fighters and reconnaissance aircraft, totalling 716 front line aircraft. A substantial proportion of this force was to be employed against the British Mediterranean Fleet.

Richthoven, who was forty-five at the time of the Crete invasion, was a fanatical Nazi and rarely enjoyed the popularity of his officers and men. He first joined the army in 1913 and fought in France, Poland and Russia before becoming a pilot in the fighter group of his famous cousin, the legendary Manfred von Richthoven. After the war he trained as an engineer then re-entered the army and won a doctorate of engineering in Berlin in 1933. In this same year he was assigned to the Air Ministry and took part in the building up of the *Luftwaffe*.

By 1938 Colonel Richthoven had become wing commander of the *Löwensgeschwader*—the Lion's Squadron—and some months later went to Spain as a Major-General in command of the famed Condor Legion. In the autumn campaign in Poland in 1939 he took command of the new close-combat air corps—the dive-bombers which later fought in Belgium.

It was Richthoven's *Fliegerkorps VIII* which, with other corps, fought so bitterly with the RAF at Dunkirk. He was much decorated for all his war service, won accelerated promotion to General and at the end of 1940 took his air corps to the Balkans in preparation for the campaign against Yugoslavia, Greece and Crete.[13]

It was the Ju 52s and towed gliders of the invasion force that Captain Morse saw from his Suda Bay HQ. At daylight that day—May 20th—when the German troop carriers on their Grecian airfields were embarking their troops the position of the British naval forces at sea was as follows:

(*a*) Force A 1—Rawlings in the *Warspite* with the *Valiant* together with the destroyers *Napier, Kimberley, Isis, Janus, Griffin* and *Imperial*—was in a position about 100 miles to the west of Crete.

(*b*) Admiral Glennie in the cruiser *Dido* accompanied by the *Orion, Ajax* and destroyers, had reached the Antikithera Strait during the night and was now proceeding to rendezvous with Force A 1.

(*c*) Admiral King in the cruiser *Naiad* with the *Perth, Kandahar, Nubian, Kingston* and *Juno,* had reached the Kaso Strait during the night and was now withdrawing to the southward.

(*d*) Force B—*Gloucester* and *Fiji*—having refuelled at Alexandria was on its way to join Rawlings in Force A 1.

Thus, at 0800 on May 20th when the German attack upon Crete began the various forces of the Mediterranean Fleet were well positioned to undertake their primary task, which they now believed to be imminent, of intercepting and destroying enemy seaborne invasion forces.

As soon as Cunningham learned of the start of the invasion he ordered all his forces to move closer to Crete but to keep out of

---

[13] Richthoven subsequently took his air corps to serve on the Russian front, notably in the Sebastopol, Leningrad and Stalingrad sectors. He was eventually captured by the Allies and died in 1945 as a prisoner of war.

sight of land and during the forenoon of the 20th he signalled his further intentions:

1. Force D, now consisting of Admiral Glennie's squadron, the flagship *Dido,* accompanied by the cruisers *Orion* and *Ajax,* and the destroyers *Isis, Kimberley, Imperial* and *Janus,* was to pass through the Antikithera Channel by 2200/20th and then sweep the Capes Malea/Hydra/Phalconera, then be off Canea at 0700/21st.
2. Force C, comprising King's squadron, the flagship *Naiad, Perth* and the destroyers *Kandahar, Nubian, Kingston* and *Juno,* was to pass through the Kaso Strait at 2200/20th, sweep along the coast towards Heraklion arriving there at 0700/21st.
3. Force B, the cruisers *Gloucester* and *Fiji,* was to pass close off Cape Matapan at 0400/21st and then proceed to join Force A 1 in a position about fifty miles west of Crete (35 degrees 20′ N, 22 degrees 25′ E) at 0700/21st.
4. The AA cruiser *Calcutta* was to pass through the Kaso Strait after Force C which she was to join off Heraklion at 0700/21st.
5. Force E, a new force comprising the 14th Destroyer Flotilla (D 14) under the command of Captain Mack in the *Jervis,* with the *Nizam* and *Ilex,* was to bombard Scarpanto aerodrome during the night of 20th–21st May, withdrawing to the southward before daylight in an effort to escape reprisal raids.
6. The AA cruiser *Carlisle* who was at Alexandria, would sail as soon as ready so as to join Force E at 0700/21st to afford better AA protection, in a position fifty miles south-east of Crete (34 degrees 30′ N, 27 degrees 00′ E).

*

Meanwhile, the German invasion flotilla intended for Maleme had assembled in the Piraeus and had threaded its way slowly to the advanced base at Milos which it reached safely on the night of the 20th. This tiny flotilla of twenty-five caiques had battled through strong head winds and rising seas to reach Milos in preparation for their assault upon Crete the following day.

British air reconnaissance located the force at sea in the Aegean as a result of which Cunningham revised his earlier intentions. At 1800 he instructed King with his Force C and Glennie with

142

his Force D to move to the north of Crete at once. The decision was then taken to cancel the two night sweeps ordered for these forces. New patrol lines more likely to result in interception of the Maleme convoy were ordered. Force C was instructed to patrol to the north of Heraklion, east of longitude 25 degrees E. Force D was ordered to guard the approaches to the general area Suda Bay/Canea/Kissamo Bay/Maleme. The Retimo danger area was to be guarded by local craft from Suda Bay.

The military situation ashore, according to early reports, was confused and complicated by baffling uncertainty. From the confusion, there emerged some clear facts. In addition to the attacks witnessed by Captain Morse from his HQ at Suda Bay, early in the morning, he reported further attacks at 1145 upon Suda Bay itself. Its defences became the target for heavy dive-bombing attacks and machinegunning which persisted throughout the whole of the afternoon and evening.

Captain M. H. S. Macdonald, the Naval Officer-in-Charge at Heraklion some sixty miles to the east of Suda Bay, was also the spectator of formidable and fateful events. He reported that the assault there began four hours after the attack at Maleme with a heavy dive-bombing attack. This was followed by an intensive aerial bombardment for two hours, then a terrifying machinegunning attack which lasted an hour. 'It is estimated that 400 planes were over the town between 1600 and 1900' Macdonald subsequently reported in his *Letters of Proceedings*.

A few minutes after this softening-up episode by Richthoven's strike aircraft, large numbers of low-flying aircraft from *Fliegerkorps XI* approached from the sea and dropped parachute troops to the west of the town and on the airfield. At about this time, too, parachute troops dropped upon Retimo.

By nightfall on May 20th Cunningham's information was that the situation at Maleme and Canea was in hand, but that 1,200 of the 3,000 estimated troops who had landed by air were unaccounted for. He was aware of the Heraklion and Retimo landings, but details were lacking. To compound the uncertainty a report was received of boats carrying troops being sighted off Heraklion.

143

It was King's Force C which was ordered to investigate these Heraklion sightings. Admiral King, in his flagship *Naiad*, had led the *Perth, Kandahar, Nubian, Kingston* and *Juno* through the Kaso Strait during the late evening of May 20th. During the passage—before nightfall—the force had fought off an ineffective attack by Italian torpedo bombers. The force was then intercepted by a patrol of five Italian motor torpedo boats and a high-speed, spirited action between this patrol and the *Naiad, Juno* and *Kandahar* ensued before the MAS boats fired their torpedoes and retired in the face of overwhelming British fire superiority. No damange was suffered by any of the combatants.

King proceeded west along the coast to investigate the reports of a seaborne invasion attempt but no evidence of any such attempt was found.

During this same night of May 20th–21st the 14th Destroyer Flotilla—Force E—consisting of Captain Mack's three destroyers, sped north to the island of Scarpanto and at 0242 on the 21st they carried out a rapid bombardment of the airfield for three minutes before speeding off to Pegadia Bay in a fruitless search for enemy shipping. His small mission accomplished, Mack led his destroyers south at speed to clear the danger zone before daylight.

CHAPTER 9

The Italian Fleet Shirks Battle

AT DAYLIGHT ON Wednesday, May 21st the British naval forces were disposed as follows:

1. Admiral Rawlings with Force A 1—the Battle Squadron—was sixty miles west of the Antikithera Strait, on a south-easterly course, steering to rendezvous with Admiral Glennie's Force D which was returning after a night of uneventful sweeps in the Maleme/Canea/Kissamo Bay area. No contact with enemy forces had been made.

2. Admiral King and his Force C had withdrawn from his patrol in the Kaso Strait and his skirmish with the MAS boats. The Force had been joined by the *Calcutta* at 0600.

3. Captain Mack with his three destroyers, Force E, was heading to join Force C after his Scarpanto mission.

4. Force B, the *Gloucester* and *Fiji,* had an uneventful night's sweep up to Cape Matapan and were now heading to join Admiral Rawlings.

5. The AA cruiser *Carlisle* had sailed from Alexandria with instructions to join Admiral King's Force C.

6. HMS *Abdiel* was on her way back to Alexandria having completed a minelaying operation.

The Commander-in-Chief's intention was that all these forces should retire to the south of Crete by day. Retirement to the south gave the hope of evading *Luftwaffe* bombers; and concentration of the forces gave greater protection by increasing the AA barrage. After dark, the intention was that these forces should resume their night sweeps. But long before nightfall was to bring its welcome darkness, the warships would have to endure intensive *Luftwaffe* attacks. The daylight hours of May 21st were to witness violent and prolonged battles between the warships and the bombers. The *Luftwaffe* believed they achieved considerable success: their contemporary report of claims indicates the severity and extent of their bombing.

The report of the Fourth Air Fleet, dated November 28th, 1941, claimed that 'Units of *Fliegerkorps VIII* sank one destroyer and severely damaged another, as well as two cruisers'. The report further claimed that on this day bomber units from various air stations in the province of Attica, Stukas from Scarpanto[1] and Italian Air Force units from Rhodes scored 'three direct hits on cruisers, one direct hit on a destroyer, one hit on a steamer and two other cruisers believed damaged'.

Such wartime claims—by both Allied and Axis Powers—were seldom substantiated. Nevertheless, the *Luftwaffe*'s determined efforts on this day were rewarded with some successes.

Throughout the daylight hours, the Fleet was subjected to heavy air attacks. Rawlings's Battle Squadron was attacked once during the forenoon and later for two and a half hours in the afternoon. No damage was suffered by the ships, but the high expenditure of AA ammunition impelled Rawlings to signal a warning to the Fleet of the need to conserve supplies.

Glennie's Force D was heavily attacked during the forenoon, during which the cruiser *Ajax* suffered near misses which caused some damage. During the afternoon, when in company with Force A 1 to concentrate AA defences, Force D also endured the same two and a half hours of bombing and the Force was attacked again in the evening.

During these attacks on both forces at least three aircraft were destroyed and another two severely damaged.

The attacks on Force C were severe and incessant during the four hours 0950 to 1350 during which King lost only one ship, the destroyer *Juno*. She was struck by bombs at about 1300 and sank in two minutes. She had survived three hours of bombing.

The *Juno* was hit by three bombs, two of which blew the after

---

[1] Captain Mack's attack on Scarpanto appears to have been ineffectual.

146

boiler room and the engine room open to the sea. The third bomb detonated her after magazine and the resulting explosion broke the ship in half and turned both parts into blazing pyres. Six officers and ninety-one ratings were rescued from the sea by the destroyers *Kingston, Kandahar* and *Nubian.* The shocked, dazed and oil-sodden men were snatched from the sea even as the attacks continued. One of the survivors was Petty Officer E. Lumley who was blown overboard by a bomb explosion and though badly burned swam forty yards into the thick layer of oil fuel to rescue a shipmate in distress.

Another survivor was the medical officer who reported:

> Suddenly there was a blinding flash, the lights went out and I could just sense redness. I have no recollection of any noise or great concussion. I and my small first aid party climbed up ladders and quickly followed others who were jumping overboard. Looking up from the water I could see the bows sliding under as the ship sank with no suction and hardly a ripple. . . . We had sunk in under a minute and soon through the pall of smoke we could see the *Kingston* and *Kandahar* returning to pick up survivors. . . . I carried on swimming for about twenty minutes and managed to get alongside *Kandahar* with some difficulty. It was only when I tried to climb up a rope which they threw me that I realised how cold and weak I felt.[2]

During the day Force A 1 remained in an area to the south-west of Kithera where it was joined by the *Gloucester* and *Fiji* and by Glennie's Force D as intended by the Commander-in-Chief. This impressive assembly of ships for the defence of Crete consisted of two battleships, the *Warspite* and *Valiant,* five cruisers, the *Gloucester, Fiji, Ajax, Orion* and *Dido* and eight destroyers, *Isis, Imperial, Kimberley, Janus, Napier, Decoy, Griffin* and *Hotspur.*

Yet even this bait failed to entice the Italian Fleet to seek battle even though the Axis Powers had the inestimable advantage of aerial reconnaissance, of exact knowledge of the position, course, speed and composition of the British forces at sea. Furthermore, these forces were known to have been hard-pressed in the hours

[2] *Medical History of the Second World War, Royal Naval Medical Services,* Vol II, Ed. J. L. S. Coulter, HMSO, 1956, p 368.

of aerial attack they had undergone during the day with the resultant high rate of consumption of fuel oil and of ammunition. All this information might have been thought worth a couple of cruisers to an adventurous admiral.

It was during this day that the Germans again attempted to persuade the Italian Fleet to put to sea, if only 'to pin down the British warships away from Crete'[3] but the authorities in Rome again refused. In March 1941 the Italians had warned Germany[4] of their urgent need for oil supplies. 'Big ships will have to be inactivated in June of this year and submarines in February 1942.' The German Chief of Armed Forces, Field Marshal Wilhelm Keitel reported that examination revealed that the Italians had 600,000 tons of stocks, 'more than we have ourselves'. This made Admiral Raeder wonder 'whether the 600,000 tons of fuel oil actually exists or whether the Italians gave this figure merely because it was the one that had been quoted by the Duce'.[5]

Commander Bragadin[6] makes no reference to the fuel oil position as a reason for the Italian Fleet's non-intervention in the dramatic naval events unfolding in the Eastern Basin. His chronicle is worthy of careful study not only for the sake of merit, but at least as much for its limitations. He attempts at some length to excuse the Italian Fleet's inaction. But he does so without conviction. His facts are disputable and the conclusions he draws wholly unconvincing. He begins his defence of *Supermarina* with the rapid collapse of the Greek front which forced the Mediterranean Fleet to carry out the emergency evacuation of British troops from the Greek coast. He reports that about 30,000[7] men took part in the evacuation which was carried out

[3] *The Invasion of Crete,* Report of Air Fleet IV, November 28th, 1941.

[4] *The Führer Conferences on Naval Affairs,* March 1941.

[5] Grand Admiral Erich Raeder, Commander-in-Chief of the German Navy, makes no reference to this in his memoirs. Indeed, he makes no reference to the naval aspects of the battle for Crete at all in his apologia for his conduct of naval affairs from 1928–43: *Struggle for the Sea,* William Kimber, 1959.

[6] *The Italian Navy in World War II,* M. Bragadin.

[7] This is patently wrong as many published British sources testify. *The Italian Navy in World War II,* M. Bragadin, p 105.

exclusively at night. 'Consequently enemy losses were very low for the German Air Force did not have any night aircraft.'

Bragadin goes on to admit that at a time when the British forces were under extreme pressure both on land and in the air an Italian naval attack in the Aegean probably could have produced excellent results. 'Nevertheless,' he continues, 'such an attack was never carried out and there are those who criticise the Navy for being as prudent in this case as it had been imprudent at the Battle of Matapan. This criticism, however, is only valid in retrospect. The fact that the British Air Force in the Eastern Mediterranean was then in a crucial situation was only discovered by the Italians later. As for the British Air Forces at Malta, they were up to strength.' These comments display an abysmal lack of intelligence by *Supermarina* at that time.

Commander Bragadin continues: 'The added fact that the British carried out their evacuation operation with only light units did not signify anything, for the Alexandria fleet was on the alert and ready to bar the way to any opposition. Also, at that time, this fleet had three battleships, while the Italians only had two available. It must also be remembered that after the experience of Matapan, the Italian Supreme Command had ordered the Navy not to operate beyond fighter plane range.'

Neither the British Admiralty, much less the harassed Commander-in-Chief Mediterranean, could indulge in such luxurious protection. 'From the 19th May to 26th May,' Admiral Cunningham later recorded in his *Despatch,* 'naval forces operating in the vicinity of Crete were without fighter protection.'

Bragadin's explanation then hints at strained Italo–German relationships: 'In the Aegean, the Navy's ships could be protected effectively only by the Fourth German Air Corps (IV CAT) just arrived from Germany. . . . The writer has reason for believing that IV CAT did not want any Italian naval assistance in the Aegean for it wished to keep for itself full credit for any and every victory.'

Turning his attention to the Battle for Crete, Bragadin asserts that the same situation was repeated. 'Again the Italian Navy did not take part in the campaign except to provide a few indispensable escort vessels. . . . Although several occasions that could have been exploited presented themselves, the means was lacking to take advantage of them. Beyond the reasons similar to those noted above, the decisive argument for the Italians not taking part in the campaign was IV CAT's definite affirmation that its planes were all that were necessary, and its ruling out of any possibility of giving the necessary air cover to the Italian naval units. In addition the IV CAT even warned that it could assume no responsibility should Italian ships appear in the Aegean, if German planes were to attack them, for the German pilots had never flown missions at sea before and were not able to distinguish between friendly and enemy ships.'

The truth of this last point was demonstrated by a flight of Stukas which attacked the Italian destroyer escort *Sagittario* which was shepherding a convoy of caiques. Another Stuka attack was directed against five Italian destroyers loaded with German troops, an attack which resulted in serious damage to the destroyer *Sella*. 'The latter ships,' Bragadin reports acidly, 'had scarcely left the Piraeus and were supposedly under German air escort.'

The Italian historian concludes his arguments: 'Finally, the fact that the Germans kept their attack plans for Crete absolutely secret and did not even reveal them to the Italian Supreme Command, proves that they wanted no rivals competing for any possible victories. The Germans thus precluded in every way any possibility of coordination with Italian naval action. The Italian Fleet, therefore, was unable to interfere with the British evacuation of Greece, and later on, of Crete.'

*

Perhaps Bragadin's report of the Fourth Air Fleet's claim that their aircraft were all that was necessary to bring about a decisive result in the battle with the British Fleet was true. Perhaps the claim was invention. But there is little doubt that the outcome of the engagements came very close to proving the truth of the claim. If the severity of the air attacks on the afternoon of May 21st, if the eager impulsion of the *Luftwaffe* pilots and the vigour

150

which characterised their efforts were to be any guide, then the British were on the threshold of being deprived of the sovereignty of the seas in the Eastern Mediterranean. Before we study the next series of air attacks, we must chronicle the rest of the naval events of this exhausting day.

CHAPTER 10

Battle for Crete: The Invasion

ON WEDNESDAY, MAY 21st, the military situation ashore continued to be cloaked in obscurity owing to the fluidity of the battle and to the conflicting reports and rumours. Above all, the scene was dominated by the *Luftwaffe* and the relentless, persistent, incessant, almost demonic, attacks—at low level, at high level, by dive-bombing and machinegunning, with a noise that stunned the senses. The day was marked, too, by the German capture of Maleme, and by the ferocity of the defenders. Such was the strength of the defence that the Germans were constantly hard-put to retain their precarious hold on the island. Their victories were often the result of desperation rather than planning. Nevertheless, they were victories, whether achieved by design or luck.

On the naval scene, the activity of the British warships earlier that day had impelled Admiral Schüster, the German Admiral South-East, to re-examine and revise his plans. He had already reported to the General Headquarters of *Fliegerkorps XI* that the Maleme flotilla had been instructed to reach its target on May 21st, and it was to do so 'regardless of enemy fleet movements'. The flotilla assembled at the island of Milos. It consisted of about twenty-five commandeered caiques or small Greek cargo and coastal steamers, under the command of naval Lieutenant Oesterlin. These frail craft were heavily laden with guns and ammunition now urgently needed ashore and each craft carried about a hundred troops. These men comprised additional battalions of German Mountain Troops together with a small token force of

Italian marines from the San Marco Regiment with their equipment, all destined for the occupation of Suda.

It is reported that the caiques and steamers were 'navigated' and controlled in convoy by lieutenants with pocket compasses and home-made megaphones.[1] The control and passage of this convoy was a creditable feat of seamanship.

Early on Wednesday 21st this squadron had sailed from Milos on the last seventy miles of its journey under the escort of the Italian destroyer *Lupo,* a modern but small vessel of 679 tons, built in 1938. She mounted only three 3.9 inch guns and four 18 inch torpedo tubes and was capable of a speed of 34 knots. She was commanded by Commander Francesco Mimbelli. Progress had been pleasant but slow. The sun shone brilliantly from a clear blue sky in which German aircraft flew unmolested. The caiques hoisted meagre sails to catch what breeze there was in an effort to aid their feeble engines, but even so, progress was no faster than a brisk walking pace, a mere four knots, and when the wind dropped even this speed fell away.

When Schüster learned of the presence of British warships patrolling in the vicinity of the flotilla's line of approach he issued instructions at 1000 ordering the convoy to return to Milos. Later reconnaissance reported no British ships north of Crete and on the assurance of Commander Mimbelli that the flotilla could reach its destination by dark, Schüster allowed the convoy to sail again at midday. The German naval historian, Admiral Ruge, implies criticism of Schüster when he records: 'Having received contradictory orders the convoy was late, and the delay was further increased by a headwind.'[2]

During the forenoon and afternoon of the 21st British aircraft spotted a number of small craft heading southwards and these were interpreted correctly as part of the invasion flotilla from

[1] Manuscript No B524–p 36-G, General von Greiffenberg, *Supplements to the Study—The Balkan Campaign (The Invasion of Greece)*, Office of the Chief of Military History, Department of the Army, Washington, DC.

[2] *Sea Warfare 1939–1945:* Admiral Ruge. No one seems to have queried Mimbelli's belief he could reach Crete 'by dark' with seventy miles to cover at about 4 knots.

Milos destined for the Maleme area in Canea Bay. Their progress was carefully logged.

Accordingly, Cunningham's Staff ordered British naval Forces B, C and D to close in through the Kaso Strait and Kithera Channel in order to prevent a seaborne landing during the night of 21st–22nd. The orders gave added directions in the event of there being no contact with the enemy during the night: Forces C and D were then to start working on a wide zig-zag sweep northwards at 0530 on the 22nd in an effort to locate the enemy flotilla.

However, at 2330, just half an hour before midnight, Force D, comprising Admiral Glennie's flagship *Dido,* with the *Orion* and *Ajax* and the three destroyers *Kimberley, Hasty* and *Hereward,* made contact with Mimbelli's troop convoy. Radar, then still known as RDF (Radio Direction Finding) proved a valuable asset to the British ships.

Mimbelli's ships had reached a point within sight of their destination, the mountains of Crete having been sighted just before darkness. Now, just eighteen[3] miles north of their landing ground, they sighted Glennie's ships and realised that their security had gone and that they were at the mercy of the British warships. Mimbelli's statement that he 'was capable of reaching Maleme before dark' was proved false. He was still heading southwards with more than four hours' steaming ahead of him when he sighted Force D steering east at twenty-eight knots, the cruisers in line ahead, the destroyers spread to screen the cruisers and to widen the area of sweep. Long fingers of searchlights probed the darkness.

The resultant skirmish, in which the conduct of Commander Mimbelli in the *Lupo* quite rightly earned the praise of his country and the grateful thanks of his Axis partners, also gained the respect of the British.

The caiques saw the approaching searchlights, lowered their sails to minimise their size and waited in silence for the ships to pass. But the destroyer, *Janus,* stationed on the flagship's port bow, was the first to sight the enemy flotilla. On receipt of the alarm bearing, Glennie led his cruisers round to the north.

[3] Reports vary between eighteen and thirty miles.

Mimbelli realised as soon as he saw the British ships that he was opposed by overwhelmingly superior forces and he immediately set about laying a smoke screen to hide the convoy and he began to engage the nearest British ships courageously. A one-sided two-hour skirmish ensued during which time Glennie's destroyers 'conducted themselves with energy and zest'. At one time the *Lupo* passed ahead of and close down the starboard side of the *Dido* and *Orion* hotly engaging both with gunfire and machineguns. She also launched two torpedoes at a range of about 700 yards, though neither struck home.

Mimbelli turned to starboard, through the cruiser line passing close under the *Orion*'s stern, ahead of *Ajax* who also joined in the general mêlée. Shells were hitting the *Lupo* all the while, and the unequal struggle could not last long. Indeed, *Ajax* claimed that the Italian destroyer was 'finished off with a complete broadside up the stern'. But in fact the damaged *Lupo,* stricken by no less than eighteen 6 inch shells, her decks riven and her hull pierced, with many dead and injured aboard, avoided destruction and made good her escape. Mimbelli even participated in the rescue of survivors from the convoy some two hours later.

Meanwhile, the cruisers and destroyers set about locating and destroying the helpless convoy, of which only three vessels, all of them Italian, managed to survive. All the other vessels, manned by German naval personnel, were destroyed. Glennie's subsequent report commented: 'When illuminated they were seen to be crowded with German troops and to be flying Greek colours. The crews, obviously pressed men, standing on deck waving white flags, and it was distasteful having to destroy them in company with their callous masters. . . . In all one or two steamers, at least a dozen caiques, a small pleasure steamer and a steam yacht were engaged and either sunk or left burning.'[4]

It was believed at the time that about 4,000 German troops had perished in the annihilation of the convoy, but this was another example of wartime over-estimation. In fact, the total strength of the German troops being transported was 2,331, com-

[4] *Letter of Proceedings: Operations off Crete 19th–23rd May, 1941,* by Rear Admiral Glennie, June 4th, 1941.

prising III Battalion 100 Mountain Regiment, Heavy Weapons Group and part of the II AA Regiment. The *Report* of the Fourth Air Fleet, remarkable for its many inaccuracies, states: 'Due to the courageous action of the *Lupo* in firing torpedoes at the enemy from a range of 2,000 metres although she herself received eighteen direct hits which put her out of action, and to the scattered formation of our ships, only a small portion of the flotilla was caught and destroyed.'

The Twelfth Army reported a few days after the skirmish on May 28th, 1941: 'The number saved from *1 Light Convoy* has increased to 1,665, including 21 Italians. It is expected that this number will be increased slightly as not all the islands have been searched yet.'

This large number of survivors owed their rescue to Italian speed boats, to the damaged *Lupo*, the destroyer escort *Lira* and to an Air Sea Rescue Service instituted by the Germans. The final casualty statement issued by Twelfth Army of thirteen officers and 311 other ranks missing, lost at sea, seems to be authentic. This was a far cry from the 4,000 originally believed to have been lost in the skirmish.

By 0200 on the 22nd as there were no more enemy vessels to engage Glennie made another sweep east and north then turned west at 0330 giving his force a rendezvous for 0600 about thirty miles west of Crete.

It will be remembered that it was Cunningham's intention that if there were no developments during the night of 21st–22nd, Forces C and D were to work to the northward commencing at 0530/22nd. These intentions were later revised by Cunningham who now ordered Forces C and D to join company and to sweep to within twenty-five miles of Milos with the object of flushing out any other invasion convoys. Because of normal time lag in despatch of this message which was timed at 0402/22nd, it did not reach Glennie till after he had withdrawn from the Aegean. Glennie's own message to the Commander-in-Chief, timed only three minutes later at 0405, reported the result of his attack on the convoy, detailed his shortage of AA ammunition and reported his intention of taking Force D to join Admiral Rawlings with the battle squadron in Force A 1. The cruisers' expenditure of AA ammunition makes interesting reading. The *Dido* had expended no less than 70%; 22% had been fired during the three and a half hours from 0600 to 0930 on the 21st. *Orion* had fired 62% and *Ajax* 58%.

Cunningham deemed that these shortages jeopardised the cruisers and agreed with Glennie's opinion that the Force might well be unable to defend itself against the expected scale of air attack. Accordingly, he instructed Glennie to withdraw Force D with all despatch to Alexandria for re-ammunitioning.

CHAPTER 11

The Luftwaffe Strikes

THURSDAY, MAY 22ND, was a day of tragedy for the Mediterranean Fleet. For the *Luftwaffe* it was a day of rejoicing.

As the sun arched across the clear blue sky the British losses in warships and personnel mounted alarmingly with no apparent reward for their sacrifices. The prime objective of the warships was the prevention of a seaborne invasion of Crete. This was a relatively intangible objective. It was not readily known to the men in the ships whether this objective was being achieved. Far more immediate problems confronted them in the shape of the menacing Stukas which dive-bombed the ships intensively. Even if the ships and the seamen were achieving their objective, they were unable to appreciate the extent of their success at the time.

For the pilots of the *Luftwaffe,* their objective was equally simply stated. It was to defeat the British Mediterranean Fleet in the waters around Crete. It was a task they accepted eagerly and enthusiastically. Again and again the high morale of the pilots is impressed upon the researcher by the zest and urgency of the men's anxiety to attack the British ships. It was an attitude of hearty but healthy respect for a tough adversary, but a feeling, too, of superiority. It was not misplaced, but it was a superiority which the pilots would have to earn in the face of fiercely fought opposition.

Ashore in Greece hundreds of Ju 87 dive-bombers, Ju 88 low-level and high-level bombers, Messerschmitt 109 fighters and twin-engined Messerschmitt 110 fighter-bombers waited on the airfields at Argos, Eleusis, Molai and Myli before taking off to do battle with the Mediterranean Fleet. Air General Freiherr von Richthoven, commanding officer of *Fliegerkorps VIII,* the same Air Corps whose Stukas and bombers helped smash the defenders of Poland and France, noted in his War Diary for May 22nd: 'Since 0500[1] hours today reports have multiplied of British cruisers and destroyers in the sea areas north and west of Crete.' Richthoven had under his command 228 bombers, 205 dive-bombers, 114 twin-engined and 119 single-engined fighters, and 50 reconnaissance aircraft: a vast air armada of 716 aircraft.

On the previous day, Wednesday 21st, German reconnaissance aircraft had carefully observed and reported all British Fleet movements. Intelligence soon revealed Cunningham's tactic of maintaining a patrolling Battle Squadron to the west of Crete to intervene itself between the island and the Italian Fleet. But on this day such was the *Luftwaffe*'s concern with supporting the hard-pressed German paratroops ashore that only a single *Stuka Gruppen* (approximating to RAF Wing) was spared to attack the British ships, with the single success we have already recorded—the sinking of the *Juno*.

But on Thursday 22nd, Richthoven's massive air fleet for use against the British ships was disposed as follows:[2]

1. *Kampfgeschwader* KG 2, with three *Gruppen* of Dornier 17s under the command of Colonel Rieckhoff based at Tatoi, north of Athens.
2. *Gruppe* I/LG and *Gruppe* II/LG 1, both equipped with Ju 88 bombers under the command of Captain Hoffmann and Captain Kollewe, based at Eleusis.
3. *Gruppe* II/KG 26 equipped with Heinkel 111 bombers also based at Eleusis.
4. *Stukageschwader* St G 2, comprising two *Gruppen* of Ju 87s under the command of Lieutenant-Colonel Dinort and nicknamed the *'Immelmann Geschwader'*, based at Mycene and

---

[1] German times quoted are one hour earlier than British times: thus this reference is to 0600.

[2] The basic operational unit in the *Luftwaffe* was the *Gruppe*. Its nearest equivalent in the RAF was a Wing, and it comprised about 30–36 aircraft. A *Geschwader*, the nearest equivalent being a Group, normally consisted of three *Gruppen* and totalled 100–120 aircraft. The *Luftwaffe* abbreviations designated a *Gruppe* by the Roman numerals which preceded the type and number of the *Geschwader*. For example, II St G 1 indicated the Second *Gruppe* of *Stukageschwader* 1.

Molai: a third *Gruppe* of Ju 87s under Captain Brücker was based on the island of Scarpanto.

5. *Zerstorer Geschwader* ZG 26, with two *Gruppen* of Me 110 twin-engined fighter-bombers under Captain von Rettberg, based at Argos.

6. *Jagdgeschwader* Jg 77, with three *Gruppen* of single-engined Messerschmitt 109 fighters under Major Woldenga. The *Geschwader* I/LG 2 under the command of Captain Ihlefeld. All were based at Molai on the Elos peninsula of the Polopouresi.

Fliegerkorps VIII was ready to seek out the British ships. 'Seldom had German airmen waited to do so with such impatience.'[3]

On Myli airfield Colonel Dinort, commander of the *Immelmann Geschwader,* had installed his HQ in a field caravan. He briefed his pilots and air crews. Reconnaissance patrols, he told them, had reported such a profusion of shipping movements that they couldn't fail to find the British Fleet.

At 0630 Captain Hitschold and Captain Sigel took off in their Ju 87s and formed up with their two Stuka *Gruppen* over the airfield before heading off south-easterly to seek out and strike at the British ships.

Similar activity was taking place at half a dozen airfields on this sunny Thursday morning and all aircraft were converging on the last reported positions of British warships. As Dinort predicted, they could not fail to make contact.

*

When the sun's first rays shone over the horizon the British naval forces were alert to the impending danger. But even the worst fears were exceeded by the intensity of the ordeal which was soon to engulf the ships and men. The ships were disposed as follows:

1. Force A 1, Admiral Rawlings's battle squadron, was in a position about forty-five miles south-west of the Kithera Channel and steering to the north-west.

2. Force B, the *Gloucester* and *Fiji,* was steaming to join Force A 1.

[3] *The Luftwaffe War Diaries* by Cajus Bekker, Macdonald & Co, 1967, p 256.

3. Force C, Admiral King's cruiser force, sweeping the north coast of Crete from the Kaso Strait, had reached a position off Heraklion at 0400 and was now steaming north sweeping for a convoy of caiques.

4. Force D, Admiral Glennie's squadron, was heading west, about thirty miles west of the Kithera Channel and about to join Force A 1. But as we have seen, Glennie was soon to receive the Commander-in-Chief's message timed at 0716 ordering his return to Alexandria.

5. The 5th Destroyer Flotilla (D 5) Captain Lord Louis Mountbatten, in the *Kelly*, with *Kashmir*, *Kipling*, *Kelvin* and *Jackal* had left Malta the previous night at 2130 with orders to join Admiral Rawlings at 1000/2nd to the west of Crete.

6. The 14th Destroyer Flotilla (D 14) Captain Mack, in the *Jervis*, with *Nizam* and *Ilex* had departed from Alexandria after refuelling and were heading for the Kaso Strait.

7. The 10th Destroyer Flotilla (D 10) Captain Waller in the *Stuart* with his old Australian destroyers *Voyager* and *Vendetta* had left Alexandria the previous day with orders to join Admiral Rawlings.

It was Admiral King's force which was to come in for more than its share of the *Luftwaffe* attention that morning. His force was steering towards Milos at 0830 when a caique carrying German troops was sighted. The *Perth* was detached to engage her and send her to the bottom. Then the *Naiad* was sent to accompany the Australian cruiser to afford greater air defence against the German aircraft which had been making sporadic attacks upon the squadron since soon after 0700.

At 0909 the *Calcutta* sighted a small merchant ship ahead and King ordered some destroyers to sink her.

By 0945 the whole British force was under mounting heavy air attacks which Cunningham later described as 'certainly on a majestic scale'.

At 1000 the force was twenty-five miles south of the eastern tip of the island of Milos, with the *Perth* having rejoined the Admiral after despatching the caique, and the *Naiad* coming up fast astern.

More small vessels were sighted ahead and King ordered some destroyers to give chase. Lieutenant-Commander P. Somerville in the *Kingston,* ahead of the cruisers, reported many more caiques having been sighted. At 1010 what appeared to be a small convoy of four or five small vessels and a destroyer escort became clearly discernible until the escort set about laying a smoke screen to help obliterate the scene from the British ships. The *Perth* and the *Naiad* engaged the escort vessel even while they were under air attack.

King's Force C had, in fact, encountered the second, and the larger, of the invasion forces. It was a considerable convoy comprising some thirty small steamers and caiques under the escort of the small destroyer *Sagittario,* commanded by Lieutenant Guiseppe Cigala Fulgosi.

The confused scene can readily be imagined. The British forces, now strung out and lacking the better defence of a compact, cohesive force, enduring incessant and fierce air attacks from numberless aircraft which droned and screamed as they dived through the noisy chatter of the smaller calibre guns, the crashing roar of the heavier guns, the explosive thuds of bombs bursting in the sea, and billowing smoke screening the ships and confusing the issues still further. Aloft, anti-aircraft shell bursts pock-marked the sky, defacing the clear Mediterranean blue.

The British force was hampered in its movements by the fact that the *Carlisle*'s top speed was 21 knots which restricted the cruisers' speed. And it was rightly considered essential to concentrate the cruisers for their mutual defence against the scores of bombers.

The convoy itself had been labouring under its own problems. It was only at 0930 that morning that Fulgosi had received orders to reverse course to the northward in view of British naval activity ahead and because of the general, precarious military situation ashore in Crete. This complicated about-turn had hardly been completed when Fulgosi sighted the masts of the British ships to the eastward. He had had no indication of the enemy's imminent appearance: 'With the sky swarming with friendly aircraft no one had informed him of the enemy's presence.'[4]

As soon as he sighted the British ships Fulgosi ordered the convoy to pull away as fast as possible, began laying a smoke screen and opened fire. The cruisers opened fire at a range of about 12,000 yards, but sighting was difficult. The *Sagittario* fired torpedoes at the second cruiser in line at about 8,000 yards but no hits were scored, though Fulgosi saw a towering column of water rise alongside the cruiser and believed he had torpedoed her. It was undoubtedly a near miss bomb burst.

Meanwhile, at 0930, Captain Cuno Hoffmann and his squadron (I/LG 1) had taken off from Eleusis near Athens after having been briefed to attack King's force. Within minutes the squadron was over the scene of the skirmishing. One of the Junkers 88 pilots, Lieutenant Gerd Stamp, described the sight far below him comprising the German midget fleet heading north with the British cruiser force in pursuit a few miles astern and in between zig-zagging to cause confusion and spreading a screen of smoke, the small Italian destroyer drawing the fire of the *Perth* and *Naiad*.

Captain Hoffmann ordered his aircraft in to the attack 'and the first Ju 88s dived into the inferno of flak'.

King was now in a perilous situation. The scale of the attacks on his ships was prodigious and almost non-stop. The dispersal of his destroyers was dangerous. High angle ammunition was being consumed at an alarming rate and the cruisers' speed was being confined to 20 knots. King had little hesitation in ordering his destroyers to abandon the chase of the fleeing convoy, to re-group with the cruisers and to withdraw to the westward. King now hoped to fight his way clear of these inhospitable waters through several hours more of daylight. It seemed only a matter of time before damage and destruction must overtake him.

As the British force withdrew, so the Heraklion invasion convoy was spared destruction. Admiral Schüster ordered the con-

---

[4] *The Italian Navy in World War II,* Bragadin, p 109.

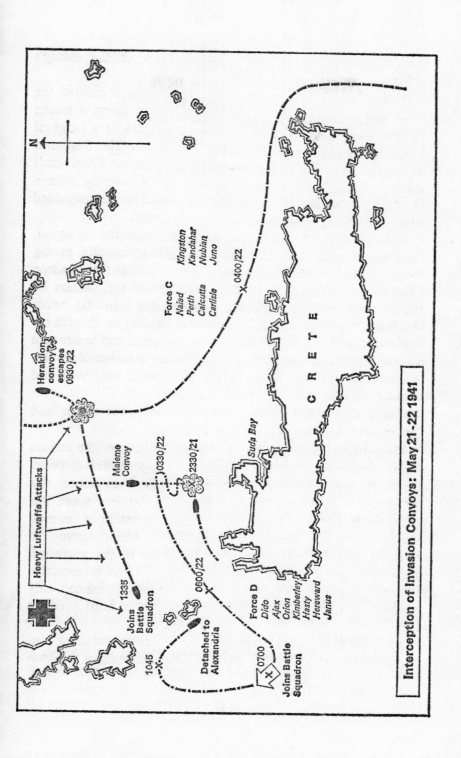

Interception of Invasion Convoys: May 21-22 1941

Heavy Luftwaffe Attacks

Heraklion
convoy
escapes
0930/22

Maleme Convoy

0330/22

2330/21

Joins Battle
Squadron 1335

Suda Bay

Force C
Naiad
Perth
Calcutta
Carlisle

0400/22

0600/22

Force D
Dido
Ajax
Orion
Kimberley
Hasty
Hereward
Janus

Detached to
Alexandria

1045

Joins Battle
Squadron

0700

CRETE

N

Force C
Kingston
Kandahar
Nubian
Juno

voy to return, not to Milos, but to the Piraeus and he abandoned the attempt to fight it through to Crete again. Although the convoy, courageously defended by such an absurdly small escort force, escaped unharmed, Cunningham claimed with justification to have prevented a seaborne landing on Crete. The Fourth Air Fleet *Report* justifiably lamented at the time: 'The problem of supplying heavy arms and reinforcement by sea therefore remains unsolved.'

The fact that the convoy was allowed to escape destruction when marauding destroyers were giving chase and the whole flotilla lay within range of the cruisers' broadsides became another issue which merits some attention. Admiral King was not, in fact, aware of the size of the enemy convoy. The Commander-in-Chief's message timed 0941/22nd which advised that the convoy was of considerable size was not seen by King until after 1100. His force was being subjected to the most intense aerial bombardment, and while no ships had yet suffered damage, it seemed only a matter of time before disaster should strike.

The Prime Minister, Winston Churchill, predictably, was critical of King's withdrawal. Cunningham, too, regarded the abandoning of the chase a mistake. In his *Despatch* he referred to the convoy and commented: 'The Rear Admiral commanding Fifteenth Cruiser Squadron was presented with a unique opportunity of effecting its destruction but unfortunately in the face of heavy air attacks, and with HA ammunition beginning to run low, he decided that he would not have been justified in pressing on to the northward and gave the order to withdraw. The situation was undoubtedly a difficult one for him, as this attack was certainly on a majestic scale but it appears that no diminution of risk could have been achieved by retirement and that, in fact, the safest place for the squadron would have been among the enemy ships. The brief action did, however, have the effect of turning back the convoy, and the troops, if they ever did reach Crete, were not in time to influence the battle.'

Cunningham's comments that the safest place for the squadron lay amid the enemy ships, a sentiment reminiscent of Nelson, had a measure of truth in it, for it was after the retirement to the

166

west that the cruiser force at last fell prey to the bombers. But Cunningham's view may not be right. The main criteria is surely the length of *time* that King's ships were to allow themselves to be attacked by the *Luftwaffe*. It mattered little whether they were in among the caiques or anywhere else at sea: the *Luftwaffe* gave them no respite when they were chasing the convoy. It would have given them none even during a confused mêlée of British warships and enemy caiques. The mood of the pilots was combative; eager to attack the British almost at any cost. The presence of a motley fleet of caiques would have brought no reprieve for King's squadron. He was doomed to endure fierce attacks for several hours whether the caiques were there or not.

The aerial activity over these Cretan waters on Thursday 22nd was so intense, the targets for the aircraft so numerous and the enthusiasm of the pilots so compelling that at the height of the air–sea battle few of the *Gruppe* formations were launched as such. No sooner had aircraft returned from a mission than they were refuelled and re-ammunitioned and they took off again in pairs or small groups, not even amounting to a *Staffel* or flight, so eager were they to resume the attack on the British ships. The consequence was that German aircraft were in the air over the ships for hour upon hour committing the British crews to man action stations for seemingly endless hours and inflicting upon them an almost unbearable, ceaseless pressure which drove them close to breaking point.

Cunningham, as in his criticism of King's withdrawal, set a high standard for both himself and the men under his command. During the next few days of the Cretan war Cunningham's flag officers were to be subjected to the greatest ordeals of their lives, calling for decisions of the utmost urgency and gravity while engaged in the bloodiest air–sea battles in history. These admirals shared the same perils of battle as did the men under their command and displayed courage of a high order: but they also miscalculated and exhibited frailties which the advantage of historical detachment enables us to spotlight. Any decisions made at the height of battle, facing peril and grave anxiety must withstand the probing and the scrutiny of critics long after the perils have passed.

*

The first British force to engage the *Fliegerkorps VIII* pilots on Thursday morning was not Admiral King's. It was Force B, now consisting of the *Gloucester,* Captain H. A. Rowley, and *Fiji,* Captain P. B. R. W. William-Powlett, plus the destroyers *Greyhound* and *Griffin.* These ships had spent an uneventful night patrolling in the vicinity of Cape Matapan. The Commander-in-Chief had signalled the *Gloucester* ordering the Force to proceed to Heraklion, but the message was received too late to implement. However, the squadron had entered the Aegean and at daylight it was about twenty-five miles north of Canea. While retiring to the westward towards Rawlings's Battle Squadron, Force B was located by the Stuka pilots. The time was 0630. For an hour and a half a series of well-directed attacks were launched upon the ships by Ju 87s and Ju 88s. The *Fiji* received slight damage as the concussive force of exploding bombs alongside churned the sea into mast-high columns of water which collapsed and cascaded aboard. The *Gloucester* was fortunate to escape with only superficial damage by fragmentation bombs which peppered her superstructure. Soon after the last dive-bomber departed Force B joined the Battle Squadron at 0830.

*

Force D, Admiral Glennie's squadron of three cruisers and four destroyers, *Dido, Orion, Ajax, Janus, Kimberley, Hasty* and *Hereward,* it will be remembered, had emerged victorious and unscathed after successfully intercepting and destroying the first invasion convoy escorted by the destroyer *Lupo.* It was now heading towards Admiral Rawlings's Force A 1. The rendezvous was achieved without further incident at 0700 on the 22nd in a position about forty-five miles south-west of the Antikithera Channel. It was a happy reunion. But it was short lived. As mentioned earlier, Glennie's squadron was ordered back to Alexandria for re-ammunitioning and refuelling. The C-in-C's message was timed 0716 and was received some time after the rendezvous.

168

Glennie and his ships were eventually detached at 1045. Their departure probably saved even greater losses than were sustained by the remaining ships during the rest of the day.

Glennie's ships were not the only ones needing re-ammunitioning. The early morning report from all ships of their assessment of remaining ammunition revealed a disturbing picture. Glennie's cruisers, *Dido, Orion* and *Ajax* signalled 25%, 38% and 40% of High Angle ammunition remaining at 0930. The figures for the *Gloucester,* 18%, and the *Fiji,* 30%, made even more sombre reading, yet neither of these ships were detached for Alexandria. The two battleships reported as follows: the *Warspite* 66% and the *Valiant* 80%.

Admiral Rawlings's Force A 1 continued to patrol between twenty and thirty miles to the west of the Antikithera Channel where, he reported laconically, he was 'serving a useful purpose by attracting enemy aircraft'. Soon after midday events began to assume graver proportions.

Admiral King, with his cruiser and destroyer Force C which had abandoned the chase of the second invasion convoy, was speeding westwards, desperately trying to fight off the hordes of German aircraft which were continuing to attack the warships with undiminished ferocity. King was hoping to reach Rawlings's position at about 1530, but long before then—at 1225—Rawlings received a signal from King reporting that Force C was in urgent need of support and that the flagship herself had been damaged.

Force C was first attacked at about 0700. Further attacks had been launched during the ill-fated convoy skirmish later in the forenoon, and from 1000 till midday the force was bombed without respite. As the squadron retired on a south-westerly course waves of Ju 88s of Captain Hoffmann's I/LG 1 and Do 17s from Colonel Rieckhoff's KG 2 rained down bombs from the clear, blue sky. At one time the *Naiad* counted thirty-six misses, many of them near ones, in a single period of ten minutes. She became damaged by the battering she was getting. Some of her hull plates started and some compartments flooded. Her speed was reduced while damage up top put several turrets out of action.

The other cruisers came in for punishment, too. The *Carlisle* received a direct hit which damaged her bridge and started a fire. Her commanding officer, Captain T. C. Hampton was killed. The destroyer *Kingston* closed the stricken cruiser to stand by in case of need but she was given a curt signal to 'Keep clear of me'. The cruiser put out the fire and fought back furiously.

The cruisers *Perth* and *Calcutta* were more fortunate and they managed to dodge every bomb aimed at them.

When Rawlings received King's plea for support he immediately decided to take his Battle Squadron into the perilous waters of the Aegean. He set course to join Force C and increased speed to 23 knots. Three-quarters of an hour later those aboard the *Warspite* sighted the AA shell burst ahead and soon the cruisers and destroyers of Force C came into view, their gun muzzles elevated, fighting off heavy *Luftwaffe* attacks.

Just twenty minutes after the first sighting and as the forces met, the *Warspite* herself came in for attention from the pilots. Dive-bombers attacked her and scored a direct hit which wrecked her starboard 4 inch and 6 inch batteries and reduced her speed. The success of this attack is attributed to a flight of Me 109 fighter-bombers of III Jg 77 under Lieutenant Wold-Dietrich Huy. The *Fliegerkorps VIII* diary entry covering this time recorded: 'The Stukas had meanwhile been brought to readiness again for an attack on the enemy fleet in the Straits of Antikithera. Aided by Me 109s with bombs or without, by Me 110s and bombers, they were to pursue a ceaseless attack.'

The executive officer[5] of the *Warspite* was stationed in the upper conning tower when the flagship was hit. He went to investigate:

> On reaching the upper deck it was apparent that one 4 inch mounting had gone overboard completely . . . There was huge hole in the deck . . . from which smoke and steam were pouring out. I then went down to the port 6 inch battery . . . to try to get at the seat of the fire through the armoured door that connected the port and starboard 6 inch battery decks . . . We had great difficulty in opening the door and had to use a sledgeham-

[5] Later Admiral Sir Charles Maddon. Taken from HMS *Warspite* by Captain S. W. Roskill, Collins, 1957.

mer. Finally, it gave, to display a gruesome scene. The starboard battery was full of flames and smoke, in among which the cries of burned and wounded men could be heard. This was very unnerving and I remember thinking how accurate were the descriptions in C. S. Forester's books of the carnage on the gun decks in Nelson's day. The flames seemed pretty fierce and I was doubtful if we would make headway against them. However, my two volunteers came either side of me with their hoses and we walked into the battery . . . I was soon joined by more fire parties . . . but was hampered by the continued cries of the burned men, which distracted the fire parties who wanted to leave their hoses to assist their comrades. I therefore concentrated on administering morphia . . . As it was dark and wounded men were thrown in all directions amidst piles of iron-work and rubbish this was not easy. . . . I then went to the starboard mess decks where a fresh scene of carnage greeted me . . . When all was under control I went to the bridge to report. The calm blue afternoon seemed unreal after the dark and smelly carnage below.

Sorting the dead out and identifying them occupied most of the dog watches, and they were then sewn up in hammocks for burial. The stout corporal of marines who served so cheerfully in the wardroom bar volunteered for and personally led this operation throughout the next two days till we returned to harbour.

All told, the *Warspite*'s casualties amounted to 8 killed, 24 missing, 11 died of wounds and 69 wounded.

As the two forces joined, the Battle Squadron now turned in astern of the damaged cruiser flagship, *Naiad*. Admiral King, senior to Admiral Rawlings, now assumed command of the combined forces. This was an unhappy circumstance, for a change in command at any time can tend to be disruptive: in the midst of battle with the enemy overhead, it is almost indefensible.

The first of a series of mistakes occurred when the destroyer *Greyhound* was detached from the fleet to intercept and sink a large caique between the islands of Pori and Antikithera. She accomplished this successfully and was returning to her station on the screen when, at 1351 she was singled out and attacked by eight dive-bombers. She was struck by three bombs in rapid suc-

171

cession and was clearly doomed. A few minutes later she sank by the stern in a position approximately five miles due west of Pori Island having managed to slip her only remaining whaler.

King ordered the *Kandahar* and *Kingston* to pick up survivors. These two destroyers reached the scene of destruction, lowered their whalers and while under savage bomb and machinegun attacks managed to pick up a number of survivors, including the commanding officer, Commander W. R. Marshall-A'Deane. To stay longer rescuing the men in the water invited destruction, so Carley floats were thrust over the side among the swimmers and the destroyers departed. The survivors clinging to rafts were machinegunned mercilessly and among those killed in this way were Lieutenant-Commander (E) R. E. G. Bremner and Warrant Gunner (T) Mr J. W. Chase. A young Ordinary Seaman in hospital in Alexandria a few days later told the Commander-in-Chief he was in the ship's whaler with the First Lieutenant (Lieutenant R. Scott) and about eighteen men aboard. When an aircraft was spotted coming in at them, the lad went over the side and swam under water. When he emerged, all aboard the whaler were dead.

A few minutes after ordering the two destroyers to assist the *Greyhound*, King ordered, at 1402, the *Fiji*, and then five minutes later, the *Gloucester*, to stand by the two rescuing destroyers to give AA support and to stand by the sinking *Greyhound* till dark. The despatch of these two cruisers with such a depleted store of HA ammunition was, of course, a gross blunder, committed unwittingly because Admiral King was unaware of the earlier returns of HA ammunition remaining in the cruisers.

The situation now was deteriorating rapidly for the British ships. All forces were under air attack and all forces were being fragmented: the *Greyhound* had disappeared but many survivors still swam awaiting rescue: the *Kandahar* and *Kingston* were trying to escape this grisly scene: the *Fiji* was hurrying to join these two destroyers and coming up astern was the *Gloucester:* Rawlings's Force A 1 was still operating as an independent division from King's Force C. The prime requirement of concentration had been lost. Dispersal invited destruction.

172

So hard-pressed was King's force at 1413, by which time his ships had nearly exhausted all their ammunition, that he ordered Rawlings to give closer support, which was accomplished even though the *Warspite* could only make eighteen knots.

Meanwhile, Rawlings who was aware of the low state of ammunition in the *Fiji* and *Gloucester* was feeling increasingly uneasy about their predicament. Accordingly he informed King who was now confronted with an agonising dilemma. He made just about the only decision open to him and signalled the two cruisers to withdraw, with any ships in company, at their discretion.

All these anguished decisions, all these ship movements, were taking place under a hail of bombs and with the deafening roar of gunfire intermingled with the concussive thud of near misses. Senses became stunned and those aboard the ships wondered how much longer these interminable attacks would continue. The *Luftwaffe* pilots went into the attack time and time again during this Thursday, no sooner expending their bomb loads than hastening back to base for refuelling and reloading with bombs so they could undertake yet another attack a few hours later.

At 1530 King must have been heartened as he sighted the *Fiji* and the *Gloucester* coming up astern, the bow waves indicating their high speed, their gun muzzles pointing skywards, still engaging *Luftwaffe* aircraft. Those aboard the two cruisers must have been even more heartened than the Admiral, for they had endured agonising moments when attacked by waves of bombers, but with only a small number of 4 inch shells to feed the guns. The pom-poms continued to put up a brisk fire, but the 4 inch were only used spasmodically. In due course, the inevitable happened. With a diminution in intensity of the 4 inch barrage, the Stuka pilots grew more courageous and pressed home their attacks to almost suicidal closeness. At 1527, just minutes before the forces sighted each other, the *Gloucester* was hit by at least two bombs. One exploded in the gunroom flat and damaged B boiler room and compressor room and the wireless office, dousing all lights in the ship. A second explosion blasted the after high angle director and the main topmast into the sea.

173

Other explosions near by in the sea thumped the hull of the cruiser with a sickening and frightening violence. A few minutes later another explosion occurred between the groups of portside torpedo tubes on the 4 inch gun deck. Fortunately the torpedoes had been fired before the explosion. Had the warheads also exploded the damage and loss of life would have been considerably greater.

The port pom-pom was wrecked when another bomb shot through its platform and exploded in the canteen flat below. In the resulting fire pom-pom ammunition began to explode adding to the dangerous situation. The cruiser began to lose steam from severed pipes and her speed fell away. At about 1545 three more violent explosions were experienced and in the turmoil of battle it is not certain whether these were bomb explosions close alongside or whether they were torpedoes from aircraft. The fine ship was now doomed. She took on a list to port and the flood water entered the main transmitting station and the second wireless office.

By now all hands had been ordered to the upper deck. Soon the order to abandon ship was given. Both port and starboard whalers were lowered but the starboard one was so damaged it filled and sank immediately. The port one was also unseaworthy. Men scrambled down the boat's falls into the sea. The *Fiji* steamed by casting overboard a number of Carley floats for the *Gloucester*'s survivors. Aboard the stricken cruiser a party of officers amidships were hurling loose wood overboard while the medical staff assisted by the chaplain comforted the wounded and dying and secured them aboard rescue rafts. Even while these acts of mercy were being enacted bombers still fell upon the crippled cruiser now blazing uncontrollably in places and listing so heavily that by 1715 her port gunwales were awash. Minutes later in a moment of nakedness the *Gloucester* turned turtle and slowly sank by the stern.

The junior medical officer[6] in his subsequent report noted that the water was agreeably warm as he stepped into it. But after a

[6] Referred to in *Medical History of the Second World War. Royal Naval Medical Services,* Vol II, Coulter, p 180.

while when the enemy had gone, and the *Fiji* no longer in company, the desolateness of the watery wastes made itself felt to the swimming survivors: 'It felt very lonely in the water after the ship had gone,' he reported.

German bombers passed overhead in the clear sky in great numbers but only one or two molested the survivors by machine-gunning them. The medical officer reported that a group of men clutched for survival to an unlikely raft which comprised two large coir fenders tied together with a length of wire. Twenty men in varying stages of exhaustion grouped together around this raft by nightfall, but the periodic capsizing and increasing choppiness of the sea caused many men to lose their hold. One by one the numbers dwindled until by daybreak only six had survived and one of these was soon to die. Later on the Friday afternoon only four men were rescued from this makeshift raft by a Greek caique manned by Germans.

The *Gloucester* had gone down in a position nine miles from Pori Island on a bearing of 294 degrees within sight of the mountains of the Peloponnese, the peaks of Crete and the island of Kithera.

Cunningham was specially grieved at the loss of this modern cruiser which had been hit by more bombs than any other ship. 'As she left Alexandria for the last time,' Cunningham wrote,[7] 'I went alongside her in my barge and had a talk with her Captain, Henry Aubrey Rowley. He was very anxious about his men, who were just worn out, which was not surprising. . . . I doubt if many of them survived as they, too, were murderously machinegunned in the water. Rowley's body, recognisable by his uniform monkey jacket and the signals in his pocket, came ashore to the west of Mersa Matruh about four weeks later. It was a long way to come home.'

When the *Fiji* signalled the *Gloucester*'s plight earlier in the afternoon, King consulted Rawlings. They considered that in view of the air attacks which continued without remission it was an unjustified risk exposing more ships to exceptional danger by tak-

[7] *A Sailor's Odyssey*, Cunningham, p 371.

ing the Battle Fleet back in support of the stricken cruiser. Accordingly the *Fiji* was ordered to leave boats and rafts for the *Gloucester* and then to withdraw. Captain William-Powlett aboard the *Fiji* was grieved at abandoning his dying consort, but after jettisoning his life rafts he turned the *Fiji* away and headed for the Battle Fleet.

In the meantime, the Battle Fleet itself had managed to survive attacks which had raged intermittently from 1320 till 1510. Further attacks were resumed some time later and the *Valiant* suffered two hits aft by medium bombs during a high-level attack at 1645, but no serious damage was sustained. By now, King's Force C had nearly exhausted all HA ammunition, there were still many hours of daylight left and the British ships were still uncomfortably close to the island of Crete. The situation was still grave. Further disaster lay in store for the British.

At 1900 William-Powlett in the *Fiji* signalled King reporting he had the *Kandahar* and the *Kingston* in company. The *Fiji*'s position was given as 305 degrees Cape Elaphonisi twenty-four miles, course 175 degrees and speed 27 knots. This position was only thirty miles due east of the Battle Fleet which had been steering south from 1830 and was now steering 215 degrees. The Battle Fleet changed course again at 2100 to ESE. But in the meantime, the *Fiji* succumbed to an air attack with tragic, twofold irony.

In the past four hours she had repulsed some twenty bombing attacks by formations of German bombers which had loosed scores of bombs at her. Now she fell victim to a single Me 109 carrying one bomb.[8]

The aircraft was one of Captain Ihlefeld's Messerschmitts of 1/LG 2 from Molai. 'The pilot, with the plane at the limit of its endurance, was about to return to base when he sighted the cruiser through a thin veil of cloud. . . . The Me 109 pilot summoned a colleague by radio.'

The aircraft flew out of the low cloud which thinly overcast

[8] At first glance it seems unlikely that an Me 109 should have scored this success. Several authorities dispute this and attribute the attack to other aircraft, but the evidence in *The Luftwaffe War Diaries* is convincing. See p 255.

the sky. Its shallow dive took it low and unseen over the cruiser. One 500 lb bomb was released which exploded close alongside on the portside amidships. The explosion blew in the cruiser's bottom, flooded several compartments and one boiler room. She heeled over to port and immediately took up a 25 degree list. She came to a stop, her engines crippled. She lay in the sea at a grotesque angle like some huge maimed animal. Thirty minutes later she was spotted by another lone aircraft which made a bombing run and released a stick of three bombs which hit the *Fiji* squarely, including one hit over A boiler room which brought the foremast crashing down. The list increased to 30 degrees and the cruiser lay careened like an ancient wooden wall. William-Powlett gave the order to abandon ship and what boats and rafts remained were got away. One hour later, at 2015 the *Fiji* rolled right over and sank without dignity.

The commanding officers of the destroyers *Kandahar* and *Kingston,* Commander W. G. A. Robson and Lieutenant-Commander P. Somerville, lowered boats and rafts then withdrew to draw clear of the area which was now filled with hundreds of survivors littering the sea. The destroyers returned after nightfall and spent two hours guided by torches from boats and rafts till the *Kingston* had rescued 339 and the *Kandahar* another 184. Even in times of great selflessness such as these the act of Commander Marshall-A'Deane, the rescued commanding officer of the *Greyhound* stands out. While aboard the *Kandahar* helping to rescue *Fiji* survivors he saw a man in difficulties, dived overboard and swam in the darkness to help. He was never seen again. For his gallantry he was awarded the Albert Medal posthumously.

At 2245 the *Kandahar* and the *Kingston,* with their 523 *Fiji* survivors, plus those from the *Greyhound,* departed from the mournful scene and set course to join the Battle Fleet at a speed of only 15 knots in order to conserve their rapidly dwindling supplies of fuel oil. During their high-speed manœuvring when they were being tormented and harried by no less than twenty-two air attacks by formations of German bombers in the four and a half hours from 1445 to 1920 their consumption of fuel

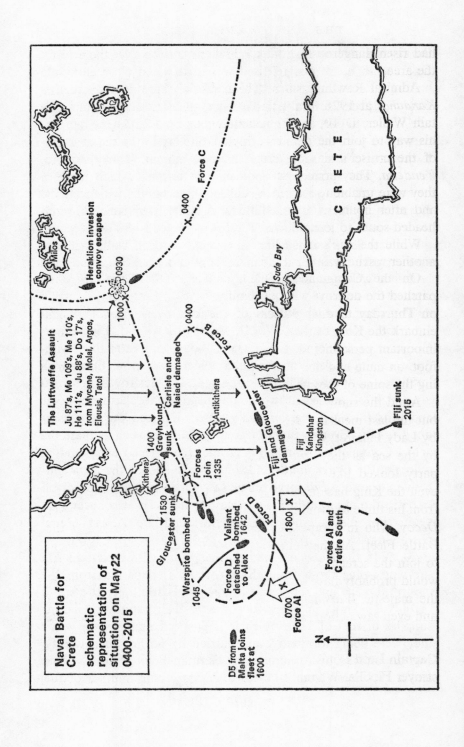

Naval Battle for Crete

schematic representation of situation on May 22
0400-2015

The Luftwaffe Assault

Ju 87's, Me 109's, Me 110's,
He 111's, Ju 88's, Do 17's,
from Mycene, Molai, Argos,
Eleusis, Tatoi

D5 from Malta joins fleet at 1600

Force C

X 0400

Heraklion invasion convoy escapes

Milos

X 0930

X 1000

X 0400

Force B

Carlisle and Naiad damaged

Antikithera

Kithera

1400 Greyhound sunk

X Forces join 1335

Fiji and Gloucester damaged

Fiji
Kandahar
Kingston

Fiji sunk 2015

1530 Gloucester sunk

Gloucester bombed 1045

Warspite bombed 1045

Force D

Valiant bombed 1642

Force D detached to Alex

Forces A1 and C retire South

X 1800

X 0700 Force A1

CRETE

Suda Bay

N

had risen dangerously, sufficiently to imperil their escape from the area.

Admiral Rawlings learned with dismay from Robson in the *Kandahar* at 1928 that the *Fiji* was doomed. He signalled Captain Waller, D 10, in the Australian destroyer *Stuart*, then on his way to join the admiral, to proceed instead to the position of the cruiser's sinking with his two destroyers *Voyager* and *Vendetta*. They arrived on the scene the following morning but they were unable to locate any signs of the *Fiji* nor her survivors and after hours of fruitless searching they were recalled and headed south to join the Battle Fleet.

While the *Fiji*'s survivors were being plucked from the sea another rescue was being effected.

On the Commander-in-Chief's instructions Rawlings despatched the destroyers *Decoy* and *Hero* from the screen at 2030 on Thursday to Ayia Roumeli on the south coast of Crete to embark the King of the Hellenes, the British Minister and other important personnel. This party had travelled for three days on foot, on mule and donkey over tortuous mountain tracks, climbing the spine of the range to a height of over 7,000 feet.

Amid the snow at this height they roasted a mountain sheep, but the last meal the King enjoyed on Grecian soil was cooked by Lady Palairet, wife of the British Minister, in the tiny village by the sea as they awaited the British destroyers. The ragged party looked like penniless refugees when they were rescued; even the King had stripped all his medal ribbons and gold braid from his tunic to avoid identification. They boarded the destroyer *Decoy*, who in company with the *Hero*, sped off to rejoin the Battle Fleet. As they neared the fleet, Rawlings ordered them to join the screen, a decision not to the liking of the King who would probably have preferred transfer to the admiral's flagship, the majestic *Warspite*. His Majesty remained in the destroyer and even saw action at sea before stepping ashore in Alexandria.

*

Captain Lord Louis Mountbatten was Captain D of the 5th Destroyer Flotilla. When his destroyer *Kelly* had been repaired and recommissioned after her North Sea torpedoing, the flotilla was despatched to the Mediterranean where it became a welcome reinforcement. When the flotilla made the passage to Malta from Gibraltar it was the first to do so for a long time, and when the destroyers led into harbour in line ahead the battlements of Valetta were black with cheering Maltese. It was an exciting welcome. But more excitement of a different nature came during the days of continuous daylight bombing while in harbour and the periodic skirmishing out to sea to maraud Rommel's supply routes from Italy to North Africa and shelling the port of Benghazi. Then came the crisis in Crete. The 5th Flotilla was released from the beleagured sandstone island to help combat the invasion.

Accordingly, Mountbatten in the *Kelly*, with the *Kashmir, Kipling, Kelvin* and *Jackal* left Malta at 2130 on Wednesday, May 21st and after an uneventful passage joined Admiral Rawlings at sea at 1600 on Thursday 22nd. Rawlings had been requested by King to detail the destroyer night activities as instructed by the Commander-in-Chief. He detached the *Kelly, Kashmir* and *Kipling* to search for *Fiji* survivors and thirty minutes later sent the *Kelvin* and *Jackal* to try to locate any more survivors from the *Gloucester*. But the Germans had rescued more than 500 *Gloucester* men, many by air–sea rescue aircraft. Rawlings later signalled new instructions to these destroyers calling off the searches and ordering them to re-group and sweep as a flotilla inside Kissamo and Canea Bays.

However, when the flotilla entered the Antikithera Channel the *Kipling* developed a steering defect which hampered her fighting efficiency. Mountbatten ordered her to rejoin the admiral. The *Kelly* and *Kashmir* encountered a troop-carrying caique in Canea Bay which they engaged with gunfire and left badly damaged. When, some minutes later, Mountbatten received a signal from NOIC Suda Bay reporting unexplained lights in Canea Bay, he detached the *Kelvin* and *Jackal* to investigate. But the lights proved to be on shore and of no sinister meaning, so the *Kelvin* and *Jackal* withdrew independently. Meanwhile, the *Kelly* and *Kashmir* had carried out a short bombardment of Maleme with a barrage of 4.7 inch shells to give support to the New Zealand troops ashore. While withdrawing they encountered another caique which they engaged and set ablaze: the caique then blew up with an explosion like a firework display. The *Kelly,* with *Kashmir* following, set course to clear the straits before daylight.

Farther along the coast, Force E, the tireless Captain Mack with his 14th Destroyer Flotilla comprising the *Jervis, Ilex, Nizam* and *Havock,* carried out another night's patrol off Heraklion. There were no incidents and the flotilla withdrew through the Kaso Strait which they had been ordered to pass at 2100 on Thursday night. Earlier in the afternoon, the Commander-in-Chief had given instruction for the *Ajax* and *Orion* who were returning to Alexandria with Admiral Glennie to rendezvous with Mack's flotilla about eighty miles south of the Kaso Strait.

Glennie duly detached these two cruisers at 1730 when about 150 miles from the Kaso Strait. But an hour or so later the *Ajax* realised she could not make the rendezvous in time, so signalled her intention—at 1843/22nd—of rejoining Glennie, which she did.

That same night the Battle Fleet—Rawlings's Force A 1 and King's Force C—was steering away from the scene of the day's disasters on an ESE course which was maintained until 0100/23rd when King with his four cruisers, two of them damaged and all practically denuded of HA ammunition parted company for Alexandria on Cunningham's orders. Rawlings remained with his force to the south of Crete until at 0400 he turned to the NW to make a rallying point for Mountbatten's destroyers off the Kithera Strait. But half an hour later a signal was received from Cunningham recalling all forces to Alexandria forthwith. We will revert to this signal later.

Before we do so and for the sake of chronology we must recount a few more movements on Thursday, May 22nd.

*

In Alexandria activity also abounded though on a less dramatic scale than in the waters around Crete. The *Glenroy* embarked

900 troops of the Queen's Royal Regiment, the HQ of the 16th Infantry Brigade and eighteen vehicles, all destined for Tymbaki in Crete. The ship sailed in the afternoon escorted by the *Coventry* and the sloops *Auckland* and *Flamingo*.

But the *Glenroy* convoy was an ill-fated little venture. Because of the intensive enemy air activity over Cretan waters the operation was postponed by Cunningham after consultation with Wavell. The convoy was ordered to return to Alexandria at 1127 on Friday 23rd. But when the Admiralty in London learned of this postponement it disapproved of the action and they intervened at 1559 and ordered the *Glenroy* to turn northwards again pending further instructions. In the meantime, Cunningham was urged by the Admiralty in a message timed 1651 to change his mind and to land the troops in Crete that night if at all possible. But the delays had now put Tymbaki out of reach by nightfall. Cunningham signalled the Admiralty to this effect at 1837. The attempt was abandoned. A further message to the Admiralty two hours later explained that the *Glenroy* would have been in the worst possible position for enemy air attacks at daylight had she proceeded northwards.

Other departures from Alexandria on Thursday the 22nd were the destroyers *Jaguar* and *Defender* who became supply vessels when they embarked ammunition urgently wanted by the army in Crete. They departed in haste with instructions to proceed to join Force A 1 on its way to the rallying point for Mountbatten's destroyers, then to proceed to Suda Bay.

At this time, too, the minelaying submarine *Rorqual* was active laying mines in the Gulf of Salonika while the modern 2,650 ton minelayer *Abdiel* capable of nearly 40 knots, laid a minefield between Cephalonia and Levkas.

*

Early in the morning of Friday 23rd, as we have seen, Rawlings received a signal from the Commander-in-Chief recalling all forces to Alexandria forthwith. It was a dramatic instruction which marked a significant development in the naval situation. Cunningham's signal, which was timed at 0408 on the 23rd, was prompted by a 'Most Immediate' signal received at 2230/22nd from Rawlings. This was the signal which gave news to the Commander-in-Chief of the loss of the *Gloucester* and the *Fiji* and detailed the ammunition remaining in the battleships and destroyers. The signal as received by Cunningham reported among other things no short-range ammunition left in the battleships. Whether this was a calligraphic or phonetic error is not known. The fact is that the first copy of the signal shown to Cunningham and his Chief of Staff indicated that the battleships were EMPTY of short-range ammunition, but the typed copy distributed the next day substituted the word PLENTY. And this was the correct word. Whether the correct wording on the original signal would have influenced Cunningham to leave the Battle Fleet in a position as a rallying point for the 5th Destroyer Flotilla or not is now mere speculation. And whether such a decision would have prevented the loss of the *Kelly* and *Kashmir* on the Friday is only further conjecture.

During the Thursday, the Commander-in-Chief had lost two modern and valuable cruisers and one destroyer, while two battleships and two more cruisers had been damaged. As far as could be ascertained with any degree of certainty the only enemy aircraft which could be claimed to have been shot down were two certain, six probable and five damaged. It was small consolation for the losses and damage sustained. Taking stock of the situation at Alexandria it is small wonder that Cunningham decided to recall the ships of the Mediterranean Fleet. Thus, another decision based on faulty information had been taken which led to more distressing losses. The net result of the faulty signal was to initiate a general retirement. The ships, tormented and harried by the *Luftwaffe* in two days of bombing with little respite, abandoned the waters of Crete and withdrew to the safety of Alexandria to lick their many wounds.

CHAPTER 12

The Flight to Alexandria

BUT A CHANGE in plans and a general retirement of the Navy to Alexandria brought small change in fortune for the Mediterranean Fleet, for another long day of peril and losses lay in store before the warships gained the sanctuary of their berths. For the sake of clarity the naval situation at daylight on Friday, May 23rd, can be summarised as follows:

1. Force A 1, Admiral Rawlings, and Force C, Admiral King, were about twenty-five miles apart and about to join each other to make the passage to Alexandria. The destroyers *Kandahar* and *Kingston* were proceeding to join Force C.

2. 5th Destroyer Flotilla, Captain Mountbatten, with the *Kelly, Kashmir* and *Kipling,* had just cleared Canea Bay having delayed departure and were retiring at full speed to clear the danger zone. Ahead of them and retiring at speed independently of their flotilla leader were the *Kelvin* and *Jackal,* in a somewhat safer area south-west of Crete.

3. Force E, Captain Mack's 14th Destroyer Flotilla, was retiring to Alexandria.

4. The destroyers *Decoy* and *Hero* were just joining Rawlings's Force A 1 with the King of the Hellenes aboard the *Decoy.*

5. Force D, Admiral Glennie's *Dido,* was just outside Alexandria harbour, being trailed by the *Ajax* and *Orion* who had failed to catch up with their flagship.

6. 10th Destroyer Flotilla, Captain Waller in the *Stuart,* with the *Voyager* and *Vendetta* was off Cape Elaphonisi still searching for *Fiji* survivors.

7. Two small forces, each carrying urgently awaited troops or supplies to the embattled island, were the only vessels not withdrawing to Alexandria in compliance with the Commander-in-Chief's order of retirement: (*a*) The destroy-

ers *Jaguar* and *Defender* having been detached from Force A 1 were now speeding for Suda Bay with ammunition for the army, (*b*) The *Glenroy* and her escorting vessels were at sea heading northwards from Alexandria: the exchange of signals revising the convoy's orders came later in the day.

*

When Rawlings received the Commander-in-Chief's message, timed at 0408/23rd, early on Friday morning, his first inclination was to continue towards Cape Elaphonisi, but instead he turned to the eastward preparatory to making the withdrawal. He decided that his force, buttressed as it was by the battleships *Warspite* and *Valiant,* should be made the rallying point for all various forces and flotillas now scattered throughout the treacherous waters south and south-west of Crete, all of them within range of German dive-bombers. Rawlings later reported that his decision was 'swayed, I believe, no little by the two fuelless destroyers (*Kandahar* and *Kingston*) and *Decoy*'s principal passenger'. He signalled his course, position and speed to all ships, then headed for Alexandria at 15 knots. Throughout the morning and forenoon of this Friday the scattered forces joined up with Force A 1, and by 1045 all were accounted for and assembled into a coherent force, except Mountbatten's three destroyers. The *Jaguar* and *Defender,* of course, detached themselves later to enter the Aegean at nightfall to make their way to Suda Bay.

During the remainder of the forenoon and afternoon the assembled fleet was kept under enemy air observation, but surprisingly no attacks developed and darkness brought safety. The fleet wearily entered harbour at Alexandria in the early hours of Saturday, May 24th, battered, bloodied and all but beaten.

*

Captain Mountbatten's fortunes must now be followed. We left the *Kelly* and *Kashmir* retiring at full speed at dawn towards the Kithera Strait after bombarding Maleme and shooting-up caiques on the night of Thursday–Friday. The *Kipling* had rejoined after repairing her steering gear. The three destroyers were spotted by aircraft early in the morning soon after daylight and soon two

186

high-level bombing attacks had been mounted by the *Luftwaffe*. These were survived by careful manœuvring of the destroyers as the bombs were seen to fall. But the attacks portended an arduous and dangerous day ahead.

The danger came earlier than expected. At 0755 when just south of Gavdos Island twenty-four Ju 87 dive-bombers of I/St G 2 under the command of Captain Hitschold located the fleeing ships and immediately launched determined attacks. The Stukas dived almost vertically, ensuring accuracy of bombing, and offering the nose and leading edges of the wings as minimal target areas for the gunners. It became the objective of the commanding officers of the destroyers to so steer their ships as to make the Stukas dive steeper and steeper and thus encourage inaccuracies in their bombing.

Despite these tactics, the *Kashmir* was struck by a bomb from the third wave of bombers which caused enormous damage. In a moment it was obvious she was doomed. She started to sink as soon as the bomb blew her open to the sea. Her commanding officer, Commander H. A. King ordered abandon ship. A young Australian Volunteer Reserve Ordinary Seaman, Ian Rhodes, struggled free from his half-submerged Oerlikon gun to another and shot down a Ju 87 as his ship sank under him. In two minutes the *Kashmir* had gone. The *Kelly* continued to fight off the aircraft but when she was making 30 knots or more under full starboard rudder, she was hit by a large bomb which exploded aft on X turret. She took on an ever-increasing list to port and finally turned turtle with considerable way on her. She floated upside down for half an hour allowing her survivors to get well clear before she sank. Not content with their victory, many dive-bombers then flew low and machinegunned the survivors struggling helpless in the sea.

Commander A. St Clair-Ford, commanding the *Kipling,* went to the rescue as soon as there was a lull in the attacks. The rescue was a skilled and dangerous operation. The *Kipling* lowered all her boats and Carley floats and picked up all the *Kelly*'s survivors, including Mountbatten. St Clair-Ford then turned his attention to the *Kashmir*'s men. No less than 152 officers and men were picked up, plus Commander King. As each bombing attack developed the *Kipling* abandoned the rescue attempt, put on speed and dodged the bomb loads while fighting off the assailants with her guns. This tactic led to a tragic incident when one attack developed. The motor boat was in the sea still secured to the falls when St Clair-Ford got the ship under way urgently. There was no time to release the boat. It dragged under, tearing the davits from the destroyer's deck and carried to their deaths the First Lieutenant of the *Kipling*, Lieutenant-Commander J. E. A. Bush, and the First Lieutenant of the *Kelly*, Lieutenant-Commander Lord Hugh Beresford, both of whom were trying to cut the falls.

St Clair-Ford handled his ship with skill and a high degree of seamanship as he nosed his ship from raft to raft for three hours before every survivor had been pulled aboard. Only then was course set for Alexandria at a speed of 17 knots. It is estimated that during the period from 0820 when the *Kashmir* and the *Kelly* had gone down and the enemy concentrated their attentions on her, till 1300 when she was left in peace, she was attacked by forty bombers which dropped a total of eighty-three bombs around her. It is a wonder that she emerged from the ordeal unscathed.

Admiral King decided reluctantly not to detach any ships from Forces A 1, and C then heading for Alexandria, to support the destroyer. Just how narrow was the margin on which these ships operated is shown by the fact that on the morning of Saturday 24th when fifty[1] miles from Alexandria, the *Kipling* finally ran out of fuel, and came to a halt. She was unable to make port and the net layer *Protector* left harbour to fuel her sufficiently for her to make base. When she finally arrived, ships' companies of the Mediterranean Fleet cleared lower deck and cheered her in.

The *Kipling*'s was an epic story of survival, but it must not conceal the fact that she was the sole survivor of three modern, fast destroyers, competently handled with plenty of searoom for

[1] Reports vary from fifty to ninety miles, but the distance itself is not important. The significance lies in the fact alone.

188

manœuvring in an engagement with German dive-bombers. It was yet another triumph for the *Luftwaffe* in its encounter with the Navy.

At the end of this busy day in the Mediterranean General Richthoven wrote in his War Diary[2] with justifiable pride: 'The result was abundantly clear. I was convinced we had scored a great and decisive victory. Six cruisers and three destroyers had certainly been sunk, with many additional hits, even on the battleships. We had at last demonstrated that a fleet at sea within range of the *Luftwaffe* was vulnerable—provided the weather permitted flying.' The General's facts were wrong. But his beliefs and the conclusions he drew were right.

During the night of May 23rd–24th the *Jaguar* and *Defender* successfully discharged their cargoes of ammunition after an uneventful dash through the night to Suda Bay and then set course for Alexandria through the Kaso Strait for the 420 miles flight to safety. They took with them 250 naval officers and men no longer needed on the island.

*

The naval situation on the morning of Saturday, May 24th, gave Admiral Cunningham small cause for satisfaction. Certainly the bulk of the ships of his fleet now lay restfully at their berths, their crews trying desperately to catch up on missing sleep and rest which perhaps more even than the clangour of pounding guns and exploding bombs and the infinite privations thrust upon them by almost continuous days at action stations, was the worst strain they endured. Captain Waller at a later date spoke of the lack of sleep as the greatest strain. The First Lieutenant of the *Hotspur* wrote of this period in his book:[3]

> It was about two in the afternoon when we finally got anchored (in Suda Bay) and managed to eat a bit and get clean. The crew were so tired by now that I only closed up the short range weapons and let everyone else sleep. Of course, at 3.30 the raid came. I was in such a deep sleep by now that it must have taken quite

[2] Quoted in *The Luftwaffe War Diaries*, Cajus Bekker.
[3] *Before the Tide Turned* by Hugh Hodgkinson, Harrap, 1944.

a few bombs to wake me, and I remember fighting to get my shoes on with the whistle and roar of bombs going on above me; and, still with a mind half conscious, I got up on deck to see a whopper go up about a hundred yards astern. . . . The most amazing thing of all was the fact that some of our sailors slept clean through the whole fiendish din.

But there was little rest or respite for the crews of the British ships. Urgent replenishment of empty fuel tanks and re-stocking of depleted ammunition magazines demanded immediate action. First aid for the ships' wounds and preparations for a speedy return to sea became prime objectives. While officers and men strove to tidy the disarray aboard their ships, the Commander-in-Chief, imbued with the same tireless spirit exhibited by his sailors, reluctantly issued orders for an immediate return to the battle zone.

At daylight on that Saturday morning, May 24th, the ships of the Mediterranean Fleet were disposed as follows: Forces A 1, C and E were all safely alongside in harbour; the *Glenroy* with her escorts were back in harbour after their abortive sortie towards Crete; the *Jaguar* and *Defender* were heading for base and the *Protector* was accompanying the gallant *Kipling,* laden with the *Kelly* and *Kashmir* survivors; HMS *Abdiel,* the modern minelayer, alone, unescorted, relying upon her high speed for safety, had departed from Alexandria during the night to carry much-needed stores and ammunition for the army in Suda: not for her the temporary sanctuary of Alexandria.

No longer did the White Ensign fly from the MTBs of the busy 10th MTB Flotilla at Suda Bay, where they had performed noble and valuable feats and had accounted for two German aircraft destroyed with another two possibles. This tiny flotilla had been hastily assembled for coastal defence at Suda Bay. The Italian Navy, over a period of many years had devoted much attention to local coast defence in the Mediterranean and had built up a force of a hundred MAS boats organised into *squadrillas* and deployed them over a wide area—Tripoli, Taranto, Naples, Leros, three ports in Sicily, Sardinia, the Adriatic, Spezia and even in Italian Somaliland in the Red Sea.

All that the British could muster was nine of the old type 55 foot Thorneycroft MTBs. These had been building for the Finnish and Philipine Navies. They were formed into the 10th MTB Flotilla and despatched to Alexandria. Five of them under the command of Lieutenant-Commander E. C. Peake, were detached for the defence of Suda. Unfortunately they suffered from lack of petrol supplies and irritating breakdowns. Nevertheless, they performed sterling work until they were all destroyed in the German air attacks of May 23rd.

When the bombers had departed on this day it was 'a melancholy sight. Beside HMS *York,* there were also two destroyers, half a dozen merchantmen and ten or twelve other craft, big or small, in a more or less disabled condition. Some of them were burning furiously and sending tall columns of black and white smoke into the sky.'[4]

It was not long before the White Ensign returned to Cretan waters in strength. If the ships were to be given no relief, nor were the aircraft to be conceded an easy victory. Each bomb-hit registered by a German aircraft had been hard-earned for the warships were defiant and retaliated fiercely in their own defence. The first ships to be thrust back into the fray barely had time to get their breath back in Alexandria before they assembled and sailed at 0800 on Saturday, May 24th.

Reports had been received of the possibility of a seaborne landing being mounted by Italian forces in the Dodecanese for an assault upon Sitia Bay at the eastern extremity of Crete during the night of Saturday–Sunday. The force ordered to deal with this contingency comprised the *Ajax* (Senior Officer), *Dido, Kimberley* and *Hotspur.* They were ordered to pass northwards through the Kaso Strait and to sweep the Sitia Bay coastal region of Crete. They were further instructed to proceed as far as Maleme if no invasion forces had been sighted and to carry out a bombardment of the airfield. But no enemy activity was encountered during the night's sweep and time did not permit of the bombardment of Maleme airfield and ensure a safe withdrawal

[4] *Climax in Crete* by Theodore Stephanides, Faber & Faber, 1946.

before daylight. The venture was abandoned, the ships turned about and went south through the Kaso Strait back to Alexandria.

In the meantime, the *Abdiel* executed her high-speed dash to the embattled island. She safely disembarked her 200 Special Service Troops, medical stores and ammunition at Suda Bay and then made good her escape to Alexandria.

Another attempt to land the HQ and two battalions of Special Service Troops (Layforce) was made by a force of three destroyers, the *Isis,* Commander C. S. B. Swinley, Senior Officer, *Hero* and *Nizam*, which left Alexandria at 0930 on Saturday 24th for Selinos Kastelli on the south-west coast of Crete. But the weather was too bad for them to complete the disembarkation, so the force was recalled, complete with the troops. The *Nizam* lost two of her 27 foot whalers during the night.

It was at this time that Captain Morse, NOIC Suda Bay, reported the growing seriousness of the military situation ashore. Continuous bombing, he recorded, had reduced the AA defences considerably, there was a shortage of ammunition, that the casualties to small craft in the harbour—such as the loss of the five MTBS—had been very heavy and that he had taken the precaution of destroying unnecessary books and papers. Morse also related that during a specially heavy bombing raid at Canea, General Freyberg's military staff had evacuated their damaged HQ and had joined Morse's naval HQ at Suda.

Cunningham had other anxieties on his mind at this time. On May 23rd he received a message from the Chiefs of Staff in London requesting an appreciation of the situation (COS No 113). The resulting exchange of messages can only have added to the burden Cunningham shouldered. His appraisal advised the Chiefs of Staff that it was no longer possible for the Navy to operate in the Aegean in the vicinity of Crete during daylight because of the scale of the enemy air attacks. Furthermore, he advised that the British command of the Eastern Mediterranean would be seriously jeopardised if further losses were suffered on the scale hitherto in preventing seaborne landings. The message was timed 1815 on Saturday 24th.

It is necessary to forego chronological order in this account if we are to comprehend the significance of the exchange of messages between the C-in-C and the Chiefs of Staff. Little will be lost by this departure and the messages will be more readily appreciated.

The Chiefs of Staff replied firmly (cos No 116) 'that unless more drastic naval action was taken than that suggested in the C-in-C Mediterranean's appreciation the enemy would be able to reinforce the island to a considerable extent'.[5] The Chiefs of Staff added it was essential that the C-in-C should concert measures for clearing up the situation without delay. In so doing, the Fleet and Royal Air Force were to accept whatever risk was entailed in preventing any considerable reinforcements reaching Crete. If enemy convoys were reported north of Crete the fleet would have to operate in that area by day although considerable losses might be expected. Experience would show for how long that situation could be maintained.

The Commander-in-Chief despatched a message to the Admiralty on May 26th explaining that the determining factor in operating in the Aegean was not the fear of sustaining losses but 'the need to avoid loss, which, without commensurate advantage to ourselves, will cripple fleet out here'.[6]

Cunningham claimed that the enemy had not succeeded in landing any seaborne reinforcements on the island so far. And he emphasised the cost of this achievement by detailing the losses: in three days the fleet had lost two cruisers and four destroyers; one battleship had been put out of action for several months while another two cruisers and four destroyers had been seriously damaged. Further the C-in-C added that even as this message had been written a report had been received of damage to the carrier *Formidable* and the destroyer *Nubian*. The C-in-C continued in his message, focusing attention on the crucial issue of the Cretan campaign, the complete mastery of the air which the *Luftwaffe* enjoyed. This fact nullified the Navy's ability to deny the German troops any seaborne reinforcements and the denial of support by

[5] Quoted in Cunningham's *Despatch*.
[6] Commander-in-Chief Mediterranean's message to Admiralty 1834C May 26th, 1941.

sea was the crux of the British strategy: 'destruction of (seaborne) convoys would win the day.'

Admiral Cunningham was at pains to rectify this erroneous impression. 'In point of fact,' his message to the Admiralty stressed, 'supply by sea has not come much into the picture, as despite loss and turning back of convoys, enemy is so prolific in air that for the moment he is able to reinforce and keep his forces supplied by air at will. This process is quite unchecked by air action on our part, and sight of constant, unhindered procession of Ju 52s flying into Crete is among factors most likely to affect morale of our forces. I feel that their Lordships should know that effect of recent operations on personnel is cumulative. Our light craft, officers, men and machinery alike are nearing exhaustion. Since Lustre started at end of February they have been kept running almost to limit of human endurance, and now, when work is redoubled, they are faced with an air concentration besides which, I am assured, that in Norway was child's play.'[7]

*

We departed briefly from chronological order to consider the exchange of messages between Cunningham and the Admiralty so we must now cast a glance back to May 25th to relate the events at sea on that day. It was, in fact, another day of considerable movement of warships and one during which a battle fleet was employed as a tactical weapon in support of the army.

At daybreak on the 25th, the minelayer *Abdiel* was speeding south having collected some sixty walking injured at Suda Bay before she left at 0240. No sooner had she reached Alexandria than she was ordered to prepare for sea again. The destroyers *Isis, Hero* and *Nizam,* it will be recalled, had abandoned their attempt to land their Special Service troops at Selinos Kastelli owing to bad weather, and had returned to Alexandria. Immediately on arrival, the troops disembarked and re-embarked aboard the *Abdiel* who then sailed early in the morning of Monday 26th for another attempt to land the men. She also took with her another 150 tons of ammunition.

[7] *Ibid.*

The *Ajax, Dido, Kimberley* and *Hotspur*, were now withdrawing south through the Kaso Strait to the south of Crete where the two destroyers were to be relieved by the *Napier, Kelvin* and *Jackal*, which had left Alexandria. This reconstituted force was to repeat the sweep of the previous night and to bombard Maleme airfield.

Yet another departure from Alexandria on the Sunday was the *Glenroy*. Her attempt to land troops a few days previously and the acidic exchange of signals resulting in Cunningham's abandonment of the venture despite Admiralty pressure from London, was to be attempted again with the same troops. She was escorted this time by Waller in the *Stuart*, with the *Coventry* and *Jaguar*. They sailed from Alexandria on Sunday evening.

Earlier in the day Alexandria was buzzing with the excitement and activity which accompanies a fleet's imminent departure from the port. The intention was to mount an attack upon the island of Scarpanto whose airfield was being used extensively for the supply of the German forces in Crete as well as accommodating the *Gruppe* of Ju 87s under Captain Brücker. It was planned that Fleet Air Arm aircraft from the *Formidable* would attack the airfield. The carrier had now managed to build up her strength to twelve Fulmars, though some were of doubtful operational standard.

Pridham-Wippell as Vice Admiral 1st Battle Squadron, was given command of the operation which was given the code name MAQ 3. At midday on Sunday the 25th, the Vice Admiral's Force A, as it was designated, left Alexandria for the flying-off position south-west of Scarpanto. The force comprised the flagship, *Queen Elizabeth*, the *Barham*, the carrier *Formidable*, and the destroyers *Jervis, Janus, Kandahar, Nubian, Hasty, Hereward, Voyager* and *Vendetta*.

Between 0500 and 0600 on Monday when the Force was about a hundred miles from the target, four Albacores and four Fulmars took off from the carrier and attacked the aerodrome. Another two aircraft were flown off but were found to be unserviceable and returned to the carrier. Yet another two were incapable of even being flown off. The Albacores approached the airfield un-

195

detected and achieved surprise which enabled them to press home their attacks against a virtually undefended target. They destroyed two aircraft on the ground and damaged many others as well as causing damage to airfield installations. The Fulmars shot up and damaged a number of Italian CR 42s and Stuka dive-bombers.

The British aircraft returned to the carrier and the Battle Squadron withdrew. Some hours later retaliatory attacks were launched by the Germans but the eight remaining Fulmars aboard the *Formidable* engaged the attackers. In the resulting dog fights one Fulmar was lost; two German aircraft were shot down and many others damaged. These eight Fulmars made twenty-four flights during the forenoon and engaged in twenty aerial skirmishes.

At 0700 the Battle Squadron was joined by the squadron comprising the *Ajax* and *Dido* and the three destroyers *Napier, Kelvin* and *Jackal,* who had only just relieved their consorts. The augmented Battle Squadron now withdrew south and west to clear the immediate danger zone. However, the *Glenroy* convoy was some distance west of Pridham-Wippell, northbound for Crete. Cunningham instructed Pridham-Wippell to provide cover. Course was altered to the west to comply soon after midday.

It was soon after 1300 when the Battle Squadron was about ninety miles north-east of Bardia that a *Gruppe* of *Stukageschwader*—II/St G 2—happened upon the force, until then completely unaware of its existence. The *Gruppe* which had been sent to support Rommel in North Africa and was on the lookout for troop transports comprised twenty dive-bombers under the command of Major Walter Enneccerus, leader of the dive-bombing squadron which crippled the carrier *Illustrious* some months previously in January 1941. He led the dive, soon followed by the formations of his First Lieutenants Jakob, Hamester and Eyer.

They singled out the *Formidable* as their main target while she turned into wind to fly off her Fulmars. Despite a heavy barrage of AA fire the carrier was hit twice and she was severely damaged. One bomb blew out her starboard side forward, between 17 and 24 bulkheads, starting a fire. The other damaged

X turret and its cable and accelerator gear. In this same fierce attack, the destroyer *Nubian* was struck by a bomb on her quarter-deck which blew off her stern. Surprisingly Commander R. W. Ravenhill managed to keep her seaworthy and even managed to achieve a speed of 20 knots.

The *Formidable* operated fighter patrols till dusk but was then detached to Alexandria with an escort of four destroyers, the *Voyager, Vendetta, Hereward* and *Decoy*. The *Formidable* underwent repairs in Alexandria for eight weeks then retired south through the Suez Canal for the United States where she spent another three months being made fit for further war service.

It was during one of the bombing attacks on the Battle Squadron in the afternoon when he was also concerned with the damaged carrier that Pridham-Wippell received a signal from Cunningham, ordering new movements. Intelligence reports indicated that Milos harbour was being used as an assembly area for small invasion craft intended for Crete. The C-in-C ordered Pridham-Wippell to detach the 14th Destroyer Flotilla, the *Nubian, Kandahar* and *Janus* to sweep north and raid the harbour during the night of Monday–Tuesday, 26th–27th. The C-in-C also intended to detach the *Ajax* and *Dido* to head north as if making to pass through the Kaso Strait at 2200/26th but then to turn about and return to Alexandria.

When Pridham-Wippell saw the signal after his preoccupation with the *Formidable,* he judged it too late for D 14 to raid Milos and be clear of Crete by daylight. He therefore cancelled both this raid and the feint by *Ajax* and *Dido*.

After the departure of the *Formidable* at dusk on Monday the 26th, the rest of the Battle Squadron operated during the night to the north-westward of Alexandria and at daylight on Tuesday the 27th proceeded towards the Kaso Strait to give cover to the *Abdiel, Hero* and *Nizam* who had landed 750 Special Service troops plus 150 tons of ammunition at Suda Bay, the last reinforcements that were to reach the island. Before departing, these ships embarked 930 men, merchant seamen, naval personnel and others no longer required in Crete.

197

But further melancholy events were to add to the Commander-in-Chief's dismay. The Battle Squadron had reached a position about 190 miles from Scarpanto on its way to the Kaso Strait by 0858 when a formation of fifteen Ju 88 and Heinkel 111s from the Dodecanese launched a determined attack upon the British ships. The battleship *Barham* was hit by a bomb which put Y turret out of action while near misses damaged her and flooded two of her bilges. A fire raged for about two hours and for that time it was necessary for the Battle Squadron to steam down wind to the south till the fire was extinguished. When she reached Alexandria safely temporary repairs were carried out which enabled her to reach Durban. There she remained for another six weeks in dockyard hands.

Soon after midday Cunningham recalled his battered Battle Squadron to Alexandria, bombed, damaged, depleted: yet another withdrawal in the face of the aerial onslaught to which his forces were being subjected.

*

Before we leave the day of the Scarpanto raid and the subsequent damage to the *Formidable* and *Barham* we have to consider another episode in the story of the naval agony in these Cretan waters. As we have seen, the assault ship *Glenroy* had left Alexandria at 2000 with the *Stuart, Coventry* and *Jaguar* making for Tymbaki with a battalion of the Queen's Regiment. The outlook for this force looked bleak when it was spotted by some reconnaisance aircraft in the forenoon on Monday 26th. These aircraft also launched some ineffective attacks. In the evening, further fiercer attacks developed. At 1820 the ships were subjected to a series of sustained dive-bombing raids during which one aircraft was shot down and others damaged. A final attack at 2050 was launched by low-flying torpedo bombers but it was not a courageous attack and the torpedoes were avoided.

When the last aircraft had departed, the *Glenroy,* now a mere fifty miles from her destination, looked a shambles. She was damaged by shrapnel and bomb blast from several near misses and from machinegunning. She had also suffered eleven casualties. Three of her landing craft were holed and useless. A large dump of petrol on the upper decks had ignited and blazed furiously for one and a half hours during which time Captain Sir James Paget had to steer his ship south to prevent the wind assisting the blaze. Despite this precaution one of the landing craft had to be cut adrift from its davits for fear of it adding to the inferno. The *Glenroy* was in serious danger. Close to enemy airfields, unprotected from above, her guardian escorts unable to prevent the enemy aircraft singling her out for attacks, an inflammable cargo blazing, with 800 troops aboard and small hope of respite or succour, save the approaching hours of darkness.

The most dangerous problem was the fire. It was tackled and brought under control, finally being extinguished an hour before the final attack, enabling a north-easterly course to be resumed. But at 2020 it was decided that the landing at Tymbaki must be cancelled because time was running short, the shortage of assault craft also jeopardised the venture, and finally, the weather made landings on to an open beach precarious. Thus, at 2115, the *Glenroy* and her escorts turned back for Alexandria.

*

By now the military situation for the British on the island had reached a crisis. A measure of the desperate nature of the situation is the fact that it was decided to run a slow convoy to Crete on Monday 26th. This decision had more than a hint of desperation about it: the risks were so outrageously high that it seems incredible to think the effort could ever have succeeded. Nevertheless, convoy AN 31 sailed from Alexandria at 0500/26th. It consisted of two ships escorted by the sloop *Auckland;* and it was planned that the *Calcutta* and *Defender* would join at 0700 the next morning. Soon after these two escorts made contact during the forenoon of the 27th, more sensible views prevailed and the convoy was turned back in view of the scale and intensity of the enemy air activity.

Phase 1 of the naval battle for Crete, the prevention of seaborne landings, had ended. The Mediterranean Fleet, almost without pause for breath, was to be flung into the fray again. For no sooner had Phase 1 ended than Phase 2, the evacuation from the island began.

CHAPTER 13

The Battering of Force B

ADMIRAL CUNNINGHAM CLAIMED, quite justifiably, that the Royal Navy prevented a seaborne invasion of Crete and, furthermore, had kept the British Army supplied with essential reinforcements of men and stores. He claimed, with as we have seen, far less justification to have inflicted considerable losses upon the German troop-carrying convoys. And finally, on the credit side, he added that twenty enemy aircraft had been shot down for certain with another eleven probably destroyed and fifteen more damaged. It has not been possible to confirm these figures, for the losses sustained by the *Luftwaffe* in action with the British warships cannot be extracted from the German records. But the British claims are modest and it is of small consequence to question them. What is more important is the effect of the prolonged strain under which the officers and men of the Mediterranean Fleet had striven so hard to combat the seemingly ever-present German bombers. It had been a demoralising experience, punctuated by grave and serious losses of valuable ships and their crews. Now, an even more harrowing prospect lay before them. With no respite from their recent ordeal the ships and crews were thrust back into the front line of battle under even greater handicaps than in Phase 1 of the battle.

Cunningham emphasised this in his *Despatch:* 'The evacuation followed without intermission on the Battle of Crete when the fleet had sustained such severe losses and threw a final almost intolerable strain on the light forces, most of whom had been operating at sea almost continuously since the beginning of Operation Lustre on March 4th, 1941.' On another occasion he wrote: 'At 3 pm on 27th the fateful decision was taken, and we wearily turned towards planning another evacuation with fewer ships, far less resources and in circumstances much more difficult. Our seamen and our ships were worn to the point of exhaustion, and now they were asked for more.'

But the need for another evacuation had been apparent long before the time mentioned by Cunningham. It had been spoken of even before battle was joined, but more immediately Captain Morse at Suda Bay put it on record on May 26th: 'General situation in Suda–Canea area very bad and General Officer Commanding decided he could no longer continue the battle. Preparations made for evacuation and movements of HQ and W/T to Sfakia. Confusion all day due to lack of definite orders. Burnt all unwanted secret papers.'

Earlier, at 1100 on Monday 26th General Freyberg signalled General Wavell that it was in his opinion 'limit of endurance had been reached by troops under my command here at Suda Bay'. He added that the fall of Suda Bay would be swiftly followed by the reduction of Retimo and Heraklion as a matter of course: moreover, Freyberg believed that a proportion of the forces might be saved if an immediate decision was taken to arrange embarkation.

Commander Bragadin[1] indicates how finely balanced were the scales of victory. When he reached Suda with his MAS squadron on May 28th, he was told by the German parachutists that on the previous night they just could not stay on their feet any longer. They said that 'they had been certain that in the attack scheduled for dawn they would have been massacred, but they had planned to carry it through for honour's sake. But the British did not know the true position and during the night-time "truce" period they withdrew to the south coast of Crete to be evacuated. Consequently, on the morning of the 28th when the Germans launched the assault they had believed to be a suicidal one, they were surprised to meet nothing but a negligible rearguard defence.'

While this rearguard defence was being organised, General Wavell informed the Prime Minister in a message timed 0825/27th that he feared we must recognise that Crete was no

---

[1] *The Italian Navy in World War II*, M. Bragadin, p 111.

longer tenable and that troops must be withdrawn as soon as possible. The Chiefs of Staff in London replied that Crete must be evacuated forthwith.

This task was beset with incalculable problems and hazards. That ancient sea route from Crete to Egypt which throughout the centuries had witnessed so many strange voyages and craft since the Minoans traded with the Pharaohs, was now to witness an even stranger procession of ships with cargoes of British and Imperial troops crammed aboard, fleeing under a deluge of screaming bombs.

Like the Greek evacuation, that from Crete was one of hurried improvisation, reliant often upon the ancient skill of seamanship inherent in the British sailor and upon the sturdy spirit of the troops who patiently awaited embarkation, battle-weary and exhausted by long marches over rugged terrain at night. A total of nearly 22,000 troops awaited evacuation.

Captain Roskill, the eminent naval historian, refers to these troops and their enormous faith in the Navy.[2]

> Buried among the mass of official documents accumulated . . . intimate human papers are rather surprisingly to be found. It appears that some of the soldiers rescued, NCOs and privates as well as officers, wrote down their personal experiences just after their escape and left them in the ships which took them off. Thence they ultimately reached the Admiralty and so came to be incorporated in the official records . . . In every one of these accounts appears the sustaining, almost blind faith that, if they could only reach the sea coast somewhere, the Navy would rescue them. One young New Zealander calls it the ever-present hope of contacting the Navy and another wrote that during all the long retreat in Greece our one hope and thought was the Navy. It is perhaps in these records that the purpose and justification of all that was endured by the maritime services at this time is to be found.

The island of Crete was not well-endowed with port facilities suited to evacuating an army. Indeed, Heraklion was the only

[2] *The War at Sea 1939–1945*, Vol I, *The Defensive*, by Captain S. W. Roskill, HMSO, 1954.

place with any port facilities at all where warships could berth alongside a jetty or quay. The bulk of the evacuation from Crete had to be made from the small open beach at Sfakia. Sfakia lay at the foot of a 500 foot escarpment, access to which was gained by a near two hour scramble down a narrow, twisting goat track in the dark. The fishing village, for that is all it was, possessed a shingle beach which it wore like an apron. About 200 yards in width, it shelved ideally for small boats to embark troops.

Communications from the beach to those on top of the cliff were virtually non-existent—except by word of mouth, with a two hour climb up the cliff face to pass the message. Communications on a broader scale were equally difficult. The HQ of both the General Officer Commanding troops in Crete and the NOIC Suda Bay had been set up in a cave near Sfakia. Captain Morse had taken the precaution of sending the portable W/T sets and naval cyphers from Suda to Sfakia in the hope of securing communications with the Commander-in-Chief at Alexandria and in case he had to control an evacuation from there.

The task of taking the equipment to Sfakia was entrusted to Lieutenant A. H. Blacke, RNR, commanding ML 1011, and Paymaster-Lieutenant B. H. Dunn, who sailed after dark on May 24th. The ML cleared the south-west corner of Crete and ran into an easterly gale. She turned for shelter into Selinos Kastelli. Soon after dawn she was sighted by a German aircraft and was attacked by four bombers and five fighters. The only gun was blown overboard by a bomb burst and Warrant Telegraphist C. A. Windebank was killed. The ML quickly sank and the crew swam for the shore while being machinegunned. Cretan guides led the survivors over the 7,000-foot mountains to Sfakia which they reached on the 27th. But the precious W/T gear was on the seabed.[3]

A replacement W/T set was sent to the new HQ by lorry but

[3] ML 1030, Lieutenant W. O. Cooksey, was also bombed and sunk west of Gavdo Pulo but most of the crew reached safety in a dinghy. ML 1032, Lieutenant E. N. Rose, fought off air attacks to reach Alexandria safely, the only ML to do so.

it arrived damaged. The RAF came to the rescue and permitted the use of their equipment at Sfakia for naval communications.

It was against this background of retreat, military defeat, of confusion and uncertainty that the evacuation from Crete had to be planned and conducted.

Cunningham sought the help of a military liaison officer on his staff, Major-General J. F. Evetts, and in particular, he set up an organisation for the coordination of fighter protection at sea. Group Captain C. B. R. Pelly was sent from HQ RAF Middle East to organise this onerous undertaking, upon the efficiency of which the safety of so many ships and the lives of so many seamen and troops depended. An Air Ministry comment to Cunningham's *Despatch* says: 'The general air situation remained much the same, with one important difference. The bulk of the troops were evacuated from bays in southern Crete during the hours of darkness and it was possible to provide some limited fighter cover to ships which by first light had proceeded some way towards the Egyptian mainland. Even then, the ranges from our airfields and the small number of aircraft available allowed no margin in hand to deal with changes in the routeing or timing of naval operations which were necessitated by enemy action.'

The message on May 27th initiating this fighter protection came from the Air Officer, Commanding-in-Chief, RAF Middle East, who stated that while all possible would be done to provide fighter cover; owing to the distance from our bases, the cover could only be meagre and spasmodic. But even this would be preferable to the complete absence of cover for the eight days of the Battle of Crete, except for the short intervention of the *Formidable*'s own aircraft on May 26th, a sortie which was costly inasmuch as it resulted in the serious damage of the carrier and its withdrawal from the theatre.

The original intentions for the evacuation from Crete provided for the following: (*a*) Troops from the Maleme/Suda Bay sector were to withdraw over the mountains and along the final poor approach road and series of hairpin bends to the assembly area at the top of the Sfakia escarpment, there to hide themselves from the prying eyes of reconnaissance aircraft. (*b*) Those from the Retimo area would have to make their way to Plaka Bay. (c) Troops at Heraklion would be embarked from the jetty in the port. (d) The small number of troops cut off in a pocket to the south of the Heraklion sector were to withdraw to Tymbaki.

It was also intended that the evacuation was to be carried out at night, invariably between the hours of midnight and 0300. This would enable the rescue ships to minimise the danger by withdrawing well to the southward before daylight; for daylight would bring reconnoitring aircraft, swiftly followed by dive-bombers.

These intentions and the ability of the Navy to extricate the troops from the island would depend upon the rearguard forces keeping the enemy at bay.

The arrangements for allocating ships for the evacuation was kept as simple as possible. The onus of signalling the number of troops for embarkation and the point of pick-up was placed upon General Freyberg. Cunningham would then consult Major-General Evetts, his military liaison officer, before deploying his ships to the point of embarkation.

Such were the intentions. In the event, the signalled numbers of troops at the embarkation points each day were substantially correct. The numbers of ships made available were generally adequate for the task. The organisation ran as smoothly as any war-time undertaking can expect to operate when subjected to the stresses and strains of aerial bombardment. But mistakes and errors—both Axis and British—occurred. German and Italian bombers notched up even more substantial successes. The Mediterranean Fleet suffered grievously. The British troops, despite their combat weariness, endured the final retreat with fortitude and patience. And, as Admiral Ruge[4] chronicled wryly, 'The Italian Fleet did not put in an appearance'.

It was decided by Cunningham's Staff that the major effort on the night of Wednesday–Thursday, May 28th–29th, should be a determined bid to rescue the besieged Heraklion garrison which had fought desperately hard for five days since May 23rd when the Germans had delivered an ultimatum to the garrison to sur-

[4] *Sea Warfare 1939–1945*, Admiral Ruge.

render. Both the British and the Greek commanders had rejected the call and had continued to resist further encroachment despite continuous enemy reinforcement by troop-carrying aircraft and heavy air raids.

Vice Admiral Rawlings was given command of Force B which was given the task of evacuating the Heraklion troops. This force comprised the following: the *Orion* (flagship), *Ajax, Dido,* and the destroyers *Decoy, Jackal, Imperial, Hotspur, Kimberley* and *Hereward.*

The force left Alexandria at 0600 on Wednesday 28th and all went well till 1700 when the force was about ninety miles from Scarpanto.

From 1700 until darkness some hours later the force underwent another ordeal of attacks from the air, high-level bombing, dive-bombing and torpedo attacking. Ten separate raids by formations of up to nine aircraft were recorded. Since some bomb explosions were seen five to ten miles away Rawlings concluded that bombs were being jettisoned 'because friendly aircraft were about'.[5]

At 1920 the destroyer *Imperial* suffered a near miss, but although shaken she appeared to be undamaged. All seemed well and she carried on. Then at 2100 the *Ajax* was near missed and the resulting explosion damaged the cruiser's side, seriously wounding twenty men and starting a small fire. When Rawlings read a damage control report from *Ajax* he immediately ordered her to return to Alexandria, a decision which also took into consideration the need for his ships to be fully operational to undertake not only the night's evacuation but also the inevitable air attacks on the morrow. Investigation of the *Ajax*'s damage when she arrived at Alexandria revealed that its extent was nowhere near as crippling as the damage control report given to the commanding officer and passed to Rawlings implied. Cunningham made it clear in his *Despatch* that he considered it 'unfortunate that HMS *Ajax* was not retained with Force B and much overcrowding thereby avoided . . . the reports given to the CO at the time were exaggerated and the ship could well have carried on with Force B.'

Soon after passing the Kaso Strait and altering course to the westward, the Force was ineffectually attacked by a solitary torpedo-carrying aircraft, then a dark, clear night with a freshening north-westerly wind shrouded its movements until it arrived safely at Heraklion at 2330.

The NOIC Heraklion, Captain Macdonald, had so organised matters that when the ships arrived all was ready for them. This was all the more creditable in view of intensive bombing and machinegunning attacks on the defensive positions by 200 aircraft during the afternoon. The British defence line encircled the harbour area and now stretched thinly over seven miles. Into this vulnerable pocket 2,000 troops, including many wounded, had been assembled near the mole ready to embark, while the outlying rearguard troops were being withdrawn to an inner defence line, thus further shrinking the perimeter.

The original intention was for the cruisers to enter the harbour and secure alongside the mole, but in view of the fresh wind Rawlings decided to keep his cruisers outside and to use his destroyers to ferry the troops out to them. He kept to this plan despite the fact the wind soon dropped and the sea calmed. Thus, the *Hotspur* led in the destroyers and they secured alongside in trots two deep. Hodgkinson described the *Hotspur*'s entry:[6] 'Like a wraith we crept in to the northern wall, and soon saw lines of troops marching along the wall towards our innermost billet, and a small flashing light to show the bollard to which we must secure our bows. We got in alongside with the minimum of light and noise, no one raising his voice to a shout, as the Germans were pretty close to the harbour . . . The *Imperial* came in alongside us and the *Jackal* and *Decoy* secured astern.'

After only thirty minutes the two outside destroyers were fully loaded with about 800 men and slipped their wires to transfer 500 of the troops to a cruiser. The two inner destroyers quickly followed suit and their berths were taken by the two remaining

[6] *Before the Tide Turned*, Hugh Hodgkinson.

destroyers, the *Hereward* and *Kimberley*. Again, all went smoothly, the British rearguard withdrawing stealthily, reducing their perimeter, till the last stragglers boarded the *Kimberley* at 0255 on the 29th. Five minutes later she slipped from the mole and joined her consorts now heading for the Kaso Strait and the run south. Captain Macdonald reported: 'It is believed that except for those in hospital none were left behind.'

A total of 4,000 troops had been lifted safely without interference from the Germans: surprisingly no parachute flares had been dropped at 2300 or 0200, which had been a regular night-time practice for several nights previously. It had been hoped to clear the harbour by 0200 but it was 0320 before the force had formed up and had set course at a speed of 29 knots. All seemed well set for a high-speed escape when misfortune struck and it set in train a number of calamities of mounting intensity for Rawlings's force.

At 0345 the *Imperial*'s steering, evidently damaged in the previous day's bomb miss, suddenly failed. Her rudder jammed hard over and she took charge, narrowly missed colliding with the *Kimberley* and then both cruisers before she disappeared in the murk astern, flashing 'My rudder' to the *Orion*. This could scarcely have happened at a worse time because further delay now would make inevitable even more time in the danger zone, within easy range of enemy aircraft soon after dawn. The *Hotspur* was despatched to investigate.

Rawlings was in a dilemma of whether to wait in the hope the *Imperial*'s steering gear could be repaired quickly or whether to transfer her troops and crew and then torpedo her. When after a prompt investigation, the *Hotspur* signalled that the *Imperial* was quite unable to steer, Rawlings reduced the speed of the Force to 15 knots and ordered the *Hotspur* to take off all the *Imperial*'s crew and troops and then to sink her. As the Admiral and his Force disappeared into the night those aboard the *Hotspur* felt they were being abandoned as they tackled the task and completed the melancholy business of torpedoing the *Imperial* at 0445. The *Hotspur* then sped off, her decks crowded with two ship's companies and about 900 troops, in pursuit of Rawlings's

Force. Soon after daylight the British ships were sighted ahead and those aboard the *Hotspur* experienced great relief for they genuinely believed that Rawlings had pushed on ahead at speed. On rejoining, the Force increased speed to 29 knots. But the delay had put the Force one and a half hours behind its timetable with the result that at sunrise the ships were only at the northern end of the Kaso Strait and about to make the southward turn. They had five or six hours to survive within Stuka range.

The attacks began at 0600 and continued intermittently throughout the day until 1500, a period, in fact, of nine hours, until the Force—or what remained of it—was only 100 miles from Alexandria. Almost as soon as the sun rose and the southward turn into the Strait was made, two dive-bombers appeared and fire was opened. 'Thereafter attacks began in earnest,' wrote Rawlings.

The *Hotspur* was still speeding to her station on the starboard wing of the Force and still had a mile to go when six Ju 87s from Scarpanto, a mere twenty-five miles away, singled her out for the first attack. She lacked the multiple pom-poms of the more modern J and K class destroyers in the force and the fact she was out of station increased her vulnerability. Lieutenant-Commander C. P. F. Brown handled his ship with skill, swinging her hard over to port then to starboard, threading the ship through the giant eruptions of water as the bombs exploded. As the Stukas dived on the destroyer he employed the tactic quickly learned by the Navy, turning the ship towards the diving aircraft to make its angle of descent steeper and steeper, forcing it to pull out of the dive early. The quicker a ship could move to achieve this the greater her chances of spoiling the pilot's aim and of surviving the attack. Aboard the *Hotspur* soldiers erected their Bren guns, others manned their Tommy guns and even rifles. Each diving Stuka was met by a hail of .50 and .303 bullets and tracers.

At 0625 when the force was in the middle of the Strait the *Hereward* on the port side of the screen came in for the next attack. The first few Stukas were evaded, but another, diving low, let go a stick of bombs, one of which exploded near her foremost funnel. She swung out of line, her speed fell away and she lost station on the screen. She was crippled and she had 450 troops aboard.

Admiral Rawlings was now faced with another grim choice, the second in only a few hours: whether to send another destroyer to assist the *Hereward* or whether to abandon her to her fate. To detach another destroyer would invite almost certain destruction, for the main hope of salvation against these aircraft attacks lay in concentration. The fact that the coast of Crete lay only five miles away helped persuade Rawlings to leave the *Hereward* to her own devices. As the force continued on its way the *Hereward* was last seen heading slowly for the coast, her guns still engaging enemy aircraft. She was commanded by Lieutenant-Commander W. J. Munn, Cunningham's flag lieutenant in the *Hood*.

Bragadin gives a different report and claims that it was an Italian torpedo-carrying aircraft which made the damaging attack upon the *Hereward* which left her dead in the water. This is difficult to accept. Later, he claims with justification, that Italian MAS boats patrolling the area moved in to give her the *coup de grace* but when they came into torpedo-launching distance the destroyer blew up and the MAS then set about rescuing survivors. The majority of both the *Hereward*'s crew and her troops were rescued by the Italians. The MAS had, in fact, helped escort the first seaborne landing on Crete's easternmost point on May 28th, but it was only a token force of Italian troops which contributed nothing to the campaign ashore.

Admiral Rawlings now ordered his remaining destroyers to close the *Orion* and *Dido* to give better mutual AA protection and no sooner had this been done than the *Decoy* came in for attention from the *Luftwaffe*. She was damaged in the engine room by a near miss which fractured her turbine feet and the speed of the force had to be reduced to 25 knots. The time was only 0645.

Some fighter protection for the force had been arranged for 0530 in the Kaso Strait. Rawlings had given a revised ETA of 0630, but the fighters which had been despatched failed to locate the British squadron.

In Alexandria Cunningham was receiving Rawlings's signals of the convulsive struggle with dismay and growing apprehension. He realised that British fighters could not have put in an appearance and every effort was made to rectify this omission, but it was not until 1200 that RAF aircraft made contact with Force B and by that time severe damage and heavy casualties had been inflicted upon yet another British cruiser.

Soon after 0700 the two cruisers were selected to bear the brunt of the attacks, but both emerged time and time again from the mushrooming columns of water and smoke. Then, during an attack at 0735 the flag captain in the *Orion,* Captain G. R. B. Back, was severely wounded by an explosive bullet from a Ju 87 which dived low and raked the cruiser with machinegun fire. Soon afterwards a near miss damaged the *Orion* and the force's speed was again reduced, to 21 knots. After this there was a lull for some minutes during which time the Germans had marshalled a considerable force of Stukas and Ju 88s which now came over in waves. The cruisers, in particular, fought off the bombers, but at 0815 the *Dido* was hit on B turret by a bomb from a Ju 87. She had experienced eight near misses in rapid succession. The ninth bomb found its target. The resulting blast wrecked the marines' mess deck which was crowded with stunned troops. Dreadful casualties occurred. Rescue was handicapped by a fire which raged after the explosion and the impossibility of reaching the dead and wounded until damage control parties had brought the fires under control and cleared some wreckage—27 sailors and 19 soldiers were killed and 10 sailors and 28 soldiers wounded.

Hodgkinson from the *Hotspur* described the episode later:[7]

A great sphere of black smoke burst out from ahead of her bridge and a single stick-like object curled up into the air, and dropped smoking into the sea. It was one of her guns from a fore turret. Then she seemed to come steaming out of the blackness like a miracle and she was engaging aircraft with her after guns, and one gun missing from B turret with its twin bent nearly double.

Forty-five minutes later the flagship, *Orion,* suffered a similar

[7] *Before the Tide Turned,* Hugh Hodgkinson.

212

blow when a Ju 87 dropped a bomb on to A turret. The pilot of the Stuka made a suicidal attack. He dived steeper and steeper and observers aboard the cruiser and other ships in the force stared unbelievingly as the aircraft screamed down closer and closer till it seemed he was determined to crash aboard the target like a Kamikaze pilot. At the last moment a bomb was released, but the pilot failed to recover from the velocity of his descent and the Stuka dived into the sea barely missing the bows of the *Dido*. The bomb exploded with devastating effect upon A turret, blasting away the whole of the armoured casing, destroying the guns and crippling B turret immediately astern as well.

Then at 0930 the flagship, *Orion,* was near missed, soon after which her wounded Captain died. Rawlings recorded the circumstances of his death.[8] The bomb explosions, he reported, 'must have brought him back to a more conscious condition as he tried to sit up, calling upon everyone to "keep steady". When the attack ceased he called out "It's all right men—that one's over". Then he died.' Command of the crippled cruiser now devolved upon Commander T. C. T. Wynne.

A lull in the assault, lasting for about forty-five minutes, enabled the damage control parties to extinguish fires and the medical staff to tend the wounded. Then, at 1045 the assault was resumed. The *Orion* was again the target for a concentrated attack by eleven yellow-nosed Ju 87s when the force was about 100 miles from the Kaso Strait. The *Orion* had 1,090 passengers aboard her, including thirteen cot cases and four women. During action stations these people patiently congregated between decks. In this attack, the Stukas dived one after the other till the exploding bombs obscured the target and the cruiser disappeared from view behind the barrage of erupting water. The last few bombers could only have aimed their bombs at the maelstrom of seething water, spray and smoke.

From this deluge of bombs, one passed right through the bridge, through the sick bay bathroom and exploded under the crowded stokers' mess deck. The result of this catastrophe was

8 *Letter of Proceedings,* by Admiral Rawlings.

indescribable carnage. For a time darkness concealed the horror. Screams of the wounded and dying added to the horror. Fires, smoke, jagged and torn steelwork, hampered the work of the damage control parties. The first lieutenant had been killed, so Lieutenant-Commander Miller, commanding officer of the *Salvia,* who had taken passage in the *Orion* on account of his local knowledge, to act as pilot at Heraklion, organised fire parties, helped restore communications and saw that medical parties extricated and tended the wounded.

It is believed that the total number of casualties amounted to 262 killed and 300 wounded.[9]

The damage to the flagship was extensive. She was out of control. The lower conning tower was put out of action; three boiler rooms were damaged; the steering gear was damaged; bridge compasses had gone; all normal communications between the bridge and the engine room were destroyed and oil fuel tanks became contaminated with salt water. Three of the five engineer officers died in the holocaust. Commander (E) H. F. Atkins, in charge of the engineering department subsequently described with understatement what 'was perhaps the least pleasant moment of a disagreeable day. The heavy list, lack of light, ship not being under control due to destruction of steering gear, the fires still burning forward, filling the machinery space with smoke, the fact that only one shaft was turning, tended to cause uneasiness.'[10]

The flagship steamed out of control, off course and for a moment headed back for Kaso. Hodgkinson recorded[11] that while the *Orion* was 'pouring yellow and black smoke, she was swinging round towards the Kaso Strait . . . The whole squadron waited breathlessly, and then she began altering slowly round, and limped back towards us. We (in the *Hotspur*) dropped back and round the wounded ship, and steamed on with her. Sometimes great clouds of yellow smoke would come from her funnel, and

[9] Figures published vary from different sources. These are taken from Coulter whose authority is dominant. He quotes 107 sailors killed and 84 wounded; 155 soldiers killed and 216 wounded.

[10] Quoted in *The Mediterranean Fleet,* HMSO, 1944.

[11] *Before the Tide Turned,* Hugh Hodgkinson.

she would drop right down in speed owing to the sea water seeping into her oil tanks.'

Frantic efforts were made by those aboard the *Orion* to get her under control. She managed to resume course as soon as the steering gear had been reinstated and a chain of men stationed to pass orders for the emergency conning position to the wheel. Speed varied between 12 and 25 knots but averaged a respectable 21 knots. Fortunately for the British force, this was the last dive-bombing attack of the day, though other high-level attacks were to be launched later.

After *Orion*'s forenoon ordeal there was a respite during which, at midday, two friendly Fulmar fighters put in an appearance, the first to be seen by the force. RAF aircraft had made several attempts to locate the naval units and in a number of engagements with German aircraft had destroyed two Ju 88s for the loss of one Hurricane fighter. Ships' gunfire had managed to shoot down only one Ju 87. The high-level bombing attacks occurred at 1300, 1330 and 1500, but were all survived without incident.

When the force finally drew away from the danger zone and reached the sanctuary of Alexandria it disembarked a total of 3,486 troops. Another estimated 600 were killed or captured on passage. Admiral Rawlings recorded 'From my own observation,' he wrote—and his vantage point aboard his own battle-scarred flagship, wounded himself, and his Flag Captain mortally wounded on the bridge, made his eye-witness account a valuable contribution—'the conduct of the military units embarked in my flagship was admirable, and they remained remarkably steady and helpful throughout. I very much regret the heavy casualties they sustained.'[12]

The battered Force B steamed into Alexandria at 2000, the flagship *Orion* with only two rounds of her 6 inch HE ammunition left and a mere ten tons of fuel oil remaining. She was utterly played out.

[12] HMS *Orion* not only survived Crete, she also survived the war during which she served at Sicily, Salerno, Anzio, the Normandy and South of France invasions. All told the *Orions* of the Navy collected almost as many battle honours (22) as the *Warspites* (25).

Cunningham watched the squadron return to harbour. He described the scene in his memoirs:[13] 'I shall never forget the sight of those ships coming up harbour, the guns of their fore-turrets awry, one or two broken off and pointing forlornly skyward, their upper decks crowded with troops, and the marks of their ordeal only too plainly visible. I went on board at once and found Rawlings cheerful but exhausted. The ship was a terrible sight and the mess deck a ghastly shambles.'

*

While the Heraklion evacuation on this first night of retreat from Crete was suffering misfortunes and casualties under seemingly endless, relentless and implacable *Luftwaffe* attacks, a naval operation was in progress to the south of the island. Sfakia, it will be recalled, became the second of the evacuation points. NOIC Suda Bay, Captain Morse, had now set up HQ in a cave near the village, sharing it with the GOC troops in Crete.

It was to this tiny fishing village that Cunningham despatched Force C, the 7th Destroyer Flotilla, under the command of Captain Arliss in the *Napier* with the *Nizam*, *Kelvin* and *Kandahar*. The flotilla embarked additional whalers at Alexandria to supplement their own small craft for ferrying the troops from the beach. The flotilla left Alexandria at 0800 on Wednesday 28th and made an uneventful passage to Crete. Embarkation started half an hour after midnight. While troops were ferried out to the destroyers, urgently needed stores and rations for 15,000 men were landed. By 0300 on Thursday, 744[14] troops had been taken aboard and the destroyers called off the operation for the night and turned for Alexandria.

Soon after 0900 the force was located by the enemy and four Ju 88s attacked from high level, one bomb near missing the *Nizam* and causing minor damage. No British fighters were seen in spite of air protection for the force being arranged for 0545,

---

[13] *A Sailor's Odyssey*, Cunningham.

[14] The figures are made up as follows: *Napier* 296, *Kandahar* 213, *Kelvin* 101, *Nizam* 114: this totalled 724 and there were another 20 'miscellaneous'. *Napier*'s load comprised the following: 36 officers, 260 other ranks, 3 women, 1 Greek, 1 Chinaman, 10 merchant seamen, 2 children and 1 dog.

but some hours later a crashed enemy aircraft was sighted which was believed to have been shot down by fighters. No other incidents occurred and the flotilla entered Alexandria harbour at 1700 on Thursday evening.

*

While the 7th Destroyer Flotilla was embarking its troops at Sfakia on the night of Wednesday–Thursday, another force, Force D, had assembled at Alexandria in preparation for the following night's evacuation. This force, under the command of Admiral King, comprised the flagship cruiser *Phoebe* with HMAS *Perth*, the *Glengyle*, the *Coventry* and *Calcutta* and the destroyers *Jervis, Janus* and *Hasty*. They left Alexandria at 2100 on Wednesday, May 28th.

Later that night a message was received from Captain Morse at Sfakia advising that up to 10,000 troops would be available for evacuation on the following night—29th–30th. A separate message from CREFORCE, General Freyberg, warned that it was unlikely that the troops on Crete could hold out until the night of May 30th–31st and he gave it as an optimistic view that only 2,000 troops could be lifted, but there would be some stragglers.

Cunningham deduced from these conflicting reports that the situation ashore on the island was confused and tangled, but that probably 10,000 troops remained for evacuation, of which probably only 2,000 would be in an organised body. On Thursday 29th, Major-General Evetts, Cunningham's military liaison officer, flew to Cairo to acquaint General Wavell of the naval situation and to discuss the progress of the evacuation. General Wavell consulted General Blamey and Air Marshal Tedder, then sent Cunningham a personal message giving their combined views: they thought it ill-advised to risk the *Glen* ships and cruisers but that destroyers should continue the evacuation.

Admiral Cunningham thereupon signalled the Admiralty a Most Immediate signal summarising the evacuation to date. Three cruisers and one destroyer had been damaged so far and casualties to the closely packed troops on board amounted to some 500. Cunningham continued: 'It is evident that tomorrow we must expect further casualties to ships accompanied with extremely (heavy) casualties to men particularly in the case of *Glengyle* if she is hit with 3,000 men on board. The fighter protection available is very meagre.' His message went on to ask if he was justified in risking heavy casualties and accepting a scale of loss and damage to his already weakened fleet which 'may make us so weak we cannot operate . . . I am ready to continue with the evacuation as long as we have a ship with which to do so, but I feel it my duty to put these considerations before their Lordships.'

The Admiralty reply to this gloomy summary, timed at 1900, was received by Cunningham at 2026 on Thursday 29th. It ordered the *Glengyle* to turn back and the remaining ships to proceed. This change in attitude (some days earlier the Admiralty had urged the sending of a *Glen* ship to Crete) was probably occasioned by a remark Cunningham made about the many men who would remain alive as prisoners but might well be dead if they embarked. However, because of the time lapse in exchanging signals, Cunningham now considered it too late to recall the *Glengyle*. Nevertheless, still feeling apprehensive for the ship's safety, he decided to despatch another three destroyers to join the *Glengyle*. The Admiralty gave its blessing to this compromise.

Accordingly, Waller in the *Stuart* with the *Jaguar* and *Defender,* was instructed late on Thursday night to meet Force D south of Crete the following morning. The intention was that in addition to providing additional AA defence these destroyers should act as rescue ships to take off evacuated troops in the event of the *Glengyle* being sunk.

Admiral King's Force D reached Sfakia at 2330 on Thursday night, after an uneventful passage except for a lone Ju 88 which dropped a stick of bombs near the *Perth* in the forenoon. The *Glengyle* and the cruisers anchored off the fishing village while the AA cruisers and destroyers patrolled to seaward. It was not intended that the AA cruisers should embark troops. The destroyers left their patrol stations one at a time to embark their quota of troops. The *Glengyle*'s landing craft and two assault craft specially carried by the *Perth* for the evacuation were excellent vessels for the job of ferrying the soldiers from the confined, shingled beach.

By 0320/30th 6,029 troops[15] had been embarked. The force assembled then set course for Alexandria at 19½ knots. Three of the landing craft were left behind for use on a later occasion. At 0645 the force was joined by the *Stuart, Jaguar* and *Defender,* south of Gavdos Island. During the passage to Alexandria there were three attacks, the first of which occurred at 0930 when the *Perth* was hit by a bomb abaft the bridge which exploded in her foremost boiler room. Four ship's company and nine passengers were killed. Warrant Officer H. C. Hill and Stoker Petty Officer W. J. H. Reece showed great gallantry in remaining in the boiler room in scalding steam to save a stoker. They were both badly scalded. It is sad to relate that they both lost their lives when the *Perth* went down in the Sunda Strait off Java in 1942.

In the next two attacks between midday and 1300 the *Perth* and *Jaguar* were both selected as targets and both suffered near misses which shook them considerably. Thereafter, the force was unmolested, a fact due, without doubt, to the presence of two or three RAF fighter aircraft which gave cover to the force for many hours during the day. In one engagement these fighters drove off a group of twenty Ju 88s and Ju 87s. The force finally reached the safety of Alexandria soon after midnight. Considerable relief was felt in naval quarters.

Meanwhile, another force had assembled in Alexandria and left at 0915 on Friday 30th. It was designated Force C. It was commanded by Captain Arliss and consisted of the destroyers *Napier, Nizam, Kelvin* and *Kandahar.* Its destination, again, was Sfakia where the situation was deteriorating rapidly. During this night of Friday–Saturday, General Freyberg and Captain Morse, acting on instructions from their respective Commanders-in-Chief in Egypt, embarked in a Sunderland flying boat near Sfakia and were flown to Egypt. Major-General Weston, Royal Marines, was

---

[15] Figure quoted is taken from Army authorities' figures based on a count of heads as troops landed at Alexandria. King's approximate figure of 3,400 is considered wildly under-estimated.

left in command of all the British and Imperial troops still on the island.

On this day, too, Cunningham sent the First Sea Lord, Admiral Sir Dudley Pound, a long letter in which he referred to the state of fatigue to which the men of his Fleet had been reduced after prolonged sea time and constant harassment from the air. The *Dido,* he pointed out, was typical of most of the other cruisers and destroyers and she had spent only one night in harbour out of twenty-one. Cunningham revealed a personal glimpse of fatigue by writing: 'It may be that the Admiralty would like a change in command of the Fleet out here. If this is so I shall not feel in any way annoyed, more especially as it may be that the happenings of the last few days may have shaken the faith of the personnel of the Fleet in my handling of affairs.' The offer of resignation was never given consideration.

*

Force C's progress to Sfakia was dogged by misfortune. At 1245 the *Kandahar,* who had performed such miracles in the past few weeks, encountered some mechanical trouble. Rather than have to contend with a lame duck Captain Arliss sent her back to Alexandria.

At 1530 more problems arose. A surprise bombing attack by three Ju 88s which swooped in unseen from astern of the force dropped their bombs and near missed the *Kelvin* causing her to reduce speed to 20 knots. Arliss decided to detach her, too. Thus he was left with only the two Australian destroyers *Napier* and *Nizam.*

A few hours later these two fine destroyers met the home-bound Force D, itself including more Australian ships, the cruiser *Perth* and the antiquated destroyer *Stuart.* Admiral King was prepared to augment Arliss's depleted force by detaching the *Jaguar,* but she was running low on fuel. So the two Australian destroyers proceeded to Sfakia where they arrived soon after midnight.

The three landing craft left behind by the *Glengyle* were immediately put to use and the destroyer's own boats were also employed. The embarkation proceeded smoothly, 'the only pity being', Captain Arliss quoted in his *Operation Report,* 'that the Army had been informed that destroyers could only carry 250 men each'. His *Report* gave final figures of 1,403: made up from *Napier* 68 officers and 637 other ranks; *Nizam* 53 officers and 645 other ranks. The Army figures, based on an actual count at Alexandria came to 1,510.

By 0230 the *Nizam* had filled to capacity and got under way. Half an hour later the *Napier* followed and they sped off for Alexandria. Fighter protection had been arranged with the RAF and fighters were sighted at 0625. They claimed later to have shot down three Ju 88s and one Cant 1007 during the day's engagements. Despite this cover, one bombing attack penetrated the defences and from 0850 until 0915 the two destroyers were bombed by twelve Ju 88s in the course of which the *Napier* received engine room and boiler room damage by a near miss which jolted her considerably. She came to a halt for some minutes to effect repairs after which she went ahead on one engine. In time she managed to achieve 20 knots. But this did not hamper her escape and both destroyers arrived in Alexandria at 1900 on the Saturday evening.

*

On Friday, May 30th, before he left Sfakia, General Freyberg asked Wavell for 'one last lift tomorrow night; we could embark anything up to 7,000'. Accordingly, at 0600 on the Saturday morning of May 31st, Admiral King in the *Phoebe,* with the *Abdiel, Kimberley, Hotspur* and *Jackal* left Alexandria to make the last dash for Sfakia and the final evacuation from the defeated island. While the squadron steamed northbound away from the haven of Alexandria to further unknown hazards off Crete there was intense activity behind the scenes in Egypt and much pressurising of Cunningham to make even greater efforts.

The first hint of a problem arose with the receipt by the naval Commander-in-Chief of a message from Captain Arliss on the forenoon of Saturday 31st revealing that there were still 6,500 troops ashore on the island awaiting rescue.

Arliss had seen copies of the signals during the day which mentioned the small number of troops to be lifted by King's force.

He took it upon himself to signal Cunningham, repeated to King and Wavell, outlining the situation at Sfakia 'where there are roughly 6,500 to come' and he deemed it essential that the Army be advised that King's force could lift them all: 'Destroyers can carry up to 1,000 each, *Napier* and *Nizam* have 1,700 now.' (This latter figure, as we have seen, is exaggerated.)

The Prime Minister of New Zealand, Peter Fraser, interested in the Crete battle because of the large number of New Zealanders participating discussed the progress of the evacuation with Wavell, Freyberg, Cunningham and with Evetts, the outcome of which was a signal from Cunningham to Admiral King at 2051 ordering him to fill his ships to the maximum capacity.

Cunningham then signalled the Admiralty advising them that the night of Saturday, May 31st–Sunday, June 1st, was the last night of evacuation. He pointed out that even if King's force arrived back safely, the British Mediterranean Fleet would be left with only two battleships, one cruiser, 2 AA cruisers, the *Abdiel* and nine destroyers fit for service. Against this depleted force could be ranged the might of the Italian Fleet.

Then, at about 2000 on Saturday, Cunningham was asked by GHQ Middle East to pass on to Major-General Weston in Crete a personal message from Wavell telling him that the night of Saturday–Sunday was the last night of evacuation and authorising him to capitulate. Later this same night Wavell signalled Weston to leave Sfakia and he did so by Sunderland flying boat.

At about 2030 Cunningham received a message from General Blamey which expressed his concern at the relatively small number of Australian troops so far evacuated and asked for a ship to be sent to Plaka Bay where he believed a lot of Australians awaited rescue. In fact, of the five Australian infantry battalions on Crete, two were withdrawing to Sfakia and one had been rescued from Heraklion. But the other two were cut off in the Retimo area. Three times an RAF aircraft had been sent to drop a message to tell the Retimo garrison to withdraw to Plaka Bay, but it remains a mystery whether the message was ever delivered.

Cunningham replied to Blamey regretting it was impossible to divert some of King's ships at this late hour. Accordingly, the Retimo garrison was abandoned.

*

We left Admiral King's force northbound for Crete on the Saturday embarked upon the final act in the evacuation from Crete. During the day ineffectual bombing attacks were survived and bombs were seen to be jettisoned some distance from the ships, heartening evidence to the seamen of the presence of RAF fighters.

The anchorage was reached at 2320/31st and the organisation ashore had the situation so well in hand that the *Glengyle*'s landing craft were already loaded and awaiting the ships' arrival, thus saving a valuable forty minutes. But the flow of troops down the escarpment became too slow and for a time the beach was empty and the early gain in time was nullified.

By 0300 after medical stores had been landed for those left behind, the three landing craft which had performed so capably, were sunk or disabled. A total of 3,710 troops were packed into the ships who now weighed anchor and formed up to leave the anchorage for the last time. The passage south was uneventful due to RAF fighter protection and King's squadron arrived at Alexandria safely at 1700 on Sunday afternoon, June 1st.

But the *Luftwaffe* had not yet finished with the Mediterranean Fleet. Cunningham despatched the two small AA cruisers *Calcutta* and *Coventry* from Alexandria early on Sunday, June 1st to rendezvous with King's returning squadron to provide additional air protection. It is sad that such a well-intentioned venture should have been so ill-rewarded. Cunningham recorded in his *Despatch:* 'At 0900 aircraft were detected by RDF approaching from the north, and at 0917 the ships hoisted the red warning. It was unfortunate that an 'up sun' barrage was not then fired as five minutes later two Ju 88s dived on the cruisers from the direction of the sun. A stick of bombs from the first machine just missed *Coventry* but two bombs from the second machine hit *Calcutta,* who settled fast and sank within a few minutes.' The *Calcutta,* incidentally, was the only AA cruiser without radar.

Captain W. P. Carne of the *Coventry* was able to rescue 23

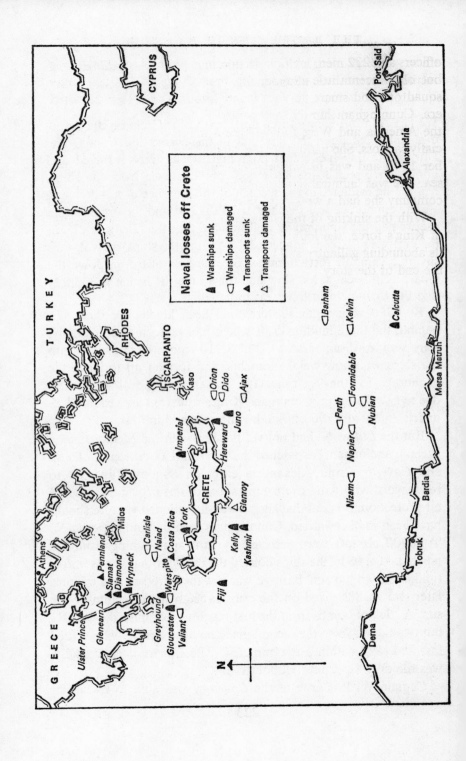

Naval losses off Crete

▲ Warships sunk
▽ Warships damaged
▲ Transports sunk
△ Transports damaged

officers and 232 men, including Captain D. M. Lees of this gallant but obsolescent little cruiser, the one-time pride of peace-day squadrons and smart flagship of an Imperial and now departed era. Cunningham himself had served in her as Flag Captain on the America and West Indies Station in 1926. Hers was a specially sad loss. She had joined the Mediterranean Fleet in September 1940 and was in action practically every time she went to sea. She was 'admirably commanded and with a first-rate ship's company she had a wonderful record of safely escorted convoys'.

With the sinking of the *Calcutta* and the return to Alexandria of King's force, the long drawn out naval battle for Crete with its abounding gallantry and courage was ended. But it is not quite the end of the story.

CHAPTER 14

The Battle Ends

WHILE ADMIRAL KING'S squadron was still at sea on its return from the sortie to Sfakia during the very early hours of Sunday, June 1st, Cunningham received a message from the First Sea Lord, Admiral Pound, announcing that the British Government considered another attempt to evacuate troops should be made on the night of June 1st–2nd, 'if reasonable prospect that any substantial formed body of men is capable of embarking'.

The situation ashore in Crete was not as happy as Cunningham might have wished. There were certainly about 5,000 troops left ashore at Sfakia and possibly the same number in the Retimo sector. Among those left behind were the gallant rearguard troops to whose self-sacrifice those so far evacuated were indebted for their salvation. Among this rearguard were a large number of the Special Service troops landed at Suda Bay as a final, sacrificial reinforcement, together with many marines of the Mobile Naval Base Defence Organisation (MNBDO). Of the original 2,000, less than 1,000 of these marines reached Alexandria.

Major-General Weston, flown out of Sfakia on the night of Saturday–Sunday, had left written orders to the 'Senior Officer left on the Island' authorising him to come to terms with the victorious Germans. Lieutenant Colonel G. A. D. Young of the Commandos was the unfortunate officer to whom this applied since Colonel Laycock declined the post. Weston also reported that the troops at Sfakia were incapable of further resistance owing to the strain of battle and the lack of food.

Cunningham embodied some of these facts in his reply to the First Sea Lord. In the circumstances, he concluded, no further ships would be sent to effect another night's evacuation. In a subsequent signal to the Admiralty despatched a few hours later Cunningham declared that the only ships he had available for a further attempt at evacuation on the night of June 1st–2nd were two battleships and five destroyers. All other ships had either been sunk, were damaged or were too slow for the undertaking. Furthermore, the moon now made night bombing of the beaches possible, further hazarding the ships and men. Fighter protection, Cunningham pointed out, was still 'thin and irregular'. He also drew attention to the sudden and belated increase, by 5,000, late on Friday, May 30th, of the number of troops still ashore on the island. Until then, all information had indicated that King's sortie on the following night would have been the final trip, leaving practically no one ashore. Finally, he informed the Admiralty that with King's arrival at Alexandria the evacuation had terminated.

The long catalogue of reasons which Cunningham could have marshalled for prohibiting any further attempts at evacuation are compelling and cogent, but they do not accord with the Commander-in-Chief's character. After the worst day of the battle —on May 22nd—his instinctive reaction to the mounting list of disaster was characteristic of the man: pugnacious, determined, aggressive. He signalled all ships at sea: 'Stick it out. Navy must not let Army down. No enemy forces must reach Crete by sea.'

It is difficult, therefore, to see why he should have refused this final plea to pluck from surrender thousands more soldiers whom he had come to respect for their bearing in adversity. The prize of rescuing them was within his grasp: and the intensity of the air attacks was known at the time to be diminishing, yet when faced with the decision to go to Sfakia once more or not, he succumbed to despair and cast aside resolve.

He had dismissed Bowyer-Smith's withdrawal from Kalamata as 'unfortunate'. He declared King's detaching of the *Greyhound, Gloucester* and *Fiji* as 'a mistake'. He considered King's decision to retire from the Aegean when engaged with the second seaborne invasion convoy and the full fury of the *Luftwaffe* as 'a faulty one'. All of these were decisions taken in the face of the enemy or threat of attack, in a moment of cruel crisis, at sea—and in King's case—under intense aerial bombardment. By the same high standards which Cunningham applied to these actions, his own decision to terminate the evacuation on the night of May 31st must be judged 'unfortunate'.

It was a melancholy end to the tragic British defeat in Crete and as Cunningham put it 'there is rightly little credit or glory to be expected in these operations of retreat'.

The Germans, for what it was worth, had won the island; and judged by any military standards, it was a matchless triumph. Never before nor since has an island been conquered from the air. It was a fruitless victory for the German paratroops: a decisive and significant success for the *Luftwaffe:* a damaging defeat for the Mediterranean Fleet: and an important signpost to the dominance of air power at sea.

Hitler's War Directive No 28
Operation Mercury

HITLER ADOPTED the policy of setting out his general programme of future events in a series of Directives. It was his seventy-four War Directives which achieved greatest historical interest.[1] The Directive announcing Operation Mercury was issued from the *Führer* Headquarters on April 25th, 1941, in Hitler's capacity as the *Führer* and Supreme Commander of the Armed Forces. This date was the day after the surrender of the Greek Government and the start of the British evacuation from Greece.

The island of Crete lay 160 miles away from Greece, enjoying a transitory peace with occupying British troops unaware of the severity of the ordeal they were about to experience.

Hitler's Directive read as follows:

1. As a base for air warfare against Great Britain in the Eastern Mediterranean we must prepare to occupy the island of Crete ('Undertaking Mercury'). For the purpose of planning, it will be assumed that the whole Greek mainland including the Peloponnese is in the hands of the Axis Powers.

2. Command in this operation is entrusted to Commander-in-Chief Air Force who will employ for the purpose, primarily, the airborne forces and the air forces stationed in the Mediterranean area.

   The Army, in cooperation with Commander-in-Chief Air Force, will make available in Greece suitable reinforcements for the airborne troops, including a mixed armoured detachment, which can be moved to Crete by sea.

   The Navy will take steps to ensure sea communications, which must be secured as soon as the occupation of the island begins. For protection of these communications and, as far as is necessary, for the provision of troop ships, Commander-in-Chief Navy will make the necessary arrangements with the Italian Navy.

3. All means will be employed to move the airborne troops and the 22nd

[1] See *Hitler's War Directives 1939–1945*, Edited by H. R. Trevor-Roper, Sidgwick & Jackson Ltd, 1964.

Division, which is under the command of the Commander-in-Chief Air Force, to the assembly area which he will designate. The necessary space for freight lorries will be put at the disposal of the Chief of Armed Forces Transport by the High Commands of the Army and Air Force. These transport movements must not entail any delay in the mounting of Operation Barbarosa (The invasion of Russia).

4. For anti-aircraft protection in Greece and Crete, Commander-in-Chief Air Force may bring up anti-aircraft units of the 12th Army. Commander-in-Chief Air Force and Commander-in-Chief Army will make the necessary arrangements for their relief and replacement.

5. After occupation of the island, all or part of the airborne forces must be made ready for new tasks. Arrangements will therefore be made for their replacement by Army units. In preparing coastal defences Commander-in-Chief Navy may if necessary draw upon guns captured by the Army.

6. I request Commanders-in-Chief to inform me of their plans and Commander-in-Chief Air Force to inform me when his preparations will be completed. The order for the execution of the operation will be given by me only.

signed ADOLF HITLER

APPENDIX B

Bibliography and Sources

BALDWIN, Hanson W., *Battles Lost and Won* (Great Campaigns of World War II), Hodder & Stoughton, 1967.

BEKKER, Cajus, *The Luftwaffe War Diarie*. Ballantine, 1972.

BRAGADIN, Commander M., *Che Ha Fatto La Marina?* Garzanti, Milan, 1959. US Edition: *The Italian Navy in World War II,* US Naval Institute, Annapolis, 1957.

BUCKLEY, Christopher, *Greece and Crete 1941,* HMSO, 1952.

BURN, Lambton, *'Down Ramps!'* Carroll & Nicholson, 1947.

CASSON, Stanley, *Greece Against the Axis,* Hamish Hamilton.

CHURCHILL, Winston S., *The Second World War,* Vol II, 'Their Finest Hour,' Bantam, 1971.

CHURCHILL, Winston S., *The Second World War,* Vol III, 'The Grand Alliance,' Bantam, 1971.

CLARK, Alan, *The Fall of Crete,* Anthony Blond, 1962.

COOPER, Bryan, *The Battle of the Torpedo Boats,* Stein and Day, 1970.

CORNEAU, M. G., *Operation Mercury,* William Kimber, 1961.

COULTER, J. L. S., Editor, *Medical History of the Second World War. Royal Naval Medical Services,* Vol II, HMSO, 1956.

CRESWELL, Captain John, *Sea Warfare 1939–1945,* University of California Press, 1967.

CRISP, Robert, *The Gods Were Neutral,* Norton, 1961.

CUNNINGHAM OF HYNDHOPE, Admiral of the Fleet, Lord, *A Sailor's Odyssey,* Hutchinson, 1951.

DAVIN, D. M., *Crete, Official History of New Zealand in the Second World War 1939–1945,* OUP, 1953.

DE BELOT, R., *The Struggle for the Mediterranean 1939–45,* OUP, 1951.

DE GUINGAND, Major-General Sir Francis, *Operation Victory,* Hodder & Stoughton, 1949.

EDWARDS, Commander Kenneth, *Men of Action,* Collins, 1943.

FARRAN, Roy, *Winged Dagger,* Collins, 1948.

GARNETT, David, *The Campaign in Greece and Crete,* HMSO, 1942.

GENTILE, R., *Storia Delle Operanziani Aere Nella Secunda Guerra Mondiale,* Firenze, Scula di Guerra Aerea, 1952.

233

GERICKE, Walter, *Da Gibt es Kein Zurück,* Fallschirmjager-Verlag, Munster, 1955.

GILL, G. Hermon, *Royal Australian Navy 1939–1942,* Series 2, Navy, Vol I, Verry.

GRAHAM, Lieutenant Colonel F. C. C., *History of the Argyll and Sutherland Highlanders 1939–1945,* Thomas Nelson, 1948.

GUEDELLA, Philip, *Middle East 1940–1942, A Study in Air Power,* Hodder & Stoughton, 1944.

GUNDELACH, Dr Karl, *The Battle for Crete, 1941,* Chronicle IV in *Decisive Battles of World War II: The German View,* Editors Dr H. A. Jacobsen and Dr J. Rohwer, Putnam, 1965.

GWYER, J. M. A., *Grand Strategy,* Vol III Part 1, Official History of the Second World War, HMSO, 1964.

HALDER, Colonel General Franz, *Halder: Kriegstagebuch,* W. Kohlhammer, Stuttgart, 1963.

HECKSTALL-SMITH, Anthony and BAILLIE-GROHMAN, Vice Admiral H. T., *Greek Tragedy '41,* Anthony Blond, 1961.

HETHERINGTON, John, *Airborne Invasion: The Story of the Battle of Crete,* Schindler, Cairo, 1943.

HEYDTE, Baron Von der, *Daedalus Returned,* Hutchinson, 1958.

HODGKINSON, Hugh, *Before the Tide Turned,* Harrap, 1944.

IACHINO, Ammiraglio D'Armata Angelo, *Gauda e Matapan,* Arnoldo Mondadori Editore, Rome, 1946.

Jane's All The World's Fighting Ships, Edited Francis E. McMurtrie, Sampson Low, Marston & Co, 1941.

KELLY, Robin A., and GRANVILLE, Wilfred, *Inshore Heroes,* W. H. Allen, 1961.

KEMP, Lieutenant-Commander P. J., *Victory at Sea,* Frederick Muller, 1958.

KENNEDY, Major-General Sir John, *The Business of War,* Morrow, 1958.

KIMMINS, Commander A., *It Is Upon the Navy,* Hutchinson, nd.

KIPPENBERGER, Major-General Sir Howard, *Infantry Brigadier,* OUP, 1949.

KUROWSKI, Franz, *Der Kampf um Kreta,* Maximilian Verlag, Herford und Bonn, 1965.

LANGMAID, Kenneth Rowland, *The Med; The Royal Navy in the Mediterranean 1939–45,* The Butterworth Press, 1948.

LEE, Air Vice Marshal A. S. G., *Special Duties,* Sampson Low, 1946.

LIDDELL-HART, B. H., *The Other Side of the Hill,* Cassell, 1948.

LONG, Gavin, *Greece, Crete and Syria: Australia in the War of 1939–45*, Series I, Vol II, Canberra, 1953.

LONGMORE, Air Chief Marshal Sir Arthur, *From Sea to Sky*, Bles, 1946.

MACINTYRE, Captain Donald, *Fighting Admiral*, Evans Bros, 1961.

MACINTYRE, Captain Donald, *The Battle for the Mediterranean*, Batsford, 1964.

MANNING, Captain T. D. and WALKER, Commander C. F., *British Warship Names*, Putnam, 1959.

MOURELLOS, J. D., *Battle of Crete*, Vol I, Erotocritous, Heraklion, 1950.

MULLER, Gunther and SCHEURING, Fritz, *Sprung uber Kreta*, Stalling Oldenberg, 1944.

PACK, Captain S. W. C., *The Battle of Matapan*, Macmillan, 1961.

PAPAGOS, General, *The Battle of Greece*, Translated by P. Eliascos, Scaziglis, Athens, 1949.

PLAYFAIR, Major-General I. S. O., with Captain F. C. Flynn, Brigadier C. J. C. Molony and Air Vice Marshal S. E. Toomer, History of the Second World War, *The Mediterranean and Middle East*, Vol II, 'The Germans came to the Help of Their Ally,' HMSO, 1956.

PLAYFAIR, Vol III, 'The British Fortunes Reach Their Lowest Ebb,' HMSO, 1960.

POOLMAN, Kenneth, *The Kelly*, Norton, 1955.

POTTER, E. B. and NIMITZ, C. W., Editors, *The Great Sea War*, Prentice-Hall, 1960.

RINGEL, General Julius, *Hurra die Gams*, Leopold Stocker Verlag, 1965.

ROSKILL, Captain S. W., *The War at Sea 1939–1945*, Vol I, 'The Defensive,' HMSO, 1954.

ROSKILL, Captain S. W., *A Merchant Fleet at War 1939–45*, Collins, 1962.

ROSKILL, Captain S. W., *HMS Warspite*, Collins, 1957.

RUGE, *Admiral Friedrich, Der Siekrieg 1939–45*, Koehler, Stuttgart, 1954: English edition *Sea Warfare 1939–45*.

SETH, Ronald, *Two Fleets Surprised, Bles*, 1960.

SINGLETON-GATES, Peter, *General Lord Freyberg VC*, Michael Joseph, 1963.

SMITH, Peter C., *The Stuka at War*, Ian Allan, 1971.

SPENCER, John Hall, *Battle for Crete*, Heinemann, 1962.

STEPHANIDES, Theodore, *Climax in Crete*, Faber, 1946.

STEWART, I. McD. G., *Struggle for Crete,* OUP, 1966.

STRABOLGI, Lord, *From Gibraltar to Suez,* Hutchinson, nd.

STUDENT, General Kurt, *Crete, 'Kommando,'* South Africa Ministry of Defence, 1952.

STYLES, Showell, *Jones's Private Navy,* Faber, 1969.

TEDDER, Lord, *With Prejudice,* Little, 1967.

TERRAINE, John, *The Life and Times of Lord Mountbatten,* Hutchinson, 1968.

THOMAS, David A., *With Ensigns Flying,* William Kimber, 1958.

TREVOR-ROPER, H. R., Editor, *Hitler's War Directives 1939–1945,* Sidgwick and Jackson, 1964.

WARNER, Oliver, *Cunningham of Hyndhope, Admiral of the Fleet,* John Murray, 1967.

WILSON, Field Marshal Lord, *Eight Years Overseas, 1939–1947,* Hutchinson, 1950.

WILSON-WASON, Betty, *Miracle in Hellas: The Greeks Fight On,* Museum Press, 1943.

WINTON, John, Editor, *Freedom's Battle,* Vol I, *'The War at Sea 1939–45,'* Hutchinson, 1967.

WISKEMANN, Elisabeth, *The Rome Berlin Axis,* Collins, 1966.

WITTMANN, Von A., *Von Kreta, der Insel der Rätsel,* Die Gebirstruppe, Vol III, Munchen, 1954.

*

The Administrative Aspect of the Campaign in Crete, Brigadier Brunskill, *The Army Quarterly,* LIV 2.

Action Against a Convoy 15–16 April 1941, Supplement to the *London Gazette,* July 14th, 1947.

Air Operations in Greece, 1940–1941, Air Vice Marshal J. H. D'Albiac's *Despatch,* Supplement to the *London Gazette,* January 9th, 1947.

Battle of Crete, Admiral Cunningham's *Despatch,* Supplement to the *London Gazette,* May 24th, 1948.

Battle of Matapan 1941, Admiral Cunningham's *Despatch,* Supplement to the *London Gazette,* July 31st, 1947.

The Campaign in Greece and Crete, Ministry of Information, HMSO, 1942.

Combined Operations 1940–42, Ministry of Information, HMSO.

East of Malta, West of Suez, The Official Admiralty account of the Mediterranean Fleet, 1939–45, HMSO.

236

Einsatz Kreta, XI Air Corps Battle Report, June 11th, 1941.

Fleet Air Arm Operations Against Taranto November 1940, Supplement to the *London Gazette,* July 14th, 1947.

Fleet Air Arm, The Admiralty account of Naval Air Operations, HMSO, 1943.

Führer's Conferences on Naval Affairs, Admiralty translation in Brassey's *Naval Annual,* 1948.

The Invasion of Crete, Report of Air Fleet IV, November 28th, 1941. (Luftflotten Kommando 4. Bericht 'Kreta'. Fuhrungsabt No 6340/1 g.Kdos.)

Letters of Proceedings, in particular those by Rear Admiral H. B. Rawlings, Rear Admiral I. Glennie, Rear Admiral E. L. S. King, Vice Admiral H. D. Pridham-Wippell and Captain M. H. S. Macdonald, NOIC, Heraklion.

Mediterranean Convoy Operations 1941–42, Cunningham, Somerville, Curteis and Syfret *Reports.* Supplement to the *London Gazette,* August 11th, 1948.

The Mediterranean Fleet, Greece to Tripoli, The Admiralty account of naval operations: April 1941 to January 1943, HMSO, 1944.

Operations in the Middle East from February 7th, 1941 to July 15th, 1941, General Wavell's *Despatch,* Supplement to the *London Gazette,* July 3rd, 1946.

The Story of HMS Glengyle *1940–1946,* The Glen Line Ltd, nd.

Supplements to the Study—The Balkan Campaign (The Invasion of Greece), MS No B524-p 36G, General von Greiffenberg, Office of the Chief of Military History, Department of the Army, Washington, DC.

Transportation of the Army to Greece and Evacuation of the Army From Greece 1941, Admiral Cunningham's *Despatch* together with *Reports* from Vice Admiral Pridham-Wippell and Rear Admiral Baillie-Grohman. Supplement to the *London Gazette,* May 19th, 1948.

War Diary, Flag Officer Southeast, Admiral Karlgeorg Schüster, May 16/31st May, 1941, 1/SKL No 14196/41 g.Kdos.

*

La Marina Italiana Nella Seconda Guerra Mondiale, Vol IX, 'La Difesa del Traffico con L'Albania, La Grecia e L'Egeo', Ufficio Storico Della Marina Militare, Roma, 1965, and Vol XIII, 'I Sommergibili in Mediterraneo', Roma, 1967.

APPENDIX C

Principal Characteristics of Ships Engaged in the Battle for Crete and Losses Suffered

Ship	Year	Tons	Guns	Speed	Damaged or Lost	Date	Dead	Missing	Wounded
Battleships									
Warspite	1915	31,100	8 – 15″ 8 – 6″ 8 – 4″	24	D	22.5	19	24	69
Valiant	1916	35,000	8 – 15″ 20 – 4.5″	24	D	22.5			
Queen Elizabeth	1915	35,000	8 – 15″ 20 – 4.5″	24					
Barham	1915	35,100	8 – 15″ 12 – 6″ 8 – 4″	25	D	26.5	7		6
Carrier									
Formidable	1940	23,000	16 – 4.5″ and 60 aircraft	31	D	26.5	12		10

	Year	Displacement	Armament	Speed	D/L	Date	Killed	Wounded	?
Cruisers									
Gloucester	1939	9,600	12 – 6″ / 8 – 4″	32.3	L	22.5	725	271	?
Fiji	1940	8,000	12 – 6″ / 8 – 4″	33	L	22.5	5	5	24
Orion	1934	7,215	8 – 6″ / 8 – 4″	32.5	D	26.4 / 29.5	1 / 115		1 / 76
Ajax	1935	7,215	8 – 6″ / 8 – 4″	32.5	D	28.4 / 28.5	5 / 6		19 / 19
Perth, RAN	1936	6,980	8 – 6″ / 8 – 4″	32.5	D	24.5 / 29.5	4		3
Dido	1940	5,450	10 – 5.25″	33	D	29.5	27		10
Phoebe	1940	5,450	10 – 5.25″	33					
Naiad	1940	5,400	10 – 5.25″	33	D	22.5	7		31
Coventry	1918	4,290	10 – 4″	29	D	17.5	2		7
Calcutta	1918	4,200	8 – 4″	29	L	1.6	9	108	40
Carlisle	1918	4,200	8 – 4″	29	D	22.5	14		25
Destroyers									
Napier, RAN	1941	1,695	6 – 4.7″	36					
Nizam, RAN	1941	1,690	6 – 4.7″	36					
Kandahar	1939	1,690	6 – 4.7″	36					
Kingston	1939	1,690	6 – 4.7″	36	D	21.5	1		2
Kimberley	1939	1,690	6 – 4.7″	36					
Kashmir	1939	1,690	6 – 4.7″	36	L	23.5	82	82	14

APPENDIX C—*continued*

Ship	Year	Tons	Guns	Speed	Damaged or Lost	Date	Dead	Missing	Wounded
Kipling	1939	1,690	6 – 4.7"	36	D	23.5	5		1
Kelvin	1939	1,690	6 – 4.7"	36	D	29.5	1		4
Kelly	1938	1,695	6 – 4.7"	36	L	23.5	3	127	17
Jervis	1939	1,695	6 – 4.7"	36	D	30.5			4
Juno	1938	1,690	6 – 4.7"	36	L	21.5	12	116	21
Janus	1939	1,690	6 – 4.7"	36					
Jackal	1939	1,690	6 – 4.7"	36					
Jaguar	1939	1,690	6 – 4.7"	36	D	26.5			2
Nubian	1938	1,870	8 – 4.7"	36.5	D	26.5	15		6
Isis	1937	1,370	4 – 4.7"	36					
Imperial	1936	1,370	4 – 4.7"	36	L	29.5			1
Ilex	1937	1,370	4 – 4.7"	36					
Hereward	1936	1,340	4 – 4.7"	36	L	29.5	5	165	
Hero	1936	1,340	4 – 4.7"	36					
Hotspur	1936	1,340	4 – 4.7"	36					
Hasty	1936	1,340	4 – 4.7"	36					
Havock	1937	1,340	4 – 4.7"	36	D	23.5	15		10
Griffin	1936	1,335	4 – 4.7"	36	D	24.5			1
Greyhound	1935	1,335	4 – 4.7"	36	L	22.5	1	83	23
Decoy	1933	1,375	4 – 4.7"	36	D	29.5	1		8

Defender	1932	1,375	4 – 4.7″	36				
Diamond	1932	1,370	4 – 4.7″	36	L	27.4	155	1
Stuart, RAN	1919	1,530	5 – 4.7″	36.5				
Voyager, RAN	1919	1,100	4 – 4″	34				
Vendetta, RAN	1919	1,100	4 – 4″	34				
Wryneck	1918	1,100	4 – 4″	34	L	27.4	108	5
Sloops								
Auckland	1938	1,200	6 – 4″					
Flamingo	1939	1,250	6 – 4″	19.25				
Minelayer								
Abdiel	1940	2,650	6 – 4.7″	40				
Assault Ships								
Glenearn	1938	9,869		18	D	25.4		4
Glengyle	1939	9,865		18	D			
Glenroy	1938	9,871		18	D	26.5		1

The total of 2,261 killed and missing naval personnel excludes the numerous casualties among those who served aboard transports and auxiliary ships of the merchant navy.

Index

244